FINANCIAL
Infidelity

FINANCIAL
Infidelity

Seven Steps to Conquering the #1 Relationship Wrecker

Bonnie Eaker Weil, PhD

HUDSON
STREET
PRESS

HUDSON STREET PRESS
Published by Penguin Group
Penguin Group (USA) Inc., 375 Hudson Street, New York, New York 10014, U.S.A. • Penguin
Group (Canada), 90 Eglinton Avenue East, Suite 700, Toronto, Ontario, Canada M4P 2Y3
(a division of Pearson Penguin Canada Inc.) • Penguin Books Ltd., 80 Strand, London WC2R
0RL, England • Penguin Ireland, 25 St. Stephen's Green, Dublin 2, Ireland (a division of
Penguin Books Ltd.) • Penguin Group (Australia), 250 Camberwell Road, Camberwell, Victoria
3124, Australia (a division of Pearson Australia Group Pty. Ltd.) • Penguin Books India Pvt.
Ltd., 11 Community Centre, Panchsheel Park, New Delhi – 110 017, India • Penguin Group
(NZ), 67 Apollo Drive, Rosedale, North Shore 0632, New Zealand (a division of Pearson
New Zealand Ltd.) • Penguin Books (South Africa) (Pty.) Ltd., 24 Sturdee Avenue, Rosebank,
Johannesburg 2196, South Africa

Penguin Books Ltd., Registered Offices: 80 Strand, London WC2R 0RL, England

First published by Hudson Street Press, a member of Penguin Group (USA) Inc.

First Printing, April 2008
10   9   8   7   6   5   4   3   2   1

REGISTERED TRADEMARK—MARCA REGISTRADA
HUDSON
STREET
PRESS

LIBRARY OF CONGRESS CATALOGING-IN-PUBLICATION DATA

Eaker Weil, Bonnie.
   Financial infidelity : seven steps to conquering the #1 relationship wrecker / Bonnie Eaker Weil.
      p. cm.
   Includes bibliographical references and index.
   ISBN 978-1-59463-045-3 (hardcover : alk. paper)
   1. Marriage—Economic aspects. 2. Man-woman relationships—Economic aspects. 3. Married
people—Finance, Personal. I. Title.
   HQ734E15 2008
   332.0240086'55—dc22   2007052689

Printed in the United States of America
Set in Bembo

In memory of my father, Hyman Eaker: "The Best," who taught me
you can always make more money; relationships come first.
You've got to know when to hold 'em and know when to fold 'em.

To my husband, Dr. Jeffrey M. Weil, who I treasure and cherish for
all you have given and continue to give and teach me.
I'm so lucky I found you.

In memory of Thomas F. Fogarty, M.D., my mentor, friend, and
guiding light, and the originator of the pursuer/distancer theory,
whose wisdom has guided me, my parents, my brother,
my husband, and my patients.
"The only need in life is connectedness."

And to my patients, whose courage in facing the infidelity and financial
infidelity in their lives and relationships inspired me to begin this
journey to light the way!

"No price is too high to pay for the privilege of owning yourself."

—Freidrich Nietschze

"There have been many terrible worries in my life but most of them never happened. So too with money."

—Arianna Huffington paraphrasing
Michel de Montaigne

CONTENTS

PART III: *The Biochemical Component*

FOREWORD

Betrayed! A word that strikes horror in the breast of humankind. We don't see ourselves as financial infidels! But are we? We don't see our partner or future partner as a person with the capacity to be financially faithless. But are they? Maybe we really are selfish. Perhaps we shouldn't feel betrayed if he looks at the top-of-the-line new cars after telling me to forget replacing the kitchen countertops. Right? So what if we soothe ourselves on snack food when she returns home with shopping bags akimbo. It's better than more of the same argument. Right?

Dr. Bonnie Eaker Weil, author and muse of Financial Infidelity, has written an outrageous, courageous, and mind-blowing book that peels away the innocence that blinds us to our own and our partner's acts of financial infidelity. She invites us to peek through the places in our soul that are empty, frightened, and lonely, even as we relentlessly, endlessly stuff those places with things money can buy. Even when we end up no fuller than before. We will control, placate, abandon, shut out, lie, cheat, steal, deny, hide, and flee in order to feel satiated. We will do this to our partner. Especially our partner.

We don't see ourselves as financially unfaithful. Yet financial infidelity is the money we hide when we can't find our partner's heart. It describes those acts we perform daily so as not to repeat our parents' financial history. Or to replicate their financial history exactly. It is the money we hold on to so that we can feel safe, even if we've never felt safe in our lives. Financial infidelity occurs when we repeatedly ask our partner for an accounting or when we never ask where the money goes. It's there when we keep silent because they'll just be silent too, and what does that accomplish? It shows up when we fear being left and we have no choice but to buy what we can now, before we're forced to move to a smaller apartment, downsize to a skimpier wardrobe, trade in for a cheaper car, or feel relegated to a home coloring kit for our hair. It shows up when we feel controlled, when we feel speechless, when we want our partner's unavailable love, when we need to feel as happy as the people down the street who did buy that expensive car. It's the stuff we buy him when we need his comfort. It's the credit cards we ramp up, the land we buy in our name only, the new dress we stuff into the back of the closet and then insist we've had it for years. It is the way to dull the ache when we can't have what we really want.

When did things get this bad? Remember how great things were in the beginning? Perhaps he told you he would always take care of you. He meant it, at the time. She said she would never give you reason to doubt her. She meant it, at the time. At the time, we really could be honest about everything. We never felt so understood. At the time, I ached when he ached, laughed when he laughed, desired what he desired. At the time, we were the people we always knew we could be. We were the best. We want those good days back; we want those carefree laughs back even if we have to betray him to get them.

Eaker Weil explains why that kind of blind romantic love can't last. In the beginning, our brains flood us with the chemicals of desire. As long as we were under the influence, we saw each other through rose-colored glasses. We each felt as if we were the best we had ever been. If, for a moment, we saw a glimpse of less than the best, we minimized it, trivialized it, forgot it, excused it, gave it a positive spin, decided we could change it, or blamed ourselves for making something big out of something so small. The first time my fiancé, Mark, and I went to the movies, he presented his great idea: "Let's make our popcorn at home.

It's cheaper than buying it at the theater." "Great idea," I replied, over-looking the twist in my belly. The first time it snowed, Mark arrived wearing a coat so large he looked dwarfed. "It's my big brother's," he crowed. "Isn't it great—he gave it to me. Now I don't have to buy one." A smile strained through my grimace. "Great," I said, and I thought to myself that I would replace it with a luxurious, hand-tailored one as soon as we married. "What's the problem?" I reassured myself. "I'll buy it as a wedding present." "She loves me," he reassured himself. "She's thrilled I have my brother's warm coat."

Eventually, the chemicals wear off and the differences between us pile up. He sees my spending as frivolous; I see his scrimping as choosing money over my emotional well-being. Our worlds become awash in our differences. Our trust in each other frays at the seams. Financial Infidelity is about the inevitable power struggle we will have over money and the way out of that struggle toward reclaiming the trust and safety we once had for the asking.

Eaker Weil takes you step by amazing step through the language of the Smart Heart Dialogue (a derivative of the Imago Dialogue, developed by Harville Hendrix, PhD, and Helen LaKelly Hunt, PhD, founders of the Imago Relationship Theory and Therapy). *The Smart Heart dialogue is the way out of the struggle. Eaker Weil's remarkable contribution includes bringing the highly charged area of money into the dialogue, providing a structure for speaking and listening that keeps both people safe and connected.* She teaches you the **language** itself that ends the infidelities and re-stores us to our passionate, enlivened selves. The **language** she models is the **Language of Attachment**. We learn the words that stop the wounding, the deceit, and the hiding. She teaches us the language that restores our mutuality, empathy, and clarity. Once learned, this language will open the floodgates to financial and emotional healing, and growth, and freedom.

You have a right to know why I think this book is different from every book I've ever read on financial success. Within these pages, you will discover that money is a metaphor for emotional hunger. Whether we're spending too much money or wrapping our lives around the money we save, we wither in a relationship that struggles over money when what we need is love. Financial infidelity is what we do when we can't find the love and intimacy we crave. We think we'll be happy when we've paid off the mortgage, even though the mortgage never made up for the lack of love. Money never looked like love, smelled like love, or touched us like a lover. Financial Infidelity is what we do to survive, not thrive.

This is a practical book, but also a very personal one. Eaker Weil knocked my socks off with her many practical skills and exercises. But when I read the chapter on the Family Money Tree, I felt chills. My own life fell into place.

A miracle is happening in your life right now: you have found the book that will unlock your particular mystery. *Financial Infidelity* can return you to you, to your relationship, to love. Your big, gorgeous life is a mystery to be solved and my heart joins Dr. Bonnie Eaker Weil's in wishing you the journey of your lifetime. Thank you, Bonnie.

Sunny Shulkin, L.C.S.W, B.C.D.
Presenter of Imago's Getting the Love You Want Workshop
Master Trainer, Imago Relationship Therapy
Bala Cynwyd, PA

ACKNOWLEDGMENTS

Thank you to my collaborator, Jill Stern. Your energy, amazing creativity and ideas, organization, optimism, and skillful shaping of my thoughts and concepts helped make me be the best I could be. Like a good marriage, or an orchestra and conductor, we were always in sync.

To my husband, Dr. Jeffrey M. Weil: I am so lucky to have you in my life while writing this book, anticipating and solving problems before there's trouble (like the new Xerox machine!). Thank you for rescuing me from deadlines, sharing precious weekends with notes and manuscript, spending hours reading drafts, without complaining, working on exercises, and exploring our family's history with financial infidelity. Special thanks for keeping the romance alive by sharing midnight dinners when deadlines loomed.

To my parents, Hyman and Paula: the love and support you showed me and each other has made so much possible. Your example has been a guiding light on my journey to helping so many others.

To my grandparents, Sarah and David Brodkin, whose generous and loving marriage weathered the power struggles and provided me with inspiration for this book.

Many thanks to my "mother-in-love," Helen, who helped with the Moneygram and Family History for hours. Thank you for your love and support and for always putting yourself out there.

To my patients, whose courage and belief in me, Smart Heart Skills and Dialogues, and my avant-garde, groundbreaking Biochemical Craving for Connection and Brush with Death theories—and most importantly, in yourselves—propelled you to transform your relationships. You are the torchbearers for reconnection and reromanticizing, and it is your personal stories and triumphs that bring this book to life! Thank you for taking the journey with me, and passing the torch. It will brighten the way for so many others.

To Kirsten Manges, my wonderful agent, whose wisdom, diplomacy, perseverance, and amazing sixth sense guided this project from idea to book and found for me a great publisher and editor. You are so smart and always on target. Thanks for believing in this book and cheering me on every step of the way. You'd make a great therapist!

To Emily Haynes, my brilliant editor, for your continued insight and enthusiasm. From the beginning you understood why Financial Infidelity posed such a threat to relationships and why so many people would benefit from this book. Thank you for taking the adventure with me and believing in me and my groundbreaking ideas.

Thanks also to Nadia Kashper, for your cooperative attitude and attention to detail. And to Marie Coolman and Liz Keenan for your bubbling personalities, fabulous ideas, tireless brainstorming, and great PR.

Grateful thanks to Angela Muniz, my husband's assistant, for the endless patience and support and assurances that nothing was ever too much trouble. And to Stan Lotwin for your networking, humor, and wisdom. Thanks to Arlene Adler for being so generous with your time and opinions and for spreading the word. And to Nick Gravante for your wisdom and support, and Michael Braun for your hysterical and astute additions. To Pat Ambrose from Lords Valley Country Club for your openness and, as usual, wonderful advice and help, and to Jessica Parry for your amazing helpfulness and positive attitude. Thank you to my good friends Ken and Julie Kendall for your encouragement every step of the way, and to Saul Weidler and Stephanie Neigeborn.

To Myrna Post for hatching the idea, helping with the title, and supporting my efforts, and to Mitchell Waters at Curtis Brown for making the fantastic match. To Kate White and Vicki Lucia at *Cosmopolitan*, Margie Rosen at *Ladies Home Journal*, and K. C. Baker from *People*, for all of your enthusiasm, interest, and support. Thanks also to Steve Portney and André Wallace for your ideas and insights into Financial Infidelity and the DVD for Financial Infidelity.

Finally, to my colleagues and mentors: Dr. Jeffrey Morrison of the Morrison Center and Grace Lindo, his assistant, for working with so many of my patients despite serious challenges as we pioneered this journey. To Sunny Shulkin for your incredible insights and your thoughtful and intuitive forward to this book. To Dr. Helen Fisher for generously taking the time to share your research and insight on relationship dynamics, chemistry, and money. To Dr. Harvey B. Bezahler, my first therapist, for teaching me and guiding me to where I am today. You have been, and will always be, an instrumental force and a guiding light in my professional and personal success. To Dr. Harville Hendrix, for your courage in paving the way for Imago and for your inspiration and teaching; and to Dr. Thomas Fogarty, my mentor, who taught me everything I know and worked with my family, my husband, and me on Financial Fidelity and Fidelity.

INTRODUCTION

In the more than thirty years that I have been a relationship therapist, I have noticed that certain relationship dynamics seem to come in waves. Communication, connection, and all the confusion that can result between men and women are driven, to some extent, by the societal norms and culture in which they are interacting. When the women's lib movement was gaining momentum in the late sixties and early seventies, women would ask, "Is it wrong for me to want to be taken care of by a man?" and men would ask, "Will I insult her if I hold the door, or help her with her coat?" In the powerful tow of societal change, both men and women were struggling with undercurrents that wreaked havoc on the foundations of what they thought they knew about each other.

At the close of the twentieth century, I noticed that relationships between men and women were being buffeted by yet another cultural force. The money-driven, "BlackBerry mistress," status-conscious, luxury-goods-craving, "greed is good" phenomenon, fueled by booming stock markets and skyrocketing developments in technology, had introduced another layer of complexity for men and women seeking to begin, build, and sustain loving and lasting relationships. In today's culture of excess and immediate gratification, people are made to feel that it is most important to "live for today." They often fear revealing what is behind appearances.

The beginning of the twenty-first century has heralded what I call a "relational paradigm shift" between men and women. Familiar, comfortable sex roles around money are being rewritten: Women are earning more—in 25 percent of households, they're earning half the household income—and stepping (not without internal conflict) into the roles of breadwinners, making men feel demoted and obsolete. Long-term, financially stable marriages and marriages wracked by financial infidelity are dissolving, taking bank accounts down with them and leaving newly skeptical and doubly suspicious older singles to struggle with today's amorphous "rules" about dating and paying. And singles, both young and old, still struggle with age-old questions, only now with a financial twist: "If I let her pay the check will she want to see me again?" or "Will he expect me to sleep with him if I don't cover my share of the dinner?"

Corporate scandals, like the 2001 Enron debacle, have exposed the financial infidelities of the high-flying business world and those who inhabit it. There's a new call for openness in the workplace, with interoffice dating no longer a secret, and financial watchdogs guarding against corporate deceptions. These dynamics send mixed messages of openess and transparency on the one hand and deceit—not sneaking and lying, but omission—on the other.

But while the money rules may be more clearly defined in the workplace, most individuals are in more trouble than ever when it comes to how their financial situations affect their lives. The average American suffers from an excess of choice and a self-imposed mandate to "keep up with the Joneses." Meanwhile, "the Joneses" are drowning in credit card debt as nearly 24 percent of families are unable to pay off their credit balances in full and most have bills that are at least thirty days post due.

In addition to money stress at home and at work, Americans are bombarded daily with threats of terrorism, a shaky stock market, falling interest rates, failing mortgages. Hard workers become workaholics, driven by the economic mandate to attain more "things." Even children are affected. According to an article in *Newsweek*, 60 percent admitted to cheating on an exam at least once and 33 percent admitted to copying answers from the Internet. Meanwhile, teachers are under pressure to improve scores and demonstrate learning in order to get grants. If they have to fudge results to get more money, some may be willing to do so.

Furthermore, developments in neuroscience have now proven that these constant stresses wreak havoc on the chemical circuitry in our brains, causing our parasympathetic systems to jump into overdrive and inhibiting our ability to consciously engage in clear and rational thought when faced with stressful "trigger" situations, such as money conflicts. What's more, most people lack the skills to deal with these "hot button" topics. Any number of physical conditions or emotional stresses can affect your biochemical balance and result in damaging behavioral patterns. If your love life is drastically out of balance and you feel you have "fallen out of love" with your partner, or if you feel "numb" or "dead" to emotional or physical stimulation, the problem may be that you are out of sync with your biochemical self. I often see patients whose emotional crises have been triggered by out-of-whack blood sugar, chronic sleep deprivation, or an imbalance of specific neurotransmitters, hormones, and biochemical reactions.

The combination of these societal, cultural, emotional, and biochemical circumstances have created a "perfect storm" of relationship chaos and I see the fallout daily in my practice. I have singles who tell me about their internal conversations on dates as they try to guess which one of them makes more and whether an independent career woman wants—or should be expected—to pay. Women wonder if they should be the ones who take care of things, or if it is okay for them to admit they want to be taken care of. Some men feel wimpy if they do not pay, while others may take advantage if they feel they have an ax to grind, perhaps with their mother or with an ex. Of course, what's really being negotiated is a certain kind of indebtedness. It's not really about the money—it's about autonomy, power, and, of course . . . sex.

I counsel couples who live together or want to commit to living together, or who are engaged, who worry about how to deal with money issues if they take the next step and commit to marriage. "Do we really have to talk about money?" they ask. They tell me that money fights ruin their sex lives and cause resentment. Most of them admit that they prefer to keep their spending and saving habits private from their partner—essentially confessing they'd rather deceive a loved one than work through a conflict about money. For these couples, talking about money triggers a cascade of emotional issues that, if ignored, will gradually destroy trust and intimacy—and if untreated, will ultimately destroy their relationship.

Other men and women struggle with balancing money and commitment. Anticipating failure in potential relationships because of the high divorce rate, they want prenups and postnups and assurances that if their relationship ends, their finances will remain stable. Just as certain cultures send women to be married with a dowry that ensures them a degree of financial stability, these men and women want to know that they will be taken care of financially if they decide to leave a relationship.

I'm also seeing more individuals whose relationships and marriages have ended and who are just now recognizing the role that money played in creating the bitterness and lack of trust they now feel toward members of the opposite sex. Men who have lost half their net worth to an ex or to financial infidelity may overcompensate, acting out unresolved issues from their previous relationship by overcorrecting and expecting their new love interest to take care of them—both emotionally *and* financially. Hiding their resentment over supporting a woman who no longer provides them with emotional support, they use the guise of "transparency"—disclosing their financial situation immediately and expecting their newest date to do the same. Some even expect to "piggyback" on the financial success of the new woman in their life and simply be taken care of. A beta data research survey of eight hundred singles showed that twice as many men than women are dating for money.

I talk to women who no longer define their financial identity through the men they are with—women who struggle with their need to be nurtured and their fear of turning a man off with their power and wealth. They worry about excelling in high-powered jobs where they feel like promotions and business travel can compromise their ability to be good wives and mothers. They're making more money than ever, but are afraid to deal with its effect on their relationships. Money equals power and these women are afraid of disempowering the man in their life.

As confused as women are in this new financial landscape, men are not faring much better. I see men who confess that they enjoy the improved lifestyle that comes with their spouse or girlfriend's increased earning power, but, used to being the breadwinner in a relationship, they admit that their egos are bruised. As one of my patients said, "I don't want to be left behind when it comes to dealing with women and money. I want to be an emotionally modern guy, but my identity as a man is in flux. If I'm not the breadwinner, if I can't take care of a woman financially, I worry that I'm going to become obsolete."

These shifting roles, expectations, and confusions over how to allow love and money to coexist in today's world create a fertile breeding ground for Financial Infidelity. As Arianna Huffington has noted, "Irrational fears can cause financial infidelity. Money's not just money: it's a stand-in for our fears."

Financial Infidelity occurs whenever you keep a secret about money. Whether it's how you spend it, or how you save it, or how it makes you feel when you or your partner use it in any particular way. The dangerous thing about financial infidelity is not the secret itself, but the act of conscious deception in a relationship. Over time, any deception destroys intimacy, and without intimacy couples cannot have true and lasting love.

In this groundbreaking book I'll show you how to recognize your risk for, or the act of, financial infidelity in your relationship. I will tell you how to confess and confront financial infidelity and work through its challenges to make your relationship stronger, safer, and more loving, intimate, and sexy than it has ever been. I'll teach you specific "attachment language" through my Smart Heart skills and dialogues and show you how to prevent the power struggles that money issues can trigger. You will learn how to consciously let go of toxic responses and emotions to money and instead enjoy a life and love filled with gratitude and abundance.

Dr. Bonnie Eaker Weil

(Dr. Bonnie)

PART I

What Is Financial Infidelity?

Understanding
Financial Infidelity

Do you lie to your husband about the cost of those sexy new sandals you just bought for full price? Do you feel that blowing a few thousand dollars on a girls-only trip to Vegas is something you deserve because you work so hard to earn it? Do you have a credit card (and debt) that your spouse doesn't know about? Do you play the stock market without your spouse's knowledge? Do you participate in office pools, golfing bets, or other kinds of gambling? After a fight with your partner, do you add an expensive outfit to your wardrobe? Or commiserate with friends over a meal at the most expensive restaurant in town? If you manage the checkbook and household budget, would you be willing to let your partner take over the books for a few months? Or would you be afraid of what a closer examination of the household accounts might reveal? When either person in a couple starts using money, whether to fill an internal feeling of emptiness from their childhood (replacing longed-for parental love with money or material objects), or to make up for what they think is missing in their relationship, or to "get back at" or manipulate their partner, the deceit, secrecy, and sometime thrill-seeking behaviors conspire to destroy trust and intimacy. These individuals are committing financial infidelity.

There's no such thing as an innocent financial fib, and if you commit financial infidelity by deceiving your spouse or romantic partner about money, you're not alone! In a recent Harris poll, 40 percent of all adults in a committed relationship admitted to *lying* to their partner about spending habits, and a shocking 82 percent said they *hide* purchases from their partners. A 2005 survey conducted by *Redbook* magazine and Lawyers.com showed that women are slightly more inclined to practice financial deception, with 33 percent of them admitting they often withhold information about spending or saving money, while 26 percent of all men surveyed admit they do the same.

In a recent article in *Tango* magazine, writer Sara Max called financial infidelity "a type of cheating so subtle, you may be straying without knowing it." It is tempting to simply say that these secret spending habits are the inevitable results of combining and managing shared finances in today's materialistic, impulse-driven society. The statistics on debt and spending are staggering. CreditCard.com reports that for the fiscal year 2006–2007, consumer debt in the United States totaled more than $2.46 *trillion*; a typical family credit card balance is equal to 5 percent of the annual household income; and the typical consumer has an average of thirteen credit obligations. Yet many couples, both married and dating, brush away troubling money behaviors. They are afraid to engage in the often-heated dialogues about money that are increasingly common in relationships today. These couples do not understand that these financial infidelities (secrets about spending and refusals or reluctance to talk about financial matters) are red flags, signaling an insidious threat to the very foundation of their intimate relationship.

These are the couples that end up in counseling with me.

"He says he loves me, but he wants to call off the wedding," Darla sobbed as her fiancé, William, shifted uncomfortably on the couch next to her.

The young couple had called me for an appointment just six months before their wedding date. They had been together for several years and were in the midst of planning their wedding when William had discovered that—despite having agreed to stick to what he described as a "very generous" budget—

Darla had been meeting with one of the city's most expensive wedding planners and had hired him to oversee what was rapidly turning into a budget-busting event.

"She paid the guy a deposit of $10,000 and didn't even tell me about it," William said. "One month we've got a healthy balance in our money market account—money that's supposed to be for a new house—and the next month we're missing ten grand!"

"I was going to tell you," Darla said. "But you're such a control freak! I knew that you'd react like this. It's the biggest day of our lives and you're worried about how much it will cost. I never knew you could be so cheap."

"It's your mother who's putting you up to this, isn't it?" William said. "Just because she eloped and never had a big wedding, she's trying to live through you. Your parents aren't even paying for most of the wedding. We agreed that we would pay for most of it. And you agreed to stick to a budget. And I'm not asking my parents for any more help—they're already complaining about how many people we invited to the rehearsal dinner."

"Oh, well, Mr. We-Need-to-Budget, what about your bachelor party last month?" Darla said. "How much did you lose in Vegas, if you're so concerned about money?"

"I worked hard to earn that money and if I want to blow off steam with some of the guys before I get locked into supporting your expensive habits for the rest of my life, then I think I'm entitled," William shot back.

"How can you say these horrible things? I'm not sure I can love someone who is so petty," Darla said. "It's like I don't even know you."

Before things could grow more heated, I stopped the discussion. I pointed out to William and Darla how dismissive and defensive their conversation had become. "What happened to the love you had for each other? There's a lot more at stake here than how much you spend on the wedding," I warned them. "And there's a lot more trouble ahead for your relationship if you don't take the time to fully understand what is really going on. The money is not your real problem."

The couple looked shocked. As far as they were concerned, the only problem was the money!

As I counseled them over the next few months, it became clear that William and Darla's path to financial infidelity probably began as early as their first date. I wasn't surprised; 47 percent of couples do not discuss money at all before they get married. The 51 percent that say they do talk about money often don't know *how* to talk about it, and wind up in power struggles. During their courtship, William always paid. He bought Darla gifts and took her on romantic trips. He never mentioned money. For William it was the beginning of establishing the power dynamic in their relationship. He always dismissed Darla's offers to contribute financially by saying, "I make so much more than you do. I'll pay."

For Darla, who was used to being spoiled by a mother overcompensating for a childhood where money was scarce, the trade-off of her affection for gifts and excess seemed natural.

Even when they moved in together, money was an off-limits topic. As William worked longer hours and advanced his career, Darla covered the loneliness and abandonment she felt with shopping splurges after which she would guiltily hide the credit card bills or borrow money from her mother to pay them off each month. As her deception around money grew more entrenched, she felt she was betraying the mutual goals she and William had set, such as buying a house and having a big wedding, and the relationship grew increasingly strained. She withdrew emotionally and physically from William. He was burnt out and stressed and whenever he realized they hadn't had sex in a while, he'd buy Darla an expensive gift, have a romantic night, and convince himself that everything was fine. In fact, both William and Darla were increasingly unhappy in the relationship, but neither of them was able to pinpoint the cause.

When their families became financially involved in planning the wedding, William and Darla's money stresses increased. What they didn't know to acknowledge is that when you marry someone you also marry their family history with money. And as Suze Orman says, "What happens to your money affects the quality of your life and the life of all those you love."

This couple perfectly illustrates how financial infidelity can have an insidious, damaging effect on a relationship at any stage—whether dating, living together, engaged, or married. William and Darla's problems with money began long before they came to a head over the cost of the wedding. And even if they had gotten past the "wedding planner" incident without seeking help and had gotten married, over time, without intervention (or Smart Heart dialogue) their toxic money dynamic would have continued until the marriage was on the verge of breaking apart. But because they had found their way to my office sooner rather than later, I was able to work with them and with their families to help them learn how to identify and address the causes and symptoms of financial infidelity that were slowly but surely undermining their love.

Relationship therapy has become an accepted and common way for couples to face the fallout from affairs, emotional distancing, or sexual dysfunction. It has also become an increasingly popular way for newly formed couples to explore their expectations for a committed relationship. In my thirty years of counseling couples brought to the brink of ending their relationships, it has become impossible not to notice the particular patterns of behavior—often undetected by the couple—that revolve around their shared finances and their personal histories with money no matter what their declared reason for therapy might be.

There are many very good books available, written by qualified financial planners, that can teach couples *how* to manage their money. These books offer advice and information on smart saving and investing, strategies for budgeting, and planning for retirement. But even when couples are able to get the information about what to do with their money, they often continue to disagree about how money is handled. Nearly 37 percent of couples responding to a poll conducted by Harris Interactive and PayPal told researchers that they argued more about money than they did about cleaning or sex. Couples today may be informed, but they are not *in touch*. And financial infidelity flourishes whenever there is a lack of a feeling of safety about what is happening with shared finances.

What I help these couples to see is that whether their financial infidelities take the form of secretive spending—characterized by lies and deceptions—or are flaunted through an outright affair with money and wealth, the effect on their relationship is nearly always the same. This financial misbehavior provokes emotional reactions and leads to the kind of "acting out" that destroys trust and undermines intimacy in all areas of their lives. A relationship without trust or intimacy is an empty partnership at best. And for many couples who have reached this stage, the result, as I have seen all too often, is that one or the other partner seeks an emotional connection elsewhere by embarking on a physical affair outside their relationship.

This kind of crisis, arising from an unwillingness or inability to feel safe about talking openly and honestly of expectations and emotions around money, does not just take its toll on established partnerships. I have many patients who, from the beginning of a new relationship, find themselves struggling with issues of commitment, trust, power, and intimacy that have somehow become entangled with their early attempts to discuss money and finance. These patients often wonder whether it is legitimate to be concerned about the spending habits or financial patterns of the people they are becoming emotionally involved with early on. Without exception, I tell them yes. What many of them don't understand is how closely money and intimacy are connected. I contend that it takes courage to love—and it takes courage and safety in communicating to break a long-held taboo and talk plainly about money. I tell these single patients that if their relationship *breaks up* over money, it would have broken up eventually anyway.

Too many couples are torn apart over a power struggle rooted in money and materialism. In the Harris survey cited above, 57 percent of respondents felt that money is used as a means of control in their relationship and I see the results of this power struggle in my office almost daily. I have seen women who went into relationships with the expectation that they would be cared for, both romantically and financially, who relinquished their financial freedom, only to be left heartbroken and without a financial cushion when the relationship fell apart. I have seen men who suffer from devastating fear of commitment and lack of trust after bitter divorces have run down their savings and continue to eat into their earnings. And while it takes two equally invested partners to create a strong, successful relationship, it also requires a healthy amount of self-interest balanced with unselfish behavior to create and sustain the balance that allows for compromise and fairness.

As my practice has evolved over the past ten years, I have come to see that couples need very specific tools and skills to learn to safely and effectively communicate about the role money plays in their relationship. As a result, I have adapted the Smart Heart skills and dialogue that I developed nearly ten years ago in my book *Adultery: The Forgivable Sin* to help couples reconnect after the pain of an adulterous affair. Smart Heart tools and dialogues are used to create the "glue" in a new relationship with no history and to help renew the passion for established couples. They are based in "attachment language," which most couples don't know how to use, but is necessary for partners to feel secure, safe, and intimate. These techniques allow couples to strengthen emotional bonds and promote the release of the same biochemicals that triggered the euphoric bliss of the "honeymoon" stage of their relationships. As couples become practiced in the Smart Heart art of empathetic, validating, open communication with a soft approach, they simultaneously build trust and intimacy while stimulating the "feel-good" endorphins that allow romantic feelings to flourish. Using these exercises to open safe dialogues about money helps couples learn to manage their emotions, expectations, and unspoken fears surrounding money and shared finances.

Whether you are in an established, long-term relationship or are just starting to date someone, when it comes to discussing difficult topics, talking about money and the role it will play in your relationship may be the hardest thing you learn to do.

Defining Your Relationship

Anyone who has ever negotiated a long-term relationship will tell you that the process is rarely one smooth journey from infatuation to happily-ever-after. In an earlier book, *Make Up, Don't Break Up,* I defined the eight stages of love that all couples move through. Some relationships end before the couple has gone through all the stages, other couples seem stuck in one particular phase, and still others progress through all eight stages, acknowledging the dynamics that arise as the necessary growing pains caused by changes needed to reach real love. The couples that successfully negotiate all eight stages are those who use challenges to their romance as catalysts for change. These couples are the ones who are successful at reaching the securely attached, committed, loving relationships most of us strive for. The case study below is a real-life example of how a couple I worked with navigated through their own version of these eight stages.

Stage 1 When Suzanne met Richard she called it "love at first sight." The two grad students met at a free film festival and were immediately struck by how similar their tastes in movies, art, and music were. And the sex? "Unbelievable" they both agreed. After they finished their degrees, they spent several months in Europe, backpacking and soaking up culture and falling under the romantic spell of being young, poor, and in Paris.

Stage 2 When they returned to New York, they moved in together and began the hard work of establishing themselves in their respective careers. Suzanne noticed that Richard didn't seem to be as ambitious as she was. She didn't want to push him, however, and believed that if she continued to be supportive of his "artistic" side, he would eventually move on to a strong career path. Richard had moments where he would think that Suzanne reminded him of his mother— always nagging at him to pick up around the apartment. Where was her bohemian side he had loved so much?

Stage 3 Suzanne continued to make money and Richard finally found work with a prominent director. When the film he was working on received international acclaim, he found himself in high demand and his earnings skyrocketed past

Suzanne's. Feeling successful and powerful, he proposed and she accepted. Once they were married, however, Richard began to attack Suzanne for her "nagging" and she began to withhold sex as a punishment for what she perceived as his "cheapness."

Stage 4 *Feeling lonely, physically isolated, and increasingly frustrated, Richard began an affair with an actress he met on the set of one of his films. Feeling guilty for cheating, he showered Suzanne with expensive gifts and took her on vacations and out to expensive dinners. Under his guilt-motivated attentions, Suzanne would relax her ban on sex. Both of them agreed it was still fantastic and for days afterward, Richard would wonder why he was continuing to pursue the affair with the actress.*

Stage 5 *Suzanne found out about the affair and left Richard. He did not want the marriage to end and they decided to come in for counseling. Despite the tension in the relationship, they admitted they still loved each other, although Suzanne was so hurt by the betrayal of the affair that she did not know if she wanted to remain married.*

Stage 6 *Through extensive counseling with me, both Richard and Suzanne came to see how their behaviors mirrored family experiences and how their relationship was first undermined by a power struggle centered around money and sex. Richard ended the affair and Suzanne agreed to a reconciliation supported by further counseling.*

Stage 7 *Although hormones can die down after the honeymoon stage, there are ways to rev up the chemistry again. Suzanne and Richard practiced some of these attachment skills and noticed immediate results. Their physical attraction to each other returned and by focusing on physical connection along with communication techniques, they were able to reconnect in an honest and open dialogue about money and shifting power roles in their relationship over time.*

Stage 8 *Several years later, Richard and Suzanne say their marriage is stronger than ever. They value the honesty they were forced to develop and are vigilant about safe and respectful communication. They made a conscious decision to stay in love.*

The Eight Stages

In the case study above, Richard and Suzanne were able to successfully negotiate all the stages of their relationship, including working
their way through financial and physical infidelity over the course of
several years. A deeper understanding of these eight stages will help you
to assess where you are right now in your own relationship and can help
you to identify potential trouble spots that may be on the horizon.

1. *Euphoria.* Sometimes referred to as the "honeymoon stage," this
   occurs at the blissful beginning of a relationship when everything
   about your new love seems perfect. You spontaneously connect in
   unexpected ways, your infatuation with each other does not require effort, and you both focus on the other person's positive
   traits (and frequently discount the negative ones). This early
   stage, which can last from the first date up to as long as eighteen
   months, is supported by the hormone-induced release of powerful neurotransmitters (vasopressin and oxytocin), which stimulate
   feelings of euphoria and contribute to the surge of positive emotions that make new love affairs literally intoxicating. There's no
   need for special communication skills or problem-solving
   techniques—the rush of hormones *does the work* of keeping you
   together!

2. *Magical Thinking.* As the endorphin rush of your love affair begins to subside, you are able to view your partner with a more
   clear-eyed perspective. However, rather than acknowledging the
   realities of similarities and differences that may cast a new mate in
   a less-than-ideal light, you gloss over these imperfections, invok-
   ing "magical thinking" in an attempt to continue the good feelings from the first euphoric highs of the endorphin rush. When
   your intuitive alarms go off, you choose to dismiss these internal
   caution signals, ignoring them as you insist to yourself that your

relationship is still perfect. Over time, this wishful but unrealistic expectation that if you simply ignore them, problems or disappointments will simply work themselves out, takes its toll on the relationship. People who can't move beyond this stage of magical thinking often suspect that they have "fallen out of love" with their partner.

3. **The Power Struggle.** When a couple is able to move through the Magical Thinking stage of a relationship and acknowledge that there is work to be done in order to move deeper into an intimate relationship, it becomes inevitable that power struggles will occur. As psychologist Harville Hendrix, PhD, tells us, *we pick a partner who will give us the most trouble.* A number of factors contribute to this phenomenon of picking partners who will challenge us in our unfinished business of childhood. In this stage, couples tend to focus on their differences and project frustrations onto each other. It can become difficult to see the good traits in the person who now annoys you so much. Because many of these frustrations stem from childhood—and possibly former romantic relationships—to successfully negotiate this stage, a couple must be willing to risk vulnerability. I tell couples I counsel that this stage is where relationships really begin to grow. Couples that confront and emerge from the Power Struggle stage do so with greater personal insight into themselves and each other and only then reach the next level of love and commitment with a more firmly cemented bond. Don't walk away from a relationship when this stage starts. You can't reach true love without navigating the Power Struggle stage.

4. **Transition.** In this stage, couples must decide whether or not to move on together or to move on to other relationships. This stage can be precipitated by an outside change, such as deciding whether to move in together, get married, buy a house, have a

child, change jobs, or go back to school. These transition times provide couples with an opportunity to understand how their family histories may influence decision making and allow them to learn to work together to arrive at a joint solution and a greater appreciation of each partner's courage and commitment to the relationship.

5. *Breaking Up.* Most couples reach a point in their relationship where one or both of them wonders if they shouldn't break up. Temporary breakups can last for a few hours, a few days, or even longer. Often, particularly in the case of long-term, committed relationships, a breakup can occur on an emotional level, even if the couple stays together physically. For couples who will benefit from a structured, limited, temporary breakup, I have created an exercise I call the "Brush with Death" that allows couples to experience the emotions and emptiness that result from loss and appreciate the essence of their partner. In this exercise, a couple willingly embarks on a purposeful physical and emotional disconnection, behaving exactly as if their partner or relationship has "died." The brush with death forces each individual to face and embrace the resulting—often terrifying—emotions of emptiness and sense of loss. This temporary "breakup" can last anywhere from a few hours, to a few days, to several weeks, to several months, but by the end, most couples realize they are willing and able to learn the skills necessary to keep their love alive. The fear of loss is essential to loving someone. By using a "breakup to makeup," couples experience a sense of urgency that propels them to get in touch with their deepest feelings. When a relationship is in crisis, the Brush with Death exercise offers the powerful opportunity for a couple to "let go with love" in order to resolve fears, become stronger, end power struggles, and realize just how important they are to each other and move from secure attachment, to desire, to romantic love.

In my practice, I have had a 98 percent success rate using this technique with individuals who need a real "jolt" to stop taking their partner for granted. When selfish, "narcissistic" people take their partner for granted, the endorphin rush caused by the breakup and the challenge from the loss can be the most effective way of working through a relationship in crisis. When a breakup is done thoughtfully and carefully, with love and respect, it can create a crisis for positive change and be used to *breathe new life* into a relationship that has resisted all previous attempts at change. Any kind of breakup is painful as it conjures up fears and anxieties not just related to the present relationship. For this reason, I frequently remind the couples I counsel that *getting rid of a person does not get rid of their real underlying problem.* Couples that work through this intense stage are able to move on and makeup to enjoy a relationship that is stronger and more meaningful in every way.

6. *Making Up.* After a breakup—or the "Brush with Death"—has occurred, the Making Up stage offers couples a second chance at a loving, intimate relationship. For this stage to be successful, a couple must view it as a fresh start, agree to set aside old impressions and grievances, and willingly accept change. There is no more taking for granted—you must see your partner with a "new face." When making up, couples work through the issues that caused their breakup using specific tools and dialogues to understand and resolve their conflicts. This stage allows couples to experience true connection. The Making Up stage lays the foundation for a satisfying, committed relationship.

7. *Reromanticizing.* In this stage, couples use their heightened feelings from the conflict and tension of the Breaking Up stage to create positive emotions and relearn how to feel romantic and passionate toward each other. By using rituals to re-create memories and romance and "tricking" themselves into *feelings* like those

they had when they first met, these couples are able to "fall back in love *again*" and re-create the initial magic and feelings of the Euphoria stage. Most couples that get to this stage in their relationship refer to it as their "second honeymoon" or "second chance!"

8. *Real and Lasting Love.* In this final stage, couples continue to grow, both individually and together in their relationship. They have learned how to *safely* "fight fair" to address conflicts and avoid power struggles. They understand the importance of making time for romance and playfulness in their lives. And they have a deep empathy for each other's troubles and struggles. Respect, balance, validation, and acceptance are hallmarks of this stage. Many couples report that they find this stage of their relationship to be as sexy as the early Euphoria stage because of the deeply intimate, yet safe bonds they have forged together. The work of remaining a committed couple continues, even at this ultimate stage, but the couples that have gone through the previous stages have come to value their relationship. Confident in the tools and Smart Heart skills they have learned as they worked toward this ultimate relationship goal, they are able to fully concentrate on enjoying each other and life.

For more than thirty years, I have worked to help couples understand how to safely and successfully navigate through these eight stages. I have provided them with the tools and techniques for effective and safe dialogue and taught them how to establish, or reestablish, a loving, intimate connection.

The Seven Steps

Over the past ten years, as the financial boom of the nineties has continued into the twenty-first century and our society has become increasingly materialistic, I have noticed a very interesting paradigm shift in the issues facing the couples I counsel. As patients became increasingly willing to delve into traditionally taboo topics such as sex and family histories, I noticed that they would often link these problems to their perceptions of their partner's spending habits or financial patterns. Money—who had it, how they used it, what they used it for—became an increasingly important social and emotional touchstone and a hot-button issue for many couples and a trigger for power struggles.

Over time, I began to consider these deep-seated differences surrounding shared finances as the catalyst, rather than the symptom, of the stated problem (an affair, unwillingness to commit, emotional distancing, etc.) that brought the couple to my office in the first place. They were using money as the vehicle to exit the relationship. In a fragile relationship I saw how money was keeping couples together or tearing them apart. I began to refer to this constellation of issues as "financial infidelity." It wasn't long before I could see that most money problems clearly corresponded to seven of the eight stages of relationships. While I define eight stages of relationships, there are only seven steps for resolving the attendant issues. That's because there's really very little need to talk about money during the Euphoria stage—most people just enjoy that hormone-drenched free fall for as long as it lasts. In fact, it's frequently an *issue with money* that arises to signal that the Euphoria stage is fading and that acts as a trigger for Stage 2: Magical Thinking.

It should be noted that many couples today are quickly moving through—or even skipping—the Euphoria stage. Divorces, failed long-term relationships, and introductions made over the Internet have made individuals more wary of relying on a purely emotional, chemical connection. For many couples beginning to date today, their stories about past relationships, emotional baggage, sexual concerns, and financial hardships are discussed from the beginning. I've had patients tell me about first dates where the conversations included harrowing tales of divorce and exes, assurances of sexual virility, and confessions about financial losses in the volatile stock market. Believe me, conversations like these can put the damper on the Euphoria stage and launch a person straight into the Magical Thinking or even the Power Struggle stage.

In order to give a potential relationship a fighting chance, it's particularly important to know how to participate in safe and smart dialogues around sensitive subjects. In my practice, I have seen that individuals who are struggling with financial issues in new relationships are better able to make clear-headed decisions about their long-term compatibility with their new love interest when they have the right tools for confronting and dealing with the topic of money. In fact, any couple—no matter which relationship stage they are in—is capable of improving even the most at-risk relationships.

While you may instantly identify the stage of your relationship from the list above, and be tempted to turn immediately to the corresponding step, I strongly encourage you to become familiar with each of the seven steps as a relationship may revisit a particular phase over and over again, until the couple fully understands how to change and move beyond it.

Step 1: Calculate the Cost corresponds to the *Magical Thinking stage*

Step 2: Examine Your Power Dynamic corresponds to the *Power Struggle stage*

Step 3: Divest yourself of the Past corresponds to a *Transition stage*

Step 4: Break Up with Your Money corresponds to the *Breaking Up stage*

Step 5: Define the Currency of Your Relationship corresponds to the *Making Up stage*

Step 6: Refinance Your Relationship corresponds to the *Reromanticizing stage*

Step 7: Invest in Your Future corresponds to the *Real and Lasting Love stage*

Many couples who come to me don't call and schedule an appointment because they think their relationship is suffering from a lack of communication around money issues. They tell me they are having problems in the bedroom, with cheating, with distancing behavior, or with trust or commitment. Nevertheless, nine times out of ten, before the first session is over, someone has brought up the topic of finances or how their partner handles money.

Other people I see are reentering the dating pool after years of marriage or are successful, unmarried individuals who, after accumulating their own wealth and professional achievements, are seeking an emotional connection. The issue of financial infidelity is just as relevant to these singles as it is to the married couples that seek my help. Just as increased risk of AIDS and STDs make it imperative to know your date's sexual history before embarking on an intimate sexual relationship, particularly in the current age of Internet introductions, online courtships, and "inflation dating," you also owe it to yourself to be informed about your date's financial status, family money, history, and habits before making a commitment to a future together.

Whether engaged, newly married, or living together, or single and dating, a certain amount of self-interest surrounding the matter of money is not just healthy, it is *critical to the health of the relationship*. Financial infidelity is a pervasive problem for most singles and couples today. If not defined, confronted, and addressed by both partners, it can be as detrimental to love, trust, and romance as any of the more traditionally recognized relationship crises, such as adultery. *The topic of money can no longer be taboo. Every couple, whether just beginning to date, living together, engaged, or married for years, must examine their relationship for the risk of financial infidelity.*

Financial Infidelity:
Are You at Risk?

If you recognize yourself or your relationship in any of the scenarios or evaluations at any relationship stage, don't panic. You can, on your own, and at any time in a relationship's evolution, begin to open up a safe, honest dialogue about money and its role in your relationship. As you use the seven steps to learn to discuss finances with your partner in a safe and intimate way, you will be surprised at the positive repercussions in other areas of your relationship. With few exceptions, couples I have worked with have discovered that once they could discuss money and work through harmful patterns of financial infidelity, their sexual and emotional connections were strengthened and they were able to trust the commitment and honesty of their relationships. They tell me that their relationships have more "sizzle"—they've become more spontaneous, both in life and in bed, once they are no longer afraid to talk about "hard" topics like money. When a relationship is truly flourishing and functional, you can talk to each other about anything at all—including money—without reacting negatively or shutting down.

For some couples, talking about money is a relationship "deal breaker." Others tell me that an inability or unwillingness to talk about money is making them "very nervous" about their relationship. When you understand the external pressures that drive even your most volatile disagreements about finances, you will be able talk about money without bringing painful memories or hurtful emotional accusations to the table. Many couples that come to me say they are afraid that they have "fallen out of love." Often I end up asking them to examine their attitudes toward shared finances. As they begin to understand that these attitudes can act as *triggers* for damaging assumptions and emotions, they are able to begin the process of reconnection.

In the rest of this chapter I will give you an overview of warning signs and common hallmarks of financial infidelity. I will help you determine if you are at risk of committing financial infidelity. I'll explain how your financial personality can affect your behavior with both money and your partner. I'll help you to see if problems in your relationship are linked to financial infidelity and tell you the warning signs that indicate that financial infidelity is increasing the risk that you or your partner will commit other painful betrayals.

Personal Risk Factors for Financial Infidelity

So, how can you tell if that handbag in your closet with the tags still on it represents a simple moment of weakness, the need for a "novelty high," or is an indicator of a pattern that can wreak havoc in your relationship and destroy your sexual and emotional connection with your partner? The test that follows addresses some of the most common emotions and behaviors associated with financial infidelity.

FINANCIAL INFIDELITY RISK PROFILE

1. Do you regularly lie about purchases or daily spending?
2. Do you regularly create and review a budget for spending with your partner?
3. Do you stash away money or pay cash for things without telling your partner?
4. Do you review monthly income and expenses with your partner?

5. Do you sometimes punish your partner by withholding money?
6. Do you know what investments (life insurance policies, stocks, retirement funds, etc.) you and your partner hold?
7. Do you regularly omit information about your spending?
8. Do you know the current balance of your checking and saving accounts (joint and individual)?
9. Do you regularly spend money when you feel emotional— happy, sad, angry, depressed, anxious, or worried?
10. Can you discuss money with your partner without fighting?
11. Do you wish you had private bank accounts?
12. Do you discuss major purchases with your partner?

SCORING

For questions 1, 3, 5, 7, 9, and 11, give yourself 2 points for every "yes," and 0 points for every "no."

For questions 2, 4, 6, 8, 10, and 12, give yourself 0 points for every "yes" and 2 points for every "no."

If your score is 0–6, you have a healthy relationship to money and its role in your committed partnership. Focus on the one or two questions where you gained points and make a conscious effort to discuss these money behaviors with your partner. If you maintain an open, safe communication about shared finances, you will strengthen trust, enhance intimacy, and increase emotional connection.

If your score is 8–12, money is a difficult subject in your relationship and it is likely you shy away from talking about it. The seven steps in this book will help you become aware of the underlying reasons for your money behaviors and help you to comfortably engage in open dialogue with your partner. It is critically important that you begin to pay attention to your attitudes and beliefs surrounding shared finances and work toward understanding whether your behavior with money is the symptom of another problem in your relationship or is in danger of driving your relationship toward an unhealthy dynamic.

If your score is 14–24, financial infidelity is damaging your relationship, and you should be considering couples therapy to try to save it. It is likely that you characterize your relationship as lacking in emotional and sexual connection and believe you have lost your romantic connection or "fallen out of love" with your partner. You need to act quickly to address the underlying causes and effects of your toxic relationship to money and begin to heal from the patterns of betrayal that have been established.

Social Pressures for Financial Infidelity

Mary and Jim came to see me shortly after moving in together. Within months after meeting the man she had initially called her "dream partner," Mary went from believing she had found a man of substance to worrying that she had become involved with someone who was little more than a charming liar.

> *"When I first met Jim, he seemed like such a romantic. He would bring me small presents, take me to restaurants he knew I loved, order champagne for no reason other than he claimed I deserved it. He dressed beautifully and drove a new Audi. We talked all the time about taking a long, romantic vacation in Venice. He promised that he'd make all my dreams come true. But now that I am committed to him and living in his house, he's completely changed his tune. He says that Venice is too expensive and that, while he'd happily take me somewhere for a long weekend, it would be irresponsible to dash off on a three-week trip to Italy. I feel like he lied to me. He made promises and now he's using money as an excuse. What else is he going to withhold?"*

> *"Of course I wish I could give Mary anything she wanted," Jim said. "Look at her." He gestured toward Mary, who was dressed in a simple but expensive Armani suit and wearing some significant jewelry (which I knew she had inherited from her grandmother, but which Jim apparently believed was her own). "She's got expensive tastes and she's clearly used to the best. When we first met, I knew I had to make her believe that I could take care*

of her. And I intend to take care of her. But we were talking about Venice months ago. The dollar is much worse against the euro now and it's just not a smart choice financially. Just because I participated in some romantic daydreams doesn't mean I'm made of money. Maybe she thinks I'm cheap, but how can I tell that she's not just a gold digger?"

The current social climate, in which it is perfectly common, even considered acceptable, to assess a person's worth based on his or her financial status and ability to acquire status goods, has no doubt contributed to the increasing role of money as a leading cause of relationship stress.

In my practice, I am now seeing generational differences in how couples approach the topic of money. Older couples, for the most part, tend to believe that finances should be kept private. They treat money as a secret, sacred topic, often failing to disclose their full financial situation. They are reluctant to share their thoughts and expectations around finances with their partner. Younger patients tend to use their money to advertise their worth. They are more likely to become embroiled in power struggles with their partner as they struggle to balance their reliance on an appearance of wealth with the demands of shared financial security. These individuals have come to associate high-ticket items such as luxury cars, designer clothing, and status addresses with personal worth. These are the patients who quickly become disillusioned or disappointed in a relationship when their new partner—who appeared to be wealthy and free of money worries—turns out to be all show and no substance where finances are concerned. People in these types of scenarios can suffer from feelings of betrayal when they come to feel that their partner has lied or been secretive or withholding when it comes to money.

Whenever someone feels betrayed in an intimate relationship, I see the same result: a loss of trust, a sense of anger, and a questioning of the security of their bond. In today's society, where money is frequently used for show, rather than security, simply owning a status item can make you *feel* as if you have more than enough money—and can make others treat you as if you are wealthy and worthwhile. If couples do not address the issue of money and finances quickly, openly, and consistently, it is not uncommon for one person, or both people, in a relationship to eventually feel he or she has been defrauded.

External Risk Factors for Financial Infidelity

While the traits of financial infidelity are deeply rooted in an individual's *personal* history with money, there are other factors that can highlight or magnify these types of betrayals. Professional, family, and personal stress and the "mundane" attachment stage certainly contribute to these volatile money behaviors. Anytime there is a shift in financial stability—regardless of whether money is increasing or decreasing—there is a danger of miscommunication or deception. The following situations represent the range of stressful situations in our average work, family, and personal lives that may function as catalysts for acts of financial infidelity. Review these lists and note if any of the scenarios apply in your current relationship.

Work Life

- Job changes: being fired or leaving to start a new job
- Significant change in compensation due to promotion, especially for women
- Retirement
- Work-related traveling
- Change in household career dynamic (from two incomes to one or vice versa) such as man deciding to stay home and become "Mr. Mom," while woman becomes major wage earner
- Increase in professional responsibilities; being a workaholic

Family Life

- Purchase of a new home / sale of an old one
- Downsizing of home

- Children attending nursery school, private school, or college
- Recent large purchase (boat, house, luxury car)
- Empty nest
- Birth of child
- Illness, medical expenses, or death of a parent or child
- Fertility treatments

Personal Life

- Changes in relationship status
- Problems with alcohol or drugs
- Decade birthday
- Midlife crisis or "burnout" (two thirds of all women who work outside the home usually work an additional thirty hours per week performing "domestic work," including child care and house-keeping)
- Significant change in investments (increase or decrease)
- Inheritance or disinheritance
- Desire for postnup, prenup, or no-nup

Relationship Risk Factors for Financial Infidelity

The emotional dynamic of your relationship plays an important role in your risk for financial infidelity. Understanding how you and your partner perceive and react to particular behaviors will help you to detect and confront financial infidelity.

Sex, Emotion, and Money

You are probably not surprised to hear that how you behave with money can reveal a great deal about how you approach sex and emotional connection. In fact, many of the couples in my practice come to me because of sexual infidelity, but end up spending their sessions fighting about finances and spending habits. The distinct personality traits that emerge in respect to an individual's approach to money often directly translate into how he or she treats sex and intimacy. I often tell my patients that if they are having problems with their sex life, their financial life is probably in poor shape, too. Likewise, if they are having trouble talking about money, then they are probably having the same kind of problems communicating in bed.

> Joan was in shock. She and her husband, Walter, had come to me for counseling after she discovered that he was having an affair with his secretary.
>
> "It's not even that she is young and good-looking," Joan railed. "She doesn't take care of herself the way I do. She dresses like someone's spinster aunt. How could you be sleeping with her?"
>
> Walter stared at his tall, rail-thin, platinum blond wife. I could practically see him making a running tally in his head: Botox treatments every six weeks—$1,500; private Pilates trainer four times a week—$1,600 a month; status handbag—$2,500.
>
> "Of course she doesn't look as good as you do," he shot back. "How could she? She doesn't spend every cent of her income on herself."
>
> "It's my money," Joan said. "I can spend it however I like to."
>
> "But it's my money that pays for the house you picked to live in and the car you choose to drive and the expensive wines you make me order every time we go out to dinner," Walter complained. "And what do I get out of providing for you like this? You don't say 'thank you' or acknowledge how hard I work to keep you in this lifestyle you love so much. In fact, you barely talk to me. I couldn't tell you the last time you gave me a massage or a hug, or kissed me when I came home in the evening. You won't even have sex with me! Maybe with Tessa, when I give her something, she gives something back."

Once Walter and Joan revealed this aspect of their relationship to me in therapy, it became clear that their major problem was not solely Walter's adultery. Joan's withholding and selfish personality, first revealed through her attitude toward their finances, and later in their relationship through her unwillingness to engage in emotional or physical closeness, had eventually motivated Walter to seek connection elsewhere.

This next test will help you to assess your "financial personality" so you can begin to explore how your attitude toward money may be influencing your sexual and emotional life. Financial infidelity is manifested not just in your checkbook—but in your bedroom and most intimate emotional connections as well.

FINANCIAL PERSONALITY PROFILE

If I got an unexpected windfall:

a)   I would tell my partner about it, but not discuss my plans for it.

b)   I would give my partner 10 percent and keep the rest.

c)   I would make that big purchase I've been craving; after all, I deserve it and it's my money.

d)   I would put it in a private bank account I have for just such possibilities.

e)   I never get windfalls, and if I did, I'd probably do something stupid with it.

f)   I could not wait to tell my partner first and fantasize about how and when to spend it as we celebrate.

How we manage our monthly budget:

a)   We give each person an allowance and that's it. No exceptions. Ever.

b)   My partner gets an allowance and needs to account for how it's spent.

c)   Whoever gets to it first can spend it.

d)   It's online, but only I have the pass codes.

e)   We don't have a monthly budget; if we have it, we spend it.

f)   We discuss weekly or monthly expenditures together and give each other guilt-free surprises frequently.

When planning vacations:

a)   It's always last minute; I never know if I can get off of work.

b)   I choose the locations, the hotel, and the activities and my partner comes along for the ride.

c)   I like to go wherever I feel like, whenever I feel like going.

d)   I think separate vacations for couples are a good idea.

e)   I can't remember the last time we went on vacation; there's always some emergency to wreck our plans.

f)   We put our relationship first, and spontaneous *and* planned vacations are an important priority for our time together.

On birthdays and gift-giving occasions:

a)   I don't see a reason to go overboard.

b)   We have a set limit on what we can spend on each other.

c)   I get my partner something—and often get myself a little something, too.

d)   It's a point of pride to get someone a gift they'd never expect and I always snoop around until I know exactly what mine is going to be.

e)   I'm horrible about remembering these kinds of things. I usually forget to get a gift and ruin the whole day.

f)   We check in with each other's wishes and sometimes go *with* the other to pick it out before the event.

About major purchases:

a)   I usually say we can't afford them; often I don't see the need.

b)   I do the research, comparison shop, and make the final decision.

c)   I usually get them right away. There's nothing wrong with a little splurge and there's always room on the credit cards.

d)   I buy them, but hope no one notices right away. If using a credit card, I try to buy at the start of the billing cycle so there are several weeks before the bill comes.

e)   I buy off-market or secondhand. Why should I spend a lot?

f)   I surprise my partner with "pictures" or window shopping and "check in" for joint decisions.

SCORING

If you chose mostly a's, your dominant financial personality trait is withholding.

Like Joan above, withholding personalities may keep large amounts of money for private use, while expecting their partner to foot the bill for joint expenses and large purchases. They are usually hoarders who may seek to acquire either material objects or increasing amounts of wealth. Individuals who withhold money from shared finances often are not physically affectionate and may withhold both sex and more general expressions of affection, such as kissing their partner hello or good-bye. (These regular physical interactions, which I call "miniconnections," are critical to the health of a relationship.) Withholders are often described as "unemotional" and rarely use words to express affection or praise. It is difficult to talk to a withholder, as they will generally "shut down" rather than confront unpleasant or difficult situations.

If you chose mostly b's, your dominant financial personality trait is controlling.

Brad and Shannon, who appear later on, provide a good example of how a partner with a controlling financial personality can significantly damage the relationship. Individuals who are controlling with money also tend to want to control sexual activity, often refusing to have sex unless they initiate it and using sex as a way to manipulate their partner's ego or self-image. Controllers are more likely to be hoarders, keeping close track of the value of both purchases and investments. They are emotionally very composed and will often walk away from situations that threaten to become heated. An individual with a controlling personality may often boast that they "never argue" in their relationship, and may not realize anything is wrong until the relationship is in crisis.

If you chose mostly c's, your dominant financial personality trait is impulsive/self-centered.

Those who can't control their spending or debt are unlikely to be able to control their sexual impulses or emotions. When it comes to finances, impulsive / self-centered personalities are also impulsive overspenders and are often characterized as "irresponsible" by their partners. For instance, an impulsive / self-centered person may not realize that her credit card debt affects her spouse's credit rating and may unconsciously jeopardize their shared financial security. Impulsive / self-centered individuals are sometimes considered "moody" by their partners because of their habit of switching from one emotion to another without apparent provocation. Sexually, impulsive / self-centered individuals may "overconnect"—being overly flirtatious, sometimes in inappropriate situations—and are often perceived as being overtly sexy in appearance.

If you chose mostly d's, your dominant financial personality trait is secretive/sneaky.

A closet full of unworn clothes, some with price tags still attached; a mad dash to get the afternoon mail to hide the credit card bills; or a furtive rifle through a spouse's wallet that's been left unattended are some of the most obvious signs of the secretive / sneaky financial personality. It's not a big stretch to imagine that the type of person who would lie to his wife about how much a new stereo costs would have little trouble lying about where he is on the evenings he gets home late from the "office" because he is having dinner (and sex) with a coworker. Secretive / sneaky personality types are generally emotionally repressed and exhibit passive-aggressive behaviors as their way of managing conflicts. This type of individual prefers to wait and see if they are going to be confronted about their behavior, at which point they quickly take a defensive position and return questions with personal attacks of shame and blame projections. The secretive / sneaky personality is constantly trying to balance the *thrill* of the behavior with the *guilt* it induces. This type of personality tends to be an overspender and is at greatest risk of financial, physical, or emotional infidelity simply because they are so lacking in ability to communicate openly and honestly.

If you chose mostly e's, your dominant financial personality trait is self-sabotaging.

One of the most extreme cases I've seen of this self-destructive personality type was my client Sheldon.

> *When Sheldon lost his business through a string of unfortunate events and questionable decisions, he became convinced that his wife of five years, Cassandra, was staying with him out of pity and was really attracted to men who made a great deal of money. Over and over again, he put her in a dangerous situation—he would encourage her to attend parties with him at the home of their neighbor, an incredibly wealthy man who had a reputation as an incorrigible playboy. Sheldon would encourage his wife to drink heavily at these parties and would make "jokes" with the host about how attractive Cassandra found him. It was only a matter of time until the inevitable happened: Sheldon "caught" a very drunken Cassandra passionately kissing the party's host. Although she was mortified—and frankly, too drunk to realize what she was doing—Sheldon threw the incident back at her repeatedly until, in a self-fulfilling prophecy, Cassandra decided to leave him, and they found themselves at my office in a last-ditch effort to salvage their relationship.*

As in the case above, those with a self-sabotaging financial personality have a self-destructive streak that comes out around money. They may be deeply in debt; they may repeatedly lose their job or jeopardize their self-owned businesses. Underlying this destructive behavior is an attitude that says, "I am a bad person. I deserve these bad things that happen to me." Self-sabotagers will often "act out" to trigger a crisis in their relationship to "prove" that a successful intimate relationship is something they cannot achieve or maintain. They often hold grudges, expecting that a single hurtful incident will inevitably be followed by others. Sexually, self-sabotaging personalities seek instant gratification without true emotional connection and are often characterized as oversexed.

If you chose mostly f's, your dominant financial personality trait is open and balanced.

You are not afraid to discuss money and finances with your partner and can easily separate money from emotions. You consciously practice financial fidelity in both your personal life and your relationship, and you have mastered your family legacy of money. Your healthy regard for your partner's feelings and respect for your shared finances has made you secure and wealthy in both your love life and our bank account.

Warning Signs of Financial Infidelity

When either person in a couple starts using money to try to cover what is missing in *themselves* (usually from childhood and displaced onto the relationship) or in the relationship, or to "get back at" or manipulate their partner through deceit or omission, they are committing financial infidelity. Whether they are shopping to fill up themselves or the hours left empty by a workaholic spouse, soothing feelings of abandonment or anger by "revenge spending," or flaunting irresponsible financial behavior as a way of "acting out" and forcing a confrontation, the person committing the financial betrayal is usually highly aware of the behavior and usually feels justified although they also feel guilt and shame.

Just as there are particular warning signs that indicate other troubles in a relationship, certain behaviors are tip-offs that you or your partner is in danger of financial infidelity. You need to consider if there is financial infidelity in your relationship if you or your partner has:

- maxed out credit cards
- excessive credit; always applying for new cards
- recently made or changed a will, without discussion

- bank accounts with cash missing or unaccounted for
- unexplained lawyer or therapy bills
- secret withdrawals from bank account
- unexplained credit card charges or balance transfers
- been secretive about money
- unexplained selling of stocks or bonds
- refused to discuss finances or unopened bills
- practiced "revenge spending" following a fight (the number one romance wrecker)

If you or your partner regularly engages in any of the behaviors above, chances are your relationship is being compromised and is manifesting this dynamic in various ways. Following the seven steps in this book can help you to identify your issues, safely open up lines of communication, and allow you to begin to move toward necessary healing in your relationship.

Facing Financial Infidelity

There is no doubt that financial infidelity is a very real and very *serious* problem for couples today. In our society of instant gratification and pleasure on demand, it is easy to default to using money as a way to soothe hurts and mask an empty relationship. Many couples, eager to be blame-free, will tell me, "We're just not 'in love' anymore." What I tell them is what I tell all of my patients: "Falling in love is easy. But staying in love? Staying in love is not for the faint of heart." For couples working through the pain of any relationship crisis, one of the biggest challenges is the sense that they have fallen "out of love" with their partner and the despair at not regaining those feelings. What they do not realize is that those loving feelings are not gone forever, but rather, they are "dormant" and can be accessible if the couple is willing to make the effort.

In the last ten years or so in my practice, I have seen an increase in the number of single men and women (often divorced, and frequently turning to online or matchmaking services as a way of reintroducing dating into their busy lives) who are seeking my advice as they try to navigate the complicated waters of dating and committing. For these—and any—newly formed couples it can be particularly difficult to know *when and how* to bring up the topic of money and finance.

There's no doubt that the culture of the 1960s and '70s, and even early '80s, laid the groundwork for people who are dating to comfortably address the topics of sex, politics, and religion. But even as consumerism has grown increasingly pervasive in our society, I find that couples—both married and dating—are still extremely uncomfortable and not knowledgeable about the language to use to broach the "private" subject of how much they earn, how they spend, and what they expect from their partner when it comes to money fears and other concerns.

In my experience I have seen that men tend to become very uncomfortable when asked to discuss their debt, fearing that having substantial amounts of debt make them look weak or may be interpreted as having a lack of control. On the other hand, women, especially those who earn less than their partners, are often reluctant to talk about spending habits.

Whether you are single and dating, divorced and dating, in a committed relationship but not living together, living together, pre-engaged, engaged, or married, if you refuse to acknowledge and explore the role money plays in your relationship you become vulnerable to the subtle and damaging effects of financial infidelity. Learning how to talk openly, honestly, and safely about money is *critical* to the health of any intimate relationship.

What to Do If You Suspect Financial Infidelity

Secrecy and deceit enable financial infidelity to continue. But many people are reluctant to confess to financial dishonesty because of the "fallout," or to confront a loved one with evidence of relationship-damaging money behaviors. When it comes to talking about money, most people experience shame, guilt, abandoment, and fear—usually a legacy from their childhood! These feelings provoke the normal temptation, or inclination, to lie, rather than open up, to loved ones about money. Make sure you don't give money the power of *noncommunication*.

When you ignore financial problems in your relationship you are allowing the money to define the relationship. By confronting or confessing financial infidelity, you will see that it's not the money that is harming the relationship—it is the *deception* that is damaging your love and intimacy. Unfortunately, most couples lack the specific attachment language skills to be able to talk about financial infidelity without finding themselves enmeshed in a frightening power struggle that can halt intimacy and make problems worse. Confronting, discussing, and working through toxic money issues using Smart Heart dialogue and techniques is the best way to save and strengthen your relationship.

How to Confront Financial Infidelity

If you know or strongly suspect that your partner is committing financial infidelity, the sooner you confront him or her, the better. As angry or hurt as you may be, the way you handle the confrontation is critical to being able to work through the conflict and repair your relationship. Be sure that you confront using only Smart Heart dialogue, as demonstrated below, with love, caring, and empathy for secure attachment.

- Be direct, but not critical.
- Set boundaries in a loving, empathetic way.
- Offer support.
- Remember to validate your partner's feelings.
- If your partner admits financial infidelity, ask if you can talk about it. Offer to talk about it lovingly, saying things like, "I'm sorry I was not there for you."
- If your partner denies committing financial infidelity, tell him or her that you refuse to engage in a power struggle over whether they did or didn't. *If one person thinks there is a problem, then there is a problem.* Tell your partner you want to work things out and suggest that both of you get help to bring intimacy back into your relationship.

- Make your partner feel *safe* by not judging or becoming angry. Be encouraging and loving and demonstrate why it's in his or her best interest to tell the truth. If your partner admits the truth, *don't throw it back in his or her face*. Offer to help after asking permission.

- Reassure your partner that you want to work things out and allow him or her to speak, while you remain calm and listen with unconditional love. (Don't forget your emotional "bulletproof vest!")

- Be compassionate. Your partner is probably feeling guilt or pain over their actions. He or she expects anger, not reassurances. Prove him or her wrong. The more you can ease your partner's *guilt*, the more productive your discussions will be.

- Do not make threats. Do not threaten to leave, especially after your partner has opened up. Don't close yourself up.

- Allow yourself time to grapple with your anger, hurt, pain, and remorse. Twice a day, take time out to brood so you can *compartmentalize* your feelings and they do not *contaminate* the rest of your day.

Smart Heart Dialogue for Confronting Financial Infidelity

The Wrong Way: "In the desk drawer I found bills for credit cards that you didn't tell me about and I'm surprised by how much debt we have that I was unaware of."

The Fear/Defensive Response: "Why are you blaming me for running up the credit card bills? We're not in danger of losing the house, so I don't see why you suddenly think my spending is a big deal."

The Right Way: "You must be so stressed and lonely. I know my working late nights and on weekends contributed to this, big time! I want to help you with a plan for the credit card debt that's accumulated, probably from your 'weariness.' Let's sit down and make a plan together. I really love you. . . ."

The Smart Heart Reply: "I'm afraid that you're going to be angry that our debt has increased because I've been spending on myself. I'm angry that you don't feel I deserve to treat myself well, and I'm afraid that you will leave and I will lose both your love and my financial security."

The Next Step—Using Attachment Language to Change the Climate: "I understand that you have been feeling abandoned. I realize that I have not been as available to you as I should be and that you've been missing me and I've let you down. I can even see how you thought that a new Louis Vuitton pocketbook would lift your spirits—and I know you were trying to fill up the emptiness I was making you feel. Let's return the expensive bag and splurge on a romantic overnight together. I love you and realize that we need to reconnect. Later we can talk about making a plan together for getting our finances under control."

How to Confess Financial Infidelity

To prepare for this talk, remind yourself that financial infidelity is often a symptom of an existing problem in a relationship or in yourself due to childhood or present stress, and that by bringing it out into the open you will be able to get to the real underlying problem, rather than focusing solely on money issues. The shame / blame game is a no-win situation. When you confess financial infidelity, your motive should be a desire to improve your relationship, not to ease your own guilt, vent anger, or get back at you partner.

- Be sensitive to timing. Consider your partner's mood, energy level, schedule and any events or crises he or she is already dealing with. If you're afraid to tell, or keep putting it off, consider making your confession in the safety of a therapist's office.
- Reassure your partner of your love. Remember to focus on the positive events and feelings in your relationship.
- Keep talking—and listening—for as long as it takes your partner

to react and process his or her feelings. Wear your "bulletproof vest" and use time-limited "appointments."

- Validate any feelings of betrayal or abandonment your partner may express.

- Tell the truth about whether you *can* or *intend* to stop your harmful money behaviors.

- Be willing to answer questions about the financial infidelity. Do not defend your damaging behaviors. *Do not deny, minimize, or avoid* your partner's feelings about your behavior.

- Apologize and show remorse, but *don't promise what you can't deliver and do not expect immediate forgiveness*. Allow your partner to process the shock, pain, or anger.

- Stop the behavior. Change your patterns. And ask for help from your partner.

Smart Heart Dialogue for Confessing Financial Infidelity

How to Bring it Up: "I love you so and I wanted so much to be a good breadwinner and give you the lifestyle you never had growing up. You mean the world to me. I really screwed up and you have every right to be furious with me. I need to tell you that I've been investing our savings in the stock market and I've made some very bad decisions trying to make a quick buck. As a result, we won't have enough money to take a vacation this year and I'm worried about meeting some of our other bills. I should have told you before, but I was hoping I could repair the damage without you finding out."

The Angry Response: "How could you jeopardize our future in this way? That money was mine, too. I make more money than you do, but always felt that we were equal partners. Is that why you took control? It's like you've have stolen from me. How can I trust you?"

The Power Struggle Fallout: "Whoever makes the money

doesn't necessarily have the control and I'm not sure who has the power in this relationship. I make the money, but you feel free to use it as you please without consulting me. Even if you feel inadequate because you don't earn as much, that doesn't give you the right to make yourself feel better by making *unilateral* financial decisions."

The Smart Heart Reply: "You do make more than I do and while I'm proud of your career, I also feel lonely when you work long hours and unimportant when my paycheck doesn't measure up to yours. I was feeling powerless and investing in the markets seemed like a good way to boost our savings and my self-esteem. I've been feeling inadequate and don't feel good about myself at all. I understand that you are angry that I have lied to you, and you feel like I have jeopardized our future. I totally get that. I love you and want to regain your trust. Let me show you the accounts and we can talk about how to make up the losses. I want to work through this together and promise that from now on we will discuss and share financial responsibility!"

Relationships in Crisis

Once you have acknowledged that financial infidelity is present in your relationship, you must immediately work to change the patterns and habits that have allowed the dynamic to develop and continue. As I have seen with many of the couples I counsel, ignoring the signs of financial infidelity inevitably leads to a domino effect, stimulating crisis after crisis in other areas of the relationship.

If you recognize aspects of your relationship in any of the scenarios above, or are surprised by your scores on the tests, then it's time to take action, no matter how intimidating it may be, to contemplate talking honestly and openly to your partner about the role of money in your relationship!

For the couples that come to me for therapy to save their relationships, it is *undeniable* that money is a hot topic. From a therapist's point of view, this is no surprise at all. Money is a potent symbol of power, security, and potential. *Our view of money is inextricably connected to a web of emotions that reach back to childhood and become integrated into our values and beliefs as adults.* Between committed couples, disagreements about money can be more passionate than arguments about sex or emotional connection. These conflicts are often deal breakers in a relationship—though they don't have to be!

In my book *Make Up, Don't Break Up*, I talked about how affairs and infidelity affected my parents' relationship—and later the choices I made as an adult about who I would become romantically involved with. Over the years, as I came to understand more about the link between financial infidelity and other kinds of deception, I also realized that financial infidelity played a significant role in my parents' dance of betrayal.

My father had his own business, and financial stability was never a certainty in our home. While my mother certainly knew that my father's love of gambling could further destabilize the family finances, she never appeared to worry about money. Whether we had it or not, it didn't matter. She would spend whatever was there and patiently wait until my father made—or won—some more money. And then she would spend that, too. She didn't just spend on herself. She spent on us kids, the house, and lavish meals—whatever she felt like.

My father had a very similar way of thinking about money. If he had it, he'd spend it. He knew that my mother was spending as freely as he was, but he never asked her to account for it. Unless she was, in his opinion, overspending on us children. Then he might become frustrated—asking her why she was spending on us, at the risk of shortchanging herself. What others might have attributed to a profound wish to keep my mother well provided for, I now understand was influenced by the guilt of my father's own infidelities. He never confronted my mother; she never confronted him. And their vicious cycle was perpetuated for another generation, as I discovered when I was forced to come to grips with the financial infidelity that occurred in my first marriage.

For my parents, it took a severe crisis to make them admit and confront the emptiness within themselves, and within their marriage—an emptiness that had allowed them to unconsciously collude with each other in these behaviors that were so damaging to their marriage, and their family.

As I saw firsthand in my parents' marriage, it can be difficult to unravel the complexities of betrayals to determine whether financial infidelity is a symptom of another problem in the relationship or is, instead, the cause of other, more obvious types of betrayals. Financial infidelity can take either of two forms. The individual practicing financial infidelity can easily transfer those cheating behaviors into the emotional or sexual areas of the relationship. Conversely, one partner's financial indiscretions can drive the other to retaliate in other arenas.

What should be kept in mind, at all times, is that any kind of ongoing affair or betrayal can only continue through an unconscious—or occasionally conscious—collusion by all the parties involved. Financial infidelity, whether it occurs as a symptom of a larger relationship problem or it acts as a catalyst for an emotional crisis, does not occur in a vacuum. In working through the hurt and anger that underlie a betrayal, it is important to not characterize one person as the perpetrator and the other as the victim. Both perpetrator and victim must equally share the blame.

Financial Infidelity as a Symptom of a Relationship Crisis

Financial infidelity that is expressed in a power struggle over money is often an indicator that something *else* is wrong in the relationship or inside the individual. For example, when Monica found out that her husband, Eric, was having an affair, she started checking their bank account and credit card balances almost daily. Every time there was a new, unexplained expense, she would note the amount and then, once a week or so, go on a shopping spree.

"In a way, I thought spending Eric's money gave me some power over the affair," she admitted. *"I thought that the more I spent, the less he'd have for his mistress."*

Eric never confronted his wife, although it was clear her spending was rap-
idly spiraling out of control. "The fact that he knew what I was doing but
was afraid to call me on it made me feel powerful, too," she said. "He was
also having to work incredibly hard to meet all the bills. I could almost fool
myself into thinking that I didn't care if he was cheating on me because this
'money mistress' had power and revenge through his wallet."

If you can identify times when you use money because you feel angry at or hurt by your partner's actions, your financial infidelity is com-
pounding preexisting problems in your relationship. The seven steps in
this book will teach you how to separate your own relationship to
money from the issues that are damaging your relationship.

Financial Infidelity as a Cause of a Relationship Crisis

When an individual's financial personality results in a couple's shared
finances becoming the vehicle for negative communication, the result is
often "acting out" in other areas of the relationship. Dave and Lynn
came to see me because Lynn, according to Dave, "out of nowhere demanded a divorce."

"Dave makes all the money. Dave controls all the money," Lynn complained
in an early session. "He gives me an allowance, he tells me how much I can
spend for groceries—he even reviews my cell phone bill!"

"She's never said a thing about this," Dave protested. "I thought that she
liked that I took care of all the finances, that she never had to worry. It's not
an 'allowance'—it's a budget; I thought I was giving her the freedom to spend
the money we had available in the ways she thought best. When I went over
the bills with her, it was to help her see where she could manage the budget
better.

"I don't understand," Dave continued. "Lynn is a very critical person.
She is always making negative comments about the way I dress, about how I
need to lose weight, about how unimaginative I am in bed. But we never fight
about money."

When I asked Lynn why she never brought up the money issue, which obviously so deeply disturbed her, her reply was that it wasn't a matter of money—it was a matter of trust. Dave's controlling behavior made her believe he did not trust her. It wasn't long before she made the jump from not feeling *trusted* to not feeling *loved*.

When your behavior with money has a negative effect on your partner and your relationship, I can guarantee that more common betrayals are likely to follow if you don't address the issue. The seven step program that follows will teach you how to communicate clearly and honestly about the role of money in your relationship and can prevent a money crisis from triggering other betrayals.

Financial Infidelity as an Addiction

In some cases, the financial infidelity in a relationship may be indicative of the serious problem of an individual's chemical imbalance caused by a power struggle or work or life stress. When I am talking to some of the couples I counsel about their feelings when beginning an affair, they often use descriptions like "sexual chemistry" and "irresistible attraction." Some even compare their craving for their lover to an addiction. They can't get enough. They feel high. Their descriptions verge on sounding like passages from a romance novel. And yet, there's some validity to their clichés. In fact, studies have shown that certain repetitive or addictive behaviors are both caused by, and contribute to, fluctuations in mood-stimulating chemicals, called neurotransmitters, in our brains.

In part 3 of this book, I'll discuss the work I've done with a prominent physician to analyze and regulate the levels of these naturally occurring chemicals in many of my patients. There is ongoing interest in understanding the biochemical drives toward particular behaviors and new research is appearing all the time.

If you are worried that your behavior with money is out of your control, you may want to discuss with your doctor whether medical intervention may be appropriate and seek individual counseling through an addiction recovery program. Couples therapy with an emphasis on behavior modification can help to heal the wounds the addictive behaviors have caused in your relationship and teach you and your partner how to regain trust and repair intimacy.

The Risk of Physical Affairs

As you will see in the example that follows, financial infidelity is just one step in a toxic choreography. Acting out through finances is a way to wake up and shake up your relationship. Cheating on your partner with money contributes to a mindset that makes it easy to rationalize cheating on your partner with a lover. Financial infidelity is, without a doubt, a wake-up call to fix your relationship. By first giving careful consideration to whether it is a symptom or a cause of other issues, you can then determine the most effective way to approach your partner. Opening a safe and honest dialogue is the first step in healing a damaged relationship and reclaiming the true emotional intimacy necessary to maintain a committed relationship.

When a cycle of financial betrayals becomes entrenched, it is often just a matter of time before other areas of the relationship are damaged as trust is eroded, communication compromised, and emotional disconnection begins to take place.

Take, for example, the case of Brad and Shannon:

> Shannon had been working as a model when she met Brad, a successful hedge fund manager, and he was very proud of his much younger, gorgeous, sexy wife. But Brad was extremely controlling in aspects of their relationship, including how Shannon spent both her own money from her work and the money Brad contributed to their household.
>
> "Brad insisted I stop working as a model once we were married," Shannon said. "I think he was jealous when I would go out on shoots. But he demanded that I take care of myself as if I were still booking cover shots."
>
> With Brad footing all the bills, Shannon spent her days working out and taking care of her hair, her nails, and her skin. He encouraged her to spend afternoons shopping for expensive outfits, but often made her return things he

didn't like. Brad was quick to tell her if Shannon was wearing something he thought was unflattering, but he rarely gave her compliments or expressed his appreciation of her well-toned body, even when they were in bed.

The more Brad exhibited these controlling behaviors, the more resentful Shannon became.

"When Brad told me to return things, I didn't," she said. "I'd take the tags off and hang them in my closet and wear them months later—or not wear them at all."

She started going through Brad's clothes before taking them to the dry cleaner and keeping whatever money she found—twenty dollars here, a hundred dollars there. Then she would spend the money on things she knew Brad would consider frivolous.

The final straw, and what drove them in to see me, was when Shannon started a casual affair with one of the trainers at her gym, a guy who constantly gave her the positive reinforcement about her looks that she needed in order to feel attractive—and that Brad could never seem to provide.

As Brad and Shannon began the hard work of repairing the trust between them and rebuilding their relationship, they learned that all the warning signs for an affair had been present, but because they thought their tensions revolved around money—something "happy" couples didn't discuss—they were unable to communicate openly and see how Brad's controlling behavior had resulted in Shannon's financial, and later physical, infidelity.

If, after reading these pages and assessing the likelihood of the financial infidelity in your relationship, you suspect that your partner may have moved—or been pushed—from cheating with money to cheating with a lover, consider the following warning signs, listed below, that I use as hallmarks for the likelihood of adultery in a relationship.

Warning Signs of a Physical Affair

- A sudden interest in investing money in personal trainer or expensive gym

- Extreme attention to personal grooming: clothes, hair, cosmetic surgery
- Withdrawal from, or increased interest in, sex and touching, new sexual techniques
- Unexpected gifts (because of guilt)
- Doing good deeds (unprompted help with household chores)
- Unusual or extravagant presents or trips
- Regular, unexplained lateness, missed appointments, lying about whereabouts (missing in action)
- Intercepting mail and phone calls
- Increased time online and insistence on privacy while using Internet
- Increased fault-finding or provoking fights

If any of these behaviors suddenly appear in your relationship, the risk of a physical affair is very high. Your partner may not yet have acted on the impulse to seek emotional or physical fulfillment elsewhere, but ignoring these obvious danger signals or taking a passive-aggressive, grudge-holding stance will only push him or her further into dangerous territory.

In any relationship, an affair of any kind—financial, physical, or emotional—must be considered a wake-up call to action. If your relationship has moved into this crisis state, you must commit to hard work to save it.

When you work through the seven steps that follow in the next part of the book, you will learn that working at staying in love with your partner is the most rewarding work you can do. Honest, safe communication through Smart Heart dialogue between partners is the critical tool in maintaining a successful, committed, intimate relationship. By using these techniques and suggestions for opening a dialogue to help you confront the damaging cycle of financial infidelity, you and your partner can acknowledge the present and childhood wounds it has caused and begin to work together to heal the damage.

PART II

The Seven Steps

As you work through each of these seven steps, you will embark on a voyage of discovery and honesty that will strengthen the trust and intimacy in your relationship. Reclaiming the passionate feelings of romantic love is possible when you work at restoring the magic of an intimate relationship on a *daily* basis. And while your bank account will most likely benefit from discovering the importance of financial fidelity, an equally important benefit is that you will be able to reclaim—and retain—the sexual and emotional connection you crave from your partner.

Each of these steps offers exercises and dialogue modeled on the Smart Heart techniques that I created and have successfully used in counseling couples in crisis. Although the Smart Heart tools were originally created to provide guidance for couples struggling with emotional issues around fidelity, I have found them to be equally effective in dealing with the emotional and physical conflicts that surround money matters. These proven tools for intimacy can be applied at every stage of a relationship. Remember: *Smart Heart skills create the glue that holds a new relationship without history together, and they are the glue used in renewing the bonds of an established partnership.*

Smart Heart Dialogues

Psychologists agree that one of the most important components of any successful relationship is a *secure attachment*. In early childhood development, secure attachment refers to the strong emotional bond a child develops with a parent or primary caregiver. This bonding allows children to develop empathy, trust, security, and independence. In adult relationships, secure attachment is characterized by a strong emotional affiliation, trust, responsiveness, and accessibility. Securely attached couples have a relationship that serves as both a secure base and a buffer against distress.

In a relationship, when one person's need for comfort, closeness, and security are not adequately met—whether by the partner's "wounding" words or actions—their secure attachment can be injured. These "attachment injuries" can be repaired when couples learn how to use *specific attachment skills and language.*

The Smart Heart skills and dialogues teach attachment language. They promote safe, open communication that is marked by empathy, affirmation, and a sharing of emotions, meanings, and goals. Smart Heart dialogue fosters self-honesty. It disarms defensiveness, addresses concerns without damage, verbalizes the *unspoken*, and allows you to interpret *clues* of your partner's. You cannot achieve true intimacy until you can divine your partner's thoughts. Whether dating, living together, engaged, pre-engaged, or married, Smart Heart skills and dialogues *give you a window to your partner's soul*. They create the glue to hold new relationships together. With no room for game playing, hiding, or deception, Smart Heart dialogues and skills allow you to build a relationship history based on empathy and respect. *It keeps you connected and reconnected to yourself and someone else.*

Even securely attached couples can become complacent in the way they communicate. They may substitute shorthand and assumptions for meaningful, safe, and open communication. Using Smart Heart language, they are able to predict, prevent, prepare for, and overcome problems before they occur. You learn to look for feelings, intentions, and expectations that are not expressed. Communicating with Smart Heart dialogues and skills conveys a directness and genuine interest and replaces language patterns that have grown dismissive, preoccupied, or defensive. It prevents escalation of conflict by containing negative emotions and responding to concerns in a positive way. For all couples, Smart Heart skills and dialogues *renew* respect and empathy. And as my mentor, Dr. Fogarty, always said, "Without respect and empathy, there cannot be true love."

Each step also ends with suggestions for *jump-starting* a productive dialogue about finances and your relationship. These tips will help you to open discussions around hot-button topics, creating a safe space for conversation and helping you remain connected to your partner when addressing sensitive subjects.

I recommend that you work through each of these steps in order to fully explore, discuss, and understand all areas that may contribute to financial infidelity. Many of the exercises in these steps are meant to facilitate deep discussion and intense emotional exploration. Take your time and be sure to allow for times when you or your partner may need to *disconnect* if the exercise or dialogue becomes too intense, particularly for men, who have shorter attention spans due to "physiological discomfort" when it comes to conflict. Becoming "stuck" on one particular step may indicate a deeply entrenched negative pattern in your relationship. In these cases, try to look at the larger picture: Which of the eight stages of relationships characterizes your current situation? What financial personality are each of you? How might these factors be contributing to your inability to move beyond a particular behavior surrounding money?

Each time you complete one of the exercises described in these steps, be sure to reconnect with each other. Reconnect emotionally, by verbally expressing love and respect for one another. Reconnect physically with touch, hugs, wrestling, tickling, or—best of all—lovemaking. You will soon find that when discussing money and finances becomes associated with pleasurable interactions, it stops being a chore you dread.

Step 1:
Calculate the Cost

What the Balance Sheet of Your Relationship Reveals

A balance sheet can reveal at a glance the general financial health of a corporation or an individual. It allows financial managers to quickly assess assets, liabilities, and net worth, and alerts them to any potential problems that exist or are likely to occur. A business owner will usually review his or her company's balance sheet on a monthly basis, but many individuals do not follow the ebb and flow of their net worth so closely. And when it comes to shared finances, the information may not even be equally available to both partners.

When financial infidelity is present in a relationship—for instance, when one partner does not tell the other about work-related bonuses, but rather banks them in a separate account; when one partner is in the habit of overwriting checks at the grocery store and pocketing the cash; or when either partner uses money or spending as a way of "keeping score"—it is not just your bank account that is harmed. Participating in a regular review of the relationship's financial *and* emotional balance sheets is the first step in identifying and treating these issues.

Magical Thinking

In any relationship, whether a marriage of twenty years or a hot new love affair of two weeks, it is important that you pause and take stock of your connection on all levels. The fact is, once the hormone-induced Euphoria stage of a relationship begins to wane (anywhere from weeks to months into it), then being "in love" becomes an *intentional* decision. True love and intimacy take effort, yet most people are surprised when I point out to them how easily the heady euphoria of a love affair is unconsciously replaced by the potentially damaging patterns of the Magical Thinking stage.

When hormonal "love chemicals" are not clouding your brain, it is unavoidable that you begin to take a clear-eyed look at the partner you have chosen. You may have to admit that the "perfect" person you fell head over heels in love with is a mere mortal with all the flaws and weaknesses of an ordinary man or woman. Even soul mates can have differences and, ironically, it's often these *differences* that subconsciously attract us to a person in the first place.

According to Helen Fisher, PhD, a research professor and member of the Center for Human Evolutionary Studies in the Department of Anthropology at Rutgers University, who specializes in the areas of human sex, love, and marriage, we are genetically attracted to mates who are as different from us as possible. Acknowledging and accepting these differences is the key to nurturing a healthy relationship. Unfortunately, in order to avoid the admittedly challenging task of initiating or maintaining honest communication some people resort to magical thinking in order to convince themselves that their "perfect relationship" continues to be without flaw. In order to understand how magical thinking contributes to various types of financial infidelity, you must first examine the role that magical thinking may already play in your relationship.

In psychology, "magical thinking" refers to the nonscientific reasoning an individual may rely on to "wish" situations into being or to practice denial when faced with unpleasant scenarios. If you have ever worried that you've somehow "cursed" an ex by wishing bad things would happen to him or her, or daydreamed about how your current partner would suddenly—and without prompting—become a dynamic lover, then you have practiced magical thinking.

The phrase is also commonly used when discussing early childhood development. It describes the thought processes during the period between the ages of about eighteen months and about eight years old, when a child creates imaginary worlds and playmates and fully participates with these constructs. It's like magic: "Abracadabra!" When you're a child you can believe that just thinking of something will make it happen. For some this continues into adulthood: for instance, an extreme example of magical thinking in financial infidelity would be gambling.

Of course, as an adult, you might observe a child sharing his lunch with an imaginary dog that follows him everywhere. And while the child might frantically insist upon two cookies (one for him, one for his "pet") it's easy to simply ascribe the behavior to the active imagination of a developing mind. Nevertheless, it is surprising how many adults subscribe to similar behavior. If you've ever had a friend tell you to "stop fooling yourself," you can be sure you've been engaging in magical thinking.

One of the most common, and detrimental, types of magical thinking that occurs in relationships is when one partner or both partners begin to believe that specific words can directly affect their world, and that by saying things aloud, they will irrevocably change their relationship. I want to be clear that I am not talking about having a dialogue or conversation. I am talking about when one person believes that simply saying the word "sex" or "money" will irrevocably alter the relationship. This belief is common, especially in relation to money, and couples will try to avoid conflict or prevent change by *not* talking about the topic, or by using euphemisms or ignoring money responsibilities, by not opening bills or by paying cash so as not to leave a trail, for instance.

"I can no longer have this relationship," André announced. A handsome man in his late fifties, he had been living and working in the United States for the past five years. "I want to go back to France. I'm going to try to make things work with my wife."

"You promised you would take care of me," Rachel said. She and André had been involved for the past three years. A successful businesswoman, she

had given up her marriage and a flourishing career in order to travel with him and to spend the summer months in Monaco at his vacation home. I had been seeing them for the past year.

When they first came to see me, both of them claimed to be happy with the arrangement. André felt it was perfectly normal to have a mistress—after all, he was accustomed to having whatever he wanted—and Rachel was clearly enamored of his wealth and the trappings associated with it.

"I asked him straight out if he would take care of me, but now that I have given up my career, my husband, and my home, he is telling me that I need to be independent," Rachel said.

"I have taken care of you," André insisted. "I've bought you jewelry and expensive clothing. You live in my apartment in Chicago when I am in France and in my apartment in Paris when we are there."

"But now you're threatening to leave me and go back to your wife," Rachel said. "What am I supposed to do? I've given up three years of my life because you said you'd take care of me."

"I'm not legally bound to support you for the rest of your life," André said. "We are not married. I am free to be as generous with you as I choose to be. Nothing more."

When I asked Rachel if she had ever talked to André about arrangements for her care if the relationship should end or if something should happen to him, she admitted that she didn't want him to think that she was only interested in him for his money.

"I was afraid that if I mentioned money, it would ruin our romance," she said.

And it did!

By avoiding the topic of André's wealth and her expectations surrounding it, and asking instead if he would "take care of her," Rachel was able to interpret his assurances in a way that made her feel secure. When she asked him if he would take care of her, she was thinking about marriage and financial support. She really wanted to know if he was going to leave his wife and marry her. She did not want to think about what would happen to her if the relationship were to end, and was afraid to bring up the topic of money. Magical thinking kept her from asking direct questions and allowed her to believe that André's assurances that he would take care of her meant she would never have to worry about supporting herself—that even if they never married, he would treat her as if she were his wife.

While most couples do not find themselves in such an extreme situation, many people, especially in the early stages of a relationship, feel uncomfortable or believe that it is rude or unnecessary to directly address the issue of money and wealth.

Asking vague questions such as, "Are you comfortable with your quality of life?" rather than, "What is your net worth?" or, "Would you give me anything you could?" rather than, "Will you pay for my plane ticket to go to Paris with you this weekend?" allows the person asking the question to hear the answer that he or she wants to hear. This type of open-ended questioning is identified in scientific cognitive studies as "confirmation bias." It means, essentially, that people who are practicing a form of magical thinking will attempt to confirm, rather than test, what they are hoping. "Yes, I'm comfortable" may mean that your date *likes* living with his mother in her house. "Of course I'd give you anything" may mean, "Anything I can afford, which is not much."

Many couples that I counsel have lingered in damaged relationships, continuing to believe that "everything will just work out." They have held on to this belief for so long that they have become disconnected from the realities of their partnership and from each other. What I tell these individuals is that *when one of them begins to actively seek change, then the relationship will change.* I acknowledge that change can be scary and that once begun, the work of being *proactive* and direct requires courage and commitment. But it is a fact of life that if we want something, we have to give something. And it is this negotiation and compromise that is the foundation of a strong and lasting intimate relationship.

The danger of refusing to address the habit of magical thinking in a relationship is that the resulting emotional disconnection can drive one or the other partner to seek connection elsewhere. It is in this Magical Thinking stage where many people try to decide whether they should settle for the unfulfilled relationship they have found themselves stuck in. And, in fact, at this stage, many couples break up or suffer from affairs. In the case of André and Rachel, they did not have what it takes to overcome their fear of closeness. Otherwise, money would not have been the deal breaker in their relationship. It was their fear of commitment after they could no longer sustain magical thinking that caused the end of the relationship.

When magical thinking becomes the default solution to dealing with difficult money issues in a relationship, it is all too easy for patterns of financial infidelity to develop. The exercises in this step are intended to take the "magic" out of thinking about money and help you and your partner to communicate plainly about the dollars that you share.

Are You Prone to Magical Thinking?

At some point or another, almost all of us have used magical thinking to give us the confidence to go on when a relationship hits a rough patch. Most people are able to move through this stage by taking risks to confront their partners. They realize that heated discussions, arguments, even passionate fights are part of the process of negotiating the differences between two individuals. They are able to set aside the fear of abandonment and be courageous instead of comfortable, proactive instead of defensive. They realize that when two people become entrenched in a behavior pattern, one of them must change in order to break the pattern. There are no "magical solutions" (except for those people still in the honeymoon stage).

When it comes to money, most adults pride themselves on their practical approach to handling their own finances. But when it comes to cooperatively managing shared resources in an intimate relationship, I have seen even the most savvy financial managers—individuals who handle negotiations, investments, and expenditures of huge sums of money in their careers—engage in magical thinking, rather than initiate discussions about money with their partners.

To find out if you practice magical thinking to ease concerns about money, ask yourself the following questions:

- Are you a gambler?
- Do you expect to win if you buy a lottery ticket?
- Do you believe it's just as easy to find a rich spouse as a poor spouse?
- Do you believe you can influence your financial situation, or do you think that things will eventually "just work out"?
- Do you avoid discussions about money?
- Do you feel financially secure, even if you don't have money put away?
- Do you still feel nervous about your future, even though you are financially prepared?
- Do you believe that appearances let you know whether a person you are dating does or doesn't have money?
- Do you find yourself daydreaming about a sudden scenario that will change your financial picture (for better or worse)?
- Do you believe that if a bank is willing to give you a loan, you are capable of repaying it?
- Do you pick pennies up from the sidewalk because you believe you will be able to save for a vacation that way?
- Do you believe a college degree is a guarantee of a good income?
- Do you believe that as long as you are working at a responsible job you can afford a new car or other major purchase, regardless of your balance sheet?
- Do you believe colleges will give you or your children significant financial aid because you have large amounts of debt?
- Do you believe bankruptcy is a way to get out from under your personal debt with no real consequences?

- Do you believe it's okay to carry high personal debt because "everyone else does"?
- Do you believe that if you don't open a bill, you don't have to pay it that month?
- Are you late with bills, even though you have the money to pay them on time?
- Do you believe that you should always stretch yourself to have the best house, car, or personal technology available?
- Do you purchase status items because they make you feel "rich"?
- Do you put high-ticket items you really can't afford on your credit card because it's not like spending "real" money?
- Are you "keeping up with the Joneses" even if it puts you in debt?

Choosing to ignore the plain facts about the ways in which you avoid the topics of debt, spending, and saving can be just as detrimental to a relationship as engaging in magical thinking in order to deny or ignore emotional or physical red flags.

Keeping the Balance

In the case of financial infidelity, couples are not open and honest about how they are spending shared finances. In some cases, such as Monica and Eric, who I mentioned earlier, the trust in the relationship has already been eroded and one person is using money to even the score.

"I knew my husband was having an affair, but we were trying to work things out," Monica said. "Because I pay all the bills, I started thinking about how much money he was spending on his mistress, buying her things like flowers and dinners at fancy restaurants and paying for her to stay in hotels. Even though he said the expenses were all for work, I knew what those charges were really for. And for months I had to look at them. After awhile I just felt like he was throwing the fact that he had a girlfriend right in my face

day after day. I started keeping track of how much he was spending, and every time he spent on his mistress, I spent the same amount on myself (my 'money mistress') without telling him. He never knew what I was doing until he got laid off. Then he found out that I had gone through our savings and run up our credit card debt sky-high. He says losing his job was a wake-up call and he's afraid to lose me. He's left his mistress, but I don't even care. He's a cheater with no money. Why stay with him?"

"You kept separate accounts, you invested in secret, you hid money from me, and now I find that $15,000 is missing from our joint account," Eric said. "I may have committed adultery, but this is worse. I could compete with another man for your love, but how can I trust you when you have put me at such financial risk?"

Not all cases are such examples of direct payback, but for many people "revenge spending" is a way to soothe hurt feelings and convince themselves that they are finding a way to *balance* the painful behavior. In the case above, Monica's revenge spending allowed her to believe she was paying her husband, Eric, back for his bad behavior. If there is any hope for saving the relationship, she is going to have to admit that by using their shared savings to inflict financial pain as a way to get even for the emotional pain her husband caused her, she was, in effect, *cheating just as much as he was!*

In more subtle cases, one person might make a spontaneous or significant purchase that puts their shared budget in distress. The person may justify the behavior by acting like a victim of overly stringent rules about spending, or rely on guilt to manipulate his or her partner into agreeing to excuse the financial "slip." When this type of pattern is repeated over and over again, it is inevitable that *resentment* and *distrust* will begin to influence how the couple interacts around money. If one partner continues to find loopholes for spending, the other may begin to feel entitled to spend an equal amount and the shared budget will soon be in shambles. In other couples, such spending patterns engender a cycle of nagging, lies, and distrust that eventually undermines *all* aspects of the relationship.

In order to prevent financial infidelity, a couple must learn how to find a balance between love and money. Working together to set financial goals while understanding the emotional motivations behind spending and saving money can prevent magical thinking, promote "financial fitness," and eliminate "scorekeeping" in your relationship.

Your Financial Balance

The two exercises that follow will help you and your partner arrive at an equal understanding of how money is spent and saved in your relationship. When creating your balance sheet and budget, focus only on the numbers. Do not become drawn into discussions about who earns the most money, the value of household labor, or the cost of child care (for those in a one-income relationship). Don't digress into talks about the merits of spending versus saving, and do not use this time to express any fear or anger you have over how shared finances are being allocated. In this exercise you must make a conscious effort to divorce emotion from money and simply deal with the numbers without judgment.

Creating a Balance Sheet

A balance sheet is simply a listing of your liabilities against your assets. Many personal financial management programs, such as Quick-Books or Microsoft Office, have templates for balance sheets. You can use an automated version or the worksheet below.

ASSETS

Cash and Cash Equivalents

Cash on hand $_____

Checking account $_____

Savings account(s) $_____

Money market funds $_____

CDs or time deposits $_____

Savings bonds $_____

Investment Assets

Stocks $_____

Bonds $_____

Mutual funds $_____

Real estate

      Home $_____

      Other $_____

Cash value of life insurance $_____

Partnership or business interest $_____

Other:_____ $_____

Retirement Assets

IRAs $_____

Employee retirement fund $_____

Other:_____ $_____

Other Assets

Art, antiques $_____

Sport or hobby equipment $_____

Automobile, other vehicles $_____

Electronics $_____

Jewelry, furs $_____

Other:_____ $_____

Total Assets: *$_____*

LIABILITIES

Past-due bills $_____

Past-due taxes $_____

Credit card debt

_____ $_____

_____	$_____
_____	$_____
_____	$_____
_____	$_____
Loans (auto, educational, other)	
_____	$_____
_____	$_____
Real estate debt	
Mortgage	$_____
Other:_____	$_____
Charitable pledges	$_____
Total Liabilities:	$_____

Total Assets	$_____
Total Liabilities	−$_____
NET WORTH	=$_____

Creating a Budget

While a balance sheet can give you the big picture of your net worth
and help you shape your long-term financial goals, for most couples, disagreements around money arise around short-term issues of cash flow.
Taking a look at your household's monthly budget can help you identify
spending patterns that can trigger financial infidelity. Your monthly
budget can be as detail-oriented as you wish. The example below provides some common monthly categories of spending.

Item	**Monthly Expense**
Housing Costs	
Mortgage or rent	$_____
Maintenance fees	$_____

Second mortgage $\underline{\hspace{3cm}}

Property tax $\underline{\hspace{3cm}}

Utilities

    Electric $\underline{\hspace{3cm}}

    Fuel (gas or oil) $\underline{\hspace{3cm}}

    Cable $\underline{\hspace{3cm}}

Water/sewer $\underline{\hspace{3cm}}

Trash removal $\underline{\hspace{3cm}}

Repairs/maintenance $\underline{\hspace{3cm}}

Other:_____ $\underline{\hspace{3cm}}

Car

    Car loan/lease $\underline{\hspace{3cm}}

    Fuel $\underline{\hspace{3cm}}

    Maintenance/repairs $\underline{\hspace{3cm}}

    Tolls $\underline{\hspace{3cm}}

Insurance

    Auto $\underline{\hspace{3cm}}

    Homeowner's/renter's $\underline{\hspace{3cm}}

    Life $\underline{\hspace{3cm}}

    Disability $\underline{\hspace{3cm}}

    Health $\underline{\hspace{3cm}}

    Other:_____ $\underline{\hspace{3cm}}

Food

    Groceries $\underline{\hspace{3cm}}

    Dining out $\underline{\hspace{3cm}}

Entertainment/Travel

    Movies/videos $\underline{\hspace{3cm}}

    Concerts/shows $\underline{\hspace{3cm}}

    Sporting events $\underline{\hspace{3cm}}

    Vacations $\underline{\hspace{3cm}}

    Other:_____ $\underline{\hspace{3cm}}

Professional Fees

    Medical $_____

    Dental $_____

    Eye care $_____

    Veterinarian $_____

    Attorney $_____

    Therapist $_____

    Financial adviser $_____

Personal Grooming

    Clothing $_____

    Dry cleaner $_____

    Gym membership $_____

    Personal trainer $_____

    Massage $_____

    Hair stylist $_____

    Other (dermatologist,

    manicure, pedicure, etc.) $_____

Family

    Education $_____

    Child care $_____

    Elder care $_____

    Alimony / Child support $_____

    Other:_____ $_____

Loans and Credit Cards

    _____ $_____

    _____ $_____

    _____ $_____

    _____ $_____

Savings and Investments

    _____ $_____

    _____ $_____

    _____ $_____

Miscellaneous

_____	$_____
_____	$_____
_____	$_____

Total Monthly Income: $_____
Total Monthly Spending: $_____

Your Relationship Balance

Exercise: Dream Big—Five-Year Goals

This exercise is one that should be done early, and often, in a relationship. Identifying individual and shared lifestyle goals is critical to maintaining the balance between emotional needs and financial resources. I advocate beginning to talk about these goals as early as a first date, and revisiting them regularly to see what has changed and assess if your partnership in attaining them is still on track. Each partner should assign an "emotional value" from 1 to 10 for each goal. Use this evaluation to talk about why certain goals are more important to you than others. Be sure to listen to what your partner says. Understanding the emotional underpinnings of financial decisions will help you to compromise and negotiate shared goals. Planning five years ahead allows you to see the benefit of saving together and helps you to budget.

Obviously this worksheet will look different for every relationship, as each couple will start in a different place. For a young couple just beginning to date (not on a first date, please), goals might include living together within a year, owning a condo or townhouse apartment within the next three years, owning a house within the next five years, owning a vacation home within the next ten years. A couple who are married with children may be looking at selling their vacation home to finance college educations, or saving for a significant trip to mark a milestone anniversary or birthday.

The sample chart below reflects a couple that has been in an exclusive dating relationship and is talking about making a deeper commitment. But all couples should do this, no matter what stage of the relationship they are in. Don't be afraid to *dream big*. Use the categories below as a starting point for discussing aspirations and goals. Add and delete categories as your lives and relationship evolve.

Here are some suggested areas to explore as you work together on your five-year relationship goals:

- What kind of house / apartment do I want? Is it important to own? How important is geographical location?
- Do I want a second or vacation home?
- Do I want children?
   —What kind of day care is best?
   —Do I want to stay home with my children?
   —Will I choose public or private schools?
   —Will I continue to have a career?
- At what age do I wish to retire?
- How much should I spend on charitable giving?
- Where do I want to travel?
- Do I want to take vacations? How often? How exotic?
- What kind of "toys" (cars, boats, technology) do I want?
- What is a priority (and at what point): career or relationship?
- Will I accept help from parents?
- How much debt am I willing to carry?

TIME FRAME	GOAL	ESTIMATED COST	BUDGET GOALS	EMOTIONAL RANKING	
				His	**Hers**
One Year	Move in together; rent an apartment	$1,500 month	Contribute $750 each per month	8	8
	Buy a new car	$35,000	Contribute $250 each per month to payment	9	6
	Vacation in Paris	$5,000	His treat	7	7
	Make partner	48 out of 52 weekends	Increase earnings by 40%	10	8
Two Years	Get married	$55,000	Save $20,000 gift from parents for balance	5	10
Three Years	Buy starter house in suburbs	$600,000	Down payment from his grand-parents; his salary will cover mortgage	8	9
	Start family; become stay-at-home mom	$75,000	Lose one salary	7	10
Four Years	Start college savings plan	$1,500 month	Reduce dining out	4	6
	Hire part-time child care	$2,000 month	Mother will return to consulting work	3	8
Five Years	Have sec-ond child	$6,000 month	Both parents will work full time	7	7

It is likely that when you create this chart, you will become aware that you and your partner have different spending priorities and patterns. You may feel it's important to save for future security and want to put away money in the early years of your relationship. Your partner may feel that it's important to "live in the present" and may place high emotional value on creating shared experiences within the relationship, preferring to spend money on exotic vacations rather than sock it away in a shared money market account. This type of tension is extremely common among couples.

In her book *Money Harmony*, Olivia Mellan, PhD, identifies a number of "polarization patterns" that frequently occur surrounding money. Referencing the theory that "opposites attract," she explains the importance of learning to move toward the middle ground when oppositional behaviors arise around money.

The idea that opposites attract is not new in relationship theory. Harville Hendrix, PhD, says that we purposely pick the person most unlike our self. By working through the power struggles that ensue, we heal our childhood wounds and emerge as a stronger, more balanced individual. Another of my early mentors, Thomas Fogarty, MD, helped me to see how opposite personality traits ultimately have a "neutralizing effect" on each of the individuals in the relationship. While opposites may initially attract, as couples work through power struggles, they come to see their opposing traits as opposite sides of the same coin and ultimately become more alike in their thinking and values. So while you may at first be attracted to the very person who is going to give you the most trouble around money, if you continue to work at open communication, understanding, and empathy, you may both change in ways that are beneficial to you as individuals—and to the relationship as a whole. This system of emotional "checks and balances" allows you to come to an understanding of *why* you have picked a certain person to be your partner.

When working through your five-year goals, pay close attention to those categories where you and your partner record wide discrepancies in emotional values. For instance, if you are very generous and your partner is extremely thrifty and neither of you is willing to work toward a balance with the other, your ongoing opposition could be an indicator of potential trouble spots or a lack of communication in your relationship. Just as money polarization can entrap couples in harmful patterns of spending and saving, a lack of shared values can lead to an emotional power struggle that is manifested in a struggle for power over the checkbook.

Communicate honestly with your partner about the emotional value you attach to particular uses for shared money. Don't be afraid to talk about why something is or isn't important to you. You may find that the emotional or financial cost of pursuing a specific goal is too high at any one particular time. Nevertheless, try to "stretch" and go outside of your comfort zone in an effort to promote a positive behavior change (Imago Theory, à la Harville Hendrix). Taking the time to engage fully in this exercise will promote flexible thinking and compromise in your relationship, limit magical thinking, and create opportunities for honest communication about expectations around money.

Exercise: The Money Tree

Of course money doesn't grow on trees—but this exercise, which uses visualization as a tool toward realization, may help you move closer to attaining shared financial goals.

Once you have completed your list of five-year goals above, I want you and your partner to go ahead and let yourselves "dream big." Without setting any time limits for achieving your dreams, create a Money Tree like the one shown below. Begin by writing down those financial goals that represent your "root values." Build upon these by listing important core goals, and then branch out from the goals to describe the other dreams and aspirations that you and your partner have for the future. *Don't judge, disparage, or dismiss your partner's dreams, even if they are not the same as yours.* Post your Money Tree in a visible spot where you both will see it on a daily basis and whenever you feel the urge to practice a bad money behavior, instead remind yourself of your dreams. Check in with each other periodically to make sure you both remain in agreement about how to *nurture* the dreams as well as the financial realities.

SAMPLE MONEY TREE	
Unlimited travel Retire at age 55 Take the grandchildren to Disneyland Take up surfing Sell family home and downsize Vacation in Hawaii Have plastic surgery Play the stock market Buy a significant piece of jewelry Buy a boat Trade in minivan for sports car	Aspirations
Buy a vacation home Upgrade family home Invest in college funds Pay off first mortgage Eliminate consumer debt	Core Goals
Increase investment in retirement accounts Increase shared income by 25 percent Upgrade one vehicle Buy a three-bedroom house in a good neighborhood Plan for a family	Root Values

Appreciate Your Shared Resources: A Brush with Divorce

Financially breaking up is hard to do. Even though money may be at the root of a couple's conflicts, many take their financial situations for granted. They do not look at balance sheets and they ignore shared budget goals.

For couples who consistently argue about money and who cannot find a way to open an honest dialogue about what they need emotionally and financially, I recommend an exercise based upon my work with couples who take each other for granted, claim they are "not in love anymore," or are discussing separation and divorce. *Before* issuing ultimatums and causing further damage with abrupt emotional disconnections, I tell these couples to experience a "Brush with Divorce," based on the Brush with Death exercise we will use in step 4. By physically separating from each other and behaving as if their relationship has ended (without actually taking legal steps to end it), they are able to truly experience the emotional emptiness that comes with the death of a relationship, regardless of the stage of dysfunction that relationship has reached. In some cases, it takes the strong emotional *jolt* of truly experiencing the reality of life without one another to awaken one or both members of a couple to the actual value of their relationship—and their value to each other. Throughout these seven steps, I will help you to experience this dynamic exercise in a variety of ways.

In this step, where you have taken the time to create a balance sheet and a budget that accurately reflects your financial and emotional picture, the "Brush with Divorce" will allow you to take stock of the "financial emptiness" that a separation would inflict. You would be surprised at how many couples, when faced with the financial implications of divorce or separation (what I call a "financial reality check"), decide to stay together and work on the underlying problems in their relationship. It is really the emotional fallout that is stronger—they are just hiding behind "financial" excuses. They finally understand what I've been saying: "Getting rid of the person doesn't get rid of the problem."

Using your budget and balance sheet, you and your partner should each calculate, separately, the cost of living apart: two houses, two cars, childcare providers, and child support (if you have children) or alimony payment. Take a look at these new budgets. They are the hard cost of walking away from a relationship because of financial infidelity. Now, alongside the numbers, list the *emotional* costs of separating from your partner.

Together, take a look at the whole picture. What does it really mean to break apart your finances and your relationship?

Alan was pressuring Denise to commit to a relationship. They had met through an online dating service and had been seeing each other for several months. Deeply scarred by a painful divorce, Denise was thrilled to have found love again and was fearful of losing Alan's affections. When he suggested she sell her home and move in with him in his house in Pennsylvania, she brought up the subject of how they would divide expenses. He offered that they could split everything fifty-fifty. For Denise, being asked to sell her home and enter into a situation where she was 50 percent responsible for Alan's house didn't feel financially fair. I encouraged her to ask him to do the balance sheet exercise as a way to honestly share information. But he refused, saying that his finances were private. He became very defensive, saying things like, "What? Do you need to see my FICO score before you sleep with me?"

While Alan had been very generous with Denise every time she had visited, she was nervous about his refusal to openly discuss money. Alan was committing financial infidelity. He was withholding, first with money, and later, it turned out, with sex.

Denise was a successful professional, with a valuable home and significant assets of her own. Denise loved her life, and her lifestyle. But after 9/11 she had lost a lot of money in the stock market, which had made her more cautious about life in general. Losing all that money made her feel powerless in life—and love. She worried what would happen if she didn't find someone who could care for her financially. Therefore, it was very important that she find out what Alan's dialogue about money was.

She did the balance sheet exercise to evaluate what would happen if she were to sell her home and move in with Alan, and to consider the emotional impact of a breakup and the potential stresses of once again getting into the dating pool. In the end, she realized that the potential financial costs of committing to someone so secretive about money were, for her, more damaging than the emotional price of breaking up with someone she was truly fond of.

Create a Shared Perspective

Denise and Alan's situation illustrates the importance of a shared perspective and openness when it comes to decisions involving financial contribution. In order to keep a balance between financial responsibility and emotional commitment, both partners have to agree to work together toward mutual goals.

> *Kelly sat on the couch with a pile of papers resting on her lap. When I asked her why she had told her husband, Walker, that she wanted a separation, she waved the stack at me. "He never has time for me," she said. "He always uses the excuse that he has to work harder, that our lifestyle is expensive. Well, I've calculated exactly how much he has spent on 'stuff' over the last year—a fancy yard tractor, a plasma TV, a membership to a health club he never goes to. We were supposed to be saving to go on a vacation, but he had to cancel because he had yet another work crisis."*
>
> *"What about how much you spend?" Walker said accusingly. "How much have you spent on lunches and girls' nights out? And clothes? You've got things with the price tag still hanging in your closet. Every time I come home there's some UPS delivery from another Internet purchase. You spend as much as I do—maybe more. I'm working as hard as I do to support your spending as much as mine!"*
>
> *"Well, why should I deny myself when you get yourself whatever you want?" she shot back.*

No relationship can heal when the injured party is *keeping score*. Ignoring the importance of shared financial goals can simply perpetuate an existing cycle of hurt and betrayal. As Walker spends on luxury items and toys to reward himself for an increasingly heavy workload and Kelly retaliates by matching his expenditures dollar for dollar, they are not only growing increasingly disconnected emotionally, but they are siphoning off their financial security.

Both Kelly and Walker need to take responsibility for the damage their spending is causing to the relationship and agree to set some shared goals that satisfy Walker's need for recognition as the breadwinner and Kelly's desire for emotional attention. Working together, they needed to create a budget that allocates their resources to both material rewards and opportunities for time together.

This case illustrates how money can act as a substitute for closeness, so I also suggested that Kelly and Walker do the following exercise to learn how to ask each other for what they really need and avoid using money as a tool for emotional fulfillment and stop their pattern of "bartering" for love.

IOUs and Wish Lists

Instead of using money as a way to reward or revenge particular behaviors, learn to ask for what you need by reviewing your partner's wish list and issuing (and honoring) IOUs.

For example, Kelly's wish list might include:

- Instead of working on a Saturday morning, spend time together working on chores around the house.
- Date night once a week.
- Adult "playdates"—a return to simple childhood pleasures, light-hearted pursuits that release endorphins and reduce stress.
- Having sex on Sunday evening, rather than preparing for Monday at the office.
- Watching a movie instead of using the computer to check work e-mails.

Walker's list might say:

- Recognize and be proud of my work achievements.
- Play together, instead of spending free time doing chores.

- Make more time for fitness.
- Understand when I need downtime after a stressful day.

I told Kelly and Walker to exchange lists. Whenever possible, they would make immediate efforts to be conscious of each other's wish lists. If Walker was unable to spend a Saturday morning at home, he might give Kelly an IOU (actually writing his promise on a piece of paper) for three hours of his time on a specified weeknight after work. If Walker came home from work with the news that he'd just closed a big deal, Kelly might give him an IOU for a couples massage or a shopping spree at the local golf pro shop.

I also helped Kelly to learn to ask for what she needed financially by using Smart Heart dialogue. She asked Walker for a separate credit card for her own use. At first he was resistant. "Why? Are you afraid I'll see what you're doing with our money?" Kelly was tempted to back down, but instead I coached her through the proper Smart Heart reply to Walker's reaction to control her spending. "I love you and respect that you work so hard. It's difficult for me to talk to you about this. I need you to not make me feel guilty and be grumpy when I bring up the subject of money. I want our love to thrive and our bank account to do the same."

When both partners are conscientious about understanding each other's wishes and generous about distributing and honoring IOUs, they will begin to associate fulfillment with *emotional* currency, rather than trying to meet their needs through acquiring material things and spending money.

When Money Talks

Not all of the talking in a relationship is done out loud. No matter what you are saying to your partner, it is likely that you are also having private conversations in which your money is expressing an opinion— loudly and clearly. Tune in to this internal dialogue and be aware if you

are hearing the kind of negative input that can intensify magical thinking. Write down what your money says to you and how you want to respond. Share these dialogues with your partner and ask him or her to do
the same. If your money is telling you any of the following, you need to
talk back and give it a reality check:

- "You shouldn't have to deny yourself if you don't have enough
  of me to afford a special purchase. That's what credit cards are
  for."
- "The more of me you have, the more of me you should spend.
  I'll just keep flowing."
- "I know you worry when your partner takes me out gambling,
  but if you don't say anything to your partner, it will be okay. No
  matter how much they lose, they'll win it back someday."
- "You've got to spend to succeed. If you look like you're wealthy
  it's the same as being wealthy."
- "If you don't have enough of me this month, there's no need to
  open the bills. Just leave them until you have more of me. If you
  ignore the bills, they'll just go away."

Smart Heart Dialogue for Balancing Financial and Emotional Expectations

Warning: Smart Heart dialogue uses attachment language to make
your first conversations about the role of money in your relationship as
safe and nonthreatening as possible. Nevertheless, using Smart Heart dialogue hastens the end of the magical thinking stage. Be aware that, for
most couples, whether just beginning to date or together for many
years, money conversations, if not using Smart Heart dialogue, will most
likely hasten or intensify the Power Struggle stage of the relationship.
However, *don't avoid these hard conversations!* If you do, you are stopping
your relationship before it really starts.

Smart Heart Dialogue for Dating Singles

In today's world it can be very confusing to interpret the expected gender roles when dating and it is tempting to default to magical thinking about how wonderful a relationship will be. Women are making higher salaries than ever before—an August 2007 iVillage.com poll showed that 30–40 percent of wives earn more than their husbands (up more than 20 percent from twenty-five years ago), and another recent study even showed that younger working women *theoretically* value a partner who will invest more in family time than in career achievements which may help to explain why so many financially secure women are comfortable "dating down." However, when surveyed later in their career, older women expressed bitterness over the expectation on women to be the higher wage earner. At the same time, another survey showed that men seem to prefer being the breadwinners. According to the 2004 report, men would rather marry their secretaries than their bosses. The danger of avoiding money talks while dating is that magical thinking can cause you to make assumptions about how each person feels about money, power, and independence. Talking about expectations around income disparities, even as early as a first date, can help expose differing values around earning, spending, ego, and willingness to compromise.

Case #1

What he says: "I'm really attracted to you; you're such a strong, independent woman."

What he may mean: "The fact that you make so much money makes me feel like I won't be able to take care of you. And I'm a little freaked out that you make more money than I do."

The Smart Heart reply: What's more important to me is your generosity, emotionally and financially. And you seem to have ambition and drive to grow and learn, which makes for a dynamite couple. It's true that I have a good career and make a good living. I'm not judging you by how much money you make.

Case #2

What she says: "I can take care of myself and it feels good that I don't have to rely on you."

What she may mean: "If you leave me I won't have to struggle financially."

The Smart Heart reply: "I admire your desire to be financially independent, but I want you to know that you can rely on me in other ways, and I hope that I would be able to count on you if I needed to."

Case #3

What she says: "I don't mind paying; I want to go to the kinds of places I'm accustomed to."

What she may mean: "In the long term, will I be able to respect someone who cannot afford or does not choose the same standard of living as I do?"

The Smart Heart reply: "I'm perfectly comfortable if you want to pay whenever you choose the place. And I'd like to be able to take you out sometimes, if you're willing to go to the places that I can afford. When I'm making more money, I'd love to spoil you by taking you where you want to go."

Or: "I'm glad you can afford these expensive dates. I don't expect that I will ever make the kind of money where I could afford to take you somewhere like this. I hope that you'll be willing to try some of the places that I like."

Case #4

What she says: "I think it's great that you like to save. I need that because I like to spend. I'm looking for that balance of fun, pleasure, and something for a rainy day."

What she may mean: "In my last relationship, the guy I dated was too frugal. I didn't think it would be a problem, but he turned out to be emotionally limited and not spontaneous in expressing his affection. I want to know if you respect money but also know how to use it for pleasure."

The Smart Heart reply: "Since opposites attract, we shouldn't be surprised that you like to spend and I'm good at saving. How about I show you my way to handle money and you show me your way? I think we can really balance each other out."

Smart Heart Dialogue for
Married and Committed Couples

After years of behaving in one way when it comes to money in your relationship, it can be difficult to initiate discussions without you or your partner feeling threatened or off balance. But simply ignoring money tension or financial infidelity will not make conflicts go away. In fact, this is one of the most damaging types of magical thinking.

Case #1

What he says: "You spend so much money on clothes. You hardly wear them before you say they go out of style. At least I wear the stuff I buy for years."

What he may mean: "You're not showing the same regard for money as I do. You don't value my hard work. I don't appreciate it when you spend our money on frivolous things."

The Smart Heart reply: "Although you make me feel loved now, I'm worried you will not appreciate me in our relationship and grow tired of me. I fear that if I don't look beautiful you're going to find someone else. Wearing the latest styles makes me feel younger and more attractive to you."

Case #2

What she says: "I really need another coat/necklace/expensive handbag. If you really loved me you'd get it for our anniversary/my birthday/no special reason."

What she may mean: "I'm afraid of being abandoned. Prove that you love me."

The Smart Heart reply: "I want to show you in other ways that I love you. I'm not going to leave you. I'm different from the other men in your past. You can feel secure about my emotional and financial commitment to our relationship. I don't need to buy you things to order to show you I love you."

Case #3

What she says: "Now that we're married, we need to buy a *real* house."

What she may mean: "I grew up in a big house and it makes me feel grounded. A big house represents the success of our relationship. It means we are secure."

The Smart Heart reply: "I know security is important to you. In order to afford the house that you are talking about, we will have to give up some of the things we love doing together—like traveling. I'm worried that if we buy a big house we'll be house poor. If we're spending that much money on a mortgage, I worry about our financial freedom and your security. Please let me know your thoughts on this."

Smart Heart Jump Starts for Financial and Emotional Balance

The previous exercises will give you an accurate picture of the relationship between your shared finances and your expectations surrounding that money. The following Smart Heart skills will help you to keep your money relationship in balance while allowing you to avoid the pitfalls of magical thinking:

- **Don't keep score with money.** Revenge spending may make you feel better in the short term, but once the chemical "high" induced by that new Marc Jacobs bag or the latest high-tech set of golf clubs wears off, your relationship will suffer as trust and intimacy are eroded by your financial infidelity.
- **Choose to fact-find and problem-solve.** Don't "decide" what your partner's actions or inactions mean by "mind reading." Even if you've been married twenty years, don't assume you "know" what your partner is thinking. Practice nonjudgmental fact-finding. Use Smart Heart dialogue to ask in a nondefensive way why your partner has made particular choices.
- **Don't look to others for solutions.** The fact is that "trading

up" for a partner who has more money, or who spends on you more freely, is really only trading one set of problems for another. Understand why some money behaviors are deal breakers for you, before you move on to the next relationship.

- **Be open to change.** Do not cling to old patterns of behavior or spending. Do not return to damaging habits because your partner has not met your expectations for similar change.
- **Manage your expectations.** Don't practice certain behavior because you expect something in return.
- **Learn to give to your partner.** Act to make that person happier, not because of quid pro quo.
- **Keep your budget meetings productive.** Plan to meet for ten minutes a week to discuss money. Pay attention to your bills and spending habits. Don't treat money as if it isn't an issue. Agree to tell your partner when you need a brief time-out—whether emotionally or physically—if the discussion becomes heated or stressful. Be sure that you reconnect by returning to the discussion within twenty-four hours (especially important for men who want to avoid these conflicts).

A Contract for Financial Fidelity

In order to maintain a balance of love and money in our relationship, we agree to:

- **Increase our financial compatibility.** Couples who are having difficulties usually focus on all the things that are *different* between them, rather than the *similarities*. Build on your financial compatibility by working toward both long- and short-term shared goals.
- **Make budgeting a top priority.** Schedule regular weekly or monthly "budget meetings" with your partner to talk about specific

bills and expenditures. Agree to discuss financial situation unemotionally. Follow up with endorphin-enhancing "playtime," such as making love, dancing, or high-energy play. You will begin to look forward to these money meetings.

- **Avoid keeping score with money.** Be conscious of "revenge spending" and avoid making financial decisions if you are feeling hurt by your partner's behavior in *other* areas of the relationship.

- **Agree to review shared finances on a regular basis.** Check in with each other on a weekly, monthly, or quarterly basis to keep the lines of communication open. Review whether you are maintaining a balance between your emotional and financial goals and whether you need to reprioritize or revisit emotional and financial expectations.

- **Avoid magical thinking around money.** Don't be afraid to discuss financial fears and worries with your partner. Avoid euphemisms for money; always discuss finances in concrete and specific terms.

- **Practice fact-finding instead of mind reading.** Do not jump to conclusions about why your partner favors certain financial decisions. Take the time to understand all motivating factors.

Step 2:
Examine Your Power Dynamic

If Money Is Power, Is There a Balance in Your Relationship?

From two-income families to full-time mothers to stay-at-home dads to couples navigating the early phases of dating, the money dynamic in a relationship sets up emotional and financial expectations that, when not clearly understood or acknowledged by each partner, can lead to feelings of emptiness and relationship dysfunction. Whether you are married or single, you and your partner must learn to examine, understand, and negotiate the money-driven power dynamic in your relationship. Talking about who makes it and how you spend it and how you feel about sharing it is a critical step in equalizing the balance in your relationship.

Marguerite arrived to our counseling session ten minutes late. "Sorry, but the traffic was terrible," she explained. Her husband, Jared, shot her an irritated look and said, "Traffic? Didn't you take the subway, like I told you to? How much money did you spend sitting in a cab in traffic?"

Marguerite turned to me in frustration. "I had to drop the kids off at their after-school program before I could come here. It's just too complicated to do it all by train."

"Do you see what I'm talking about?" Jared asked me. "I feel like I have to tell her how to do everything. She has no respect for me or how hard I've worked to get us where we are today." He turned to his wife and said, "My job is to make the money. It's your job to take care of the kids and run the

household. You need to plan better so you're not wasting money on things like taxis to get to your appointments on time. You need to do your job better."

"I don't understand why you have to manage our accounts," Marguerite said. "You deal with our stocks, savings, and checking. You handle the taxes and pay all the bills. All I have is whatever you budget. Every time I want something extra I have to ask you for it. It makes me feel like a child. Maybe I should get my own job in order to have my own spending money?"

"I don't want you to have your own job," Jared shot back.

"Why does the idea of Marguerite working bother you so much?" I asked him.

"Her job is to take care of our family. My father told my mother to work to earn her spending money, but I resented that she was never there for me when I was growing up," Jared said.

While Jared was irritated that Marguerite was not upholding her side of their partnership, Marguerite perceived that she had no actual power at all. To Jared, working as a team meant him making the money and Marguerite managing it carefully. To him, how they shared and used money in the relationship was a symbol of his commitment to her and to goals he believed they shared. To her, it had become a symbol of power and control.

Marguerite resented Jared's insistence on knowing how, where, and why she spent the household money so much that she had begun to commit financial infidelity. Later in their session, she admitted that, when doing the weekly grocery shopping for the family, would regularly write checks for anywhere from twenty to eighty dollars over the total amount. She would also go through Jared's pants and suit pockets and keep any money that she might find. She'd then use her secret stash to buy outfits or makeup or to have a facial or lunch with friends. By covertly pocketing cash from the shared budget she experienced a feeling of power.

She considered this "found" money her little secret and would then tell a variety of lies in order to explain to Jared why the grocery bill was slightly higher on some weeks than others. Marguerite's increasing need to feel she had some power in the relationship had snowballed into a damaging case of financial infidelity.

Jared honestly didn't see himself as controlling. For him, being the sole breadwinner of the family made him feel like a manly man. Marguerite, who admitted to being attracted to Jared because she considered him "powerful," someone who "could take care of her," was chafing at feeling trapped in a trade-off between feeling secure and feeling powerless in the relationship. She had reached the point where the very traits that had initially attracted her to Jared made her resentful and angry with him.

This couple was so deeply entrenched in their subconscious power struggle that their money patterns had evolved into mirror opposites: Jared became increasingly controlling—he could not even admit that if she had taken the subway and missed the session, it would have cost around three hundred dollars, much less than a cab. And Marguerite became increasingly sneaky.

In order for them to rebalance their power dynamic around spending, Jared was going to have to become more trusting of Marguerite, perhaps agreeing that a specific amount of money each week would be hers to use as she wished. He would have to commit to breaking the habit of questioning her about her spending habits and show through his actions that he believed she was as invested in long-term financial goals as he was. Marguerite needed to communicate honestly with Jared. She needed to explain why she felt she deserved to have certain things that he considered indulgences.

Understanding the Power Dynamic

For some individuals, learning to give up the idea of "being right" and moving on to "what works" for the relationship seems nearly impossible. Many relationships come to a crashing halt as people bail out of the relationship just when the going gets tough. But in order for the relationship to grown and mature, couples need to commit to work together to find ways to connect with and nurture each other, particularly during these tough times.

In the Power Struggle stage, the very characteristics that first attracted you to your mate will begin to coalesce as the source of conflict. Olivia Mellan calls this phenomenon a "polarization pattern." In her book *Money Harmony*, she lists seven ways in which a couple can polarize around money. For instance, if you spend money freely, you may be drawn to someone with financial restraint, someone for whom saving is a priority. Or if you are struggling to meet financial obligations and are on a tight budget, you may be attracted to someone who is extremely generous.

Dr. Mellan takes her concept of polarization pattern one step further in postulating "Mellan's Law," in which she states that even couples who are incredibly similar in their money styles—for example, people who are attracted because they both like to spend, or two people who are inclined to save—will eventually polarize over time, with one person vying for the role of "superspender" or "supersaver" and the other person reacting to this extreme behavior by changing his or her own money style. Thus even a couple that starts out as a spender/spender combination will evolve into some version of a spender/saver and clash with each other over how shared finances are used.

I see this type of polarizing phenomenon manifest in a variety of ways in all of the couples I counsel. For some it may begin with differences in money styles. For others it develops around emotional and intimate behaviors. In all cases, how each person in the relationship handles money generally becomes a hot-button topic. This is not surprising. In study after study conducted on reasons for marriage distress, money is consistently named as one of the top two sources of conflict.

In any relationship, as the honeymoon stage fades, and magical thinking no longer masks the fact that you and your partner have some very real differences, you must be prepared for the power struggle to commence in earnest. Many couples avoid the money issue for just this reason. They want to perpetuate the "honeymoon loving" feelings.

Ruby and Alex had been going out for two years when they came to see me because they were on the verge of breaking up. Alex explained how he had been attracted to Ruby because of her generous nature. He'd been going through a difficult time, helping to finance his mother's heart surgery and rehabilitation, and Ruby had been an incredibly supportive source of comfort. He explained how he had been drawn to her independence—she had asked him to move in with her and had graciously accepted whatever he could contribute toward the rent. She urged him to think of the house as his own. "She was so giving in every way," he said. "Emotionally, financially, sexually. And I was completely tapped out by the demands of my mother's illness."

But recently, Alex explained, he had begun to feel as if Ruby had become another person entirely. "I've noticed that when she talks about the house she always says 'my house,'" he said. "And not a day goes by when she doesn't comment on how much I'm eating from the fridge or how many times she's paid for us to go out to dinner during a particular week." It had gotten so bad, he complained, that when she noticed him using her iPod, she had started a screaming fight that had lasted for hours. "We're not even having sex anymore," Alex said. "If we don't fix or end this relationship, I'm afraid I'm going to have an affair."

When it was Ruby's turn to talk, she told me how she had been drawn to Alex because he was so obviously in need of nurturing. "He was going through such a tough time with his family," she said. "And he was frustrated because his career had stalled while he took care of his personal obligations. But I loved how he had chosen to put family first." Ruby's family was very wealthy and she had grown up accustomed to privilege, but aware that her parents were very unhappy. Her father repeatedly cheated on her mother, and her mother compensated by ignoring her children and focusing all of her love and attention on her spouse in a series of unsuccessful bids to keep him from straying.

Ruby admitted that she expected that Alex would take care of her the same way he was taking care of his ill mother. "But then his mother died," she said, "and even after allowing for time to grieve, he was still just as needy. He didn't begin to take care of me, and continued to treat the apartment and all of the expensive things that I provided for us as something he simply expected from the relationship. He's not grateful at all. And now he says he doesn't want to be with me—after all I've done for him."

When I asked Ruby about their sex life, she admitted that she was withholding sex in an attempt to get Alex to pay more attention to her. "My mother practically killed herself to get my father's attention," she said. "I'm not going to humiliate myself like that. Alex is already draining my financial resources; I won't let him suck me dry emotionally as well." But she also pointed out that if she didn't initiate sex, weeks would go by without Alex so much as holding her hand or hugging her when she came home. "He was so tender with his mother when she was sick," Ruby said. "Why is he so cold to me?"

By constantly reminding Alex of how much he "owed" her, Ruby was attempting to control Alex through giving. She was hoping to manipulate him into providing her with the physical and emotional attention she so deeply craved from him. The more Ruby gave, the more powerless Alex began to feel. In an effort to balance the power, he tried to exert his own kind of control.

As their arguments around money grew more intense, Alex began to use sex as a power move, both by withholding physical attention and by threatening affairs to ignite Ruby's fears of abandonment. By the time they arrived in my office, their conflict had reached such intensity that both of them considered that the easiest thing to do would be to simply walk away from the relationship. For Alex and Ruby, the very things that had first attracted them to each other—Ruby's generosity and Alex's need for nurturing—had become polarizing points of conflict and the catalysts for a passive power struggle in their relationship.

When you are open to understanding the underlying dynamics of the power struggles in your relationship, instead of driving you further apart, each clash of wills can be a chance for you to learn about yourself and your partner. Instead of seeing this stage of a relationship as a reason for a breakup, you must realize that working through a power struggle offers you incredible opportunities for intimacy to grow. As I tell many of my patients who wonder if their relationship will survive this turbulent stage, "It's not ending; it's just getting good!"

For most couples, disagreements over money are often brought into sharp relief in the Power Struggle phase of a relationship. Once both partners have stopped using magical thinking as a way to avoid acknowledging differences, it is apparent that there are no effortless solutions to "magically" make their problems disappear. Initially, instead of working through conflicts and striving to reach a middle ground, each person begins to think of these differences as negatives and sources of frustration in the relationship. Power struggles are inevitable as each partner, convinced that his or her way is the "right" way, tries to change the other.

Men, Women, Power, and Money

There are no limits to the differences that can arise in a relationship. And these differences arise out of a number of factors. Scientists and researchers have discovered that there are even biochemical markers that consistently predict whether or not two people will be attracted to each other. For instance, according to Helen Fisher, PhD, individuals who are high in estrogen are attracted to types who are high in testosterone. These two hormones are responsible for certain types of sex-linked characteristics that are very different. Her research also shows that people high in the neurotransmitter dopamine exhibit behavior—such as spontaneity, creativity, and novelty seeking—that is attractive to individuals who are high in the neurotransmitter serotonin, which is associated with traits like planning, following rules, and traditionalism.

In both of these cases, it is the differences—physical, behavioral, chemical—that trigger the attraction. As relationships develop and deepen, these very differences can either become unbearable points of contention or evolve into a balance that offers stability yet provides ongoing interest and excitement to those involved.

When it comes to dealing with the role of money in a relationship, in over thirty years of counseling couples, I have found that both men and women continue to perceive their partner—and often themselves—as possessing specific gender-related attributes when it comes to actions and emotions surrounding money.

For centuries certain attributes have been considered predominately "male" or "female." And while these traditional sex roles—men are aggressive, women are supportive; men compete, women collaborate; men protect, women nurture; men seek power, women seek consensus; men provide, women accept (to list just a few)—are regularly challenged today by individuals who are refusing to be defined by historical gender roles, these archetypes remain lurking in our subconscious.

When She Earns More: Navigating a Role-Reversal Power Struggle

Today it is increasingly common for the woman to be the higher earner in a relationship. Among the couples I counsel, both men and women seem to be equally conflicted about how they feel when the traditionally male role of breadwinner is flipped on its head. Research shows that men who are breadwinners have happier marriages. Men identify through women rather than vice versa. These feelings of ambivalence most commonly manifest in power struggles centered around money. The following are some things married couples can do, individually and together, to minimize power struggles:

What Women Need to Do:

- Be his biggest advocate.
- Be discrete; don't brag about your earning power in front of others. Respect, don't damage, his (possibly fragile) ego.
- Believe he is as valuable as you are. Don't just "act as if." Really feel grateful for what he brings to the relationship.
- Be open; don't make him feel excluded. Don't neglect to talk about work; it's an important part of your life.

- Work as a team; don't try to control and don't make unilateral spending decisions.
- Discuss your paychecks but in the context of shared goals. Acknowledge that his paycheck, whatever it is, helps you to *reach* these goals.
- Watch your pronouns. Don't use "my money." Say "our money."
- Reward, admire, and appreciate him for what he brings to the relationship. He's just as important as you are!
- Don't devalue his work or accomplishments.
- Use Smart Heart dialogue when delegating child-care responsibilities and household chores to make him feel needed, not demoted. Remember, men do not like to be told what to do.

What Men Need to Do:

- Appreciate her sacrifices.
- Acknowledge what she does professionally.
- Show fondness and appreciation. Think of her several times during the day to bring this on. In a study, divorced men had no thoughts of their wives during the day.
- Focus on the positives—more free time, entrepreneurial possibilities, freedom to take economic risks if not the main breadwinner.
- Admire her work without resentment. See her making more money as *increasing* your lifestyle.
- Work as a team.
- Take "influence" without resentment. Do not see this as taking "orders." Men who can take influence have happier marriages.
- Have a guilt-free spending fund so as not to feel demoted.
- Encourage her to travel for work or work late hours to alleviate her guilt.
- Use Smart Heart dialogue to talk about role reversal without resentment. It's all how you see it!

What You Both Need to Do:

- Take turns paying the bills or pay them together.
- Be empathetic.
- Prioritize.
- Negotiate.
- Reevaluate.
- Discuss resentments immediately—use Smart Heart dialogue and high-energy physical play to defuse negativity and spike endorphins. I suggest that couples plan a weekly "walk and talk" to discuss hard subjects and to ward off role-reversal resentments.
- Create *moments* for fondness and appreciation.
- Help spender curb spending, so partner feels "part" of it, and so the one making less money doesn't spend more.

Married and single women in today's world struggle. Women are self-conscious of their success and wealth; they don't want to threaten and outshine men. They still apologize and "hide" if they make more money. They "hide" their purchases, apartments, and possessions. Men are confused by these women. They seem to want to be taken care of *and* be independent.

Pitfalls for Young, Successful Women "Dating Down":

- Want to be independent and taken care of.
- Not sure who should pay. Everything is turned on its head, which affects sex and money and who is the instigator.
- Women see themselves as being "weak" if they end up like their mothers.

Pitfalls for Married Women:

- Excessive spending because they gave up their career for children; they feel resentful and lost when they experience empty nest.

Pitfalls for Married Men:

- May feel unappreciated as breadwinner.
- Financial responsibilities for family feel like a "bottomless pit."
- If wife works or makes *more* money they may try to boost self-esteem through financial infidelity (by buying expensive "toys" or playing the stock market) or seeking gratification outside through a physical affair.

Pitfalls for Single Men:

- Feel "wimpy" if they don't pay.
- Some take advantage if they have an axe to grind with their mother or ex. They ask the woman to pay or split the bill.

These perceived gender characteristics, whether acknowledged as stereotypes or not, are frequently cited by couples I counsel today, particularly when our conversations move into the area of money and finance. Assigning any of these gender traits to an individual influences the way you approach your dealings with the opposite sex. (In step 3, "Divest Your Past," I'll show you how to look more deeply at the money patterns and gender archetypes in your family history to help you to understand how they influence your relationship in the present.)

The bottom line is that men and women have very different approaches to acquiring and wielding power and money and it's no surprise that these differences translate to conflicts over managing shared finances in their relationships. The way men and women tend to communicate, to socialize, and to assess and react to risk, as well as the values they assign to logic, emotion, and decision-making styles, are all part of the dance of equality and balance in any relationship.

Clare and Lukas came to see me because she wanted to get a divorce and he was fighting to keep their relationship going. At first, it seemed to me that Lukas was trying to hold on to a good financial situation. Clare was an attorney with a growing clientele in a successful partnership. Lukas was a sculptor who had not even finished college. When they met at an art gallery they had fallen madly in love.

"I was happy to support his art," Clare said. "I love my job and it was my dream to buy the practice so I could have more control and power over my own schedule."

Clare and Lukas had agreed that she would continue to work toward buying out her partner and going into a solo practice, even if it meant longer days and more hours apart. In exchange, Clare suggested that Lukas take on all the household responsibilities, including paying all the bills and keeping track of their budget.

It seemed to be going well until, over the past few months, Lukas began telling Clare they couldn't afford to make the two-thousand-dollar monthly contribution toward buying her business.

"I had no idea we were in money trouble," Clare said. "Lukas never said anything to me about our income. I know he sells some of his sculpture and teaches classes and keeps that money for himself. I never ask him what he does with it. I never ask him to account for it. And I don't act like the money I make is all mine, either."

"She doesn't ask me to account for the money," Lukas finally spoke up. "But if I don't give her the check for her practice each month, she stops having sex with me until she gets it. And I'm not going to give her the money until she starts treating me like her husband rather than her accountant."

I could see that they were locked in a classic power struggle, with sex and money as the weapons. As I worked with Clare and Lukas, I helped them to see that, by having Lukas take control of the bill paying, Clare was asking him to take care of her. Her father had been a wealthy stockbroker who rarely had time for his family but showered them with gifts and freely handed out cash.

While she had chosen a man who was a low-income artist—and about as different from her father as she could find—she had always equated control of money with power and she wanted her husband to have some power in their relationship. Despite being a self-made, successful businesswoman, she was willing to symbolically hand over her power, by giving Lukas control of the money.

"Men are so much better at handling money," she told me in one of our sessions.

Unfortunately for Clare, she had made an incorrect assumption that Lukas, too, viewed money as power. Instead, Lukas was not interested in managing the shared finances and resented that Clare had forced him into the role. He felt that she was using her role as breadwinner to exert power over him.

"She's trying to turn me from an artist into a businessman," he complained.

"My father always took care of financial things and that's the way I want Lukas to be, too," Clare said.

"Well, we've got a problem then," Lukas replied. "I need to feel like you're an integral part of the team when it comes to making financial decisions. I'm grateful you're willing to give me the power over the checkbook and not question my competence, but I need you to share in handling our financial responsibilities—not just make the money."

In order to improve communication with your partner as you undertake the effort of rebalancing the power dynamics in your relationship, it is helpful to know how each of you perceives and wields power. The quiz below helps to reveal your personal approach to power and how it may be affecting the dynamic of your relationship.

Quiz: Do You Need to Feel Powerful?

Answer True or False to Each of the Following:

It is important that my partner admits I am right when we argue.	T	F
I believe that every argument should end in a firm resolution.	T	F
I am good at fixing problems.	T	F
I will not engage in arguments with my partner.	T	F
I am disappointed when people do not meet my expectations.	T	F

I am comfortable with a partner who earns more than I do.	T	F
I expect people to listen when I speak to them.	T	F
There is only one right answer to a problem.	T	F
I do not share the password to my bank account or computer—even with my spouse.	T	F
It does not matter to me if people agree with what I say, as long as they still follow my direction.	T	F

SCORING

Give yourself 2 points for every time you selected *T* as your answer. For every *F*, subtract 1 point.

11–20 points: You consider yourself a powerful person and expect others to relate to you in a submissive manner.

5–10 points: You maintain a balance between healthy self-confidence and a willingness to compromise. Though you may appear overbearing at times, you are willing to listen to reason and capable of working toward shared goals.

Less than 5 points: You tend to be overly submissive. Over time you may build resentment toward those you consider to have power over you and find yourself saying "yes" when you mean "no". Consider whether your attitude manifests as episodes of passive-aggressive behavior in your relationship.

QUIZ: DOES MONEY EQUAL POWER?

Answer True or False to Each of the Following:

It is important that I make more money than my partner.	T	F
The person who makes more money should have more power and control over how it is spent.	T	F
When I make money from my investments it proves I am a good manager.	T	F
When I lose money from my investments it shows I have received bad advice.	T	F

If I reveal that I am wealthy, people will only like me for my money.	T	F
If I reveal that I have a low salary, people will judge me.	T	F
People will do anything if you offer them enough money.	T	F
The person who makes the most money should handle all financial matters in the relationship.	T	F
It doesn't matter how you make your money, just that you have plenty of it.	T	F
Platinum credit cards are better than plain credit cards, even if you have to pay a fee to get them.	T	F

SCORING

Give yourself 2 points for every time you selected **T** as your answer. For every **F**, subtract 1 point.

11–20 points: You closely equate money with power. You consciously try to control those around you by using money as a reward or punishment. Your identity is closely tied to your bank balance.

5–10 points: You understand the importance of money, but are also able to appreciate the complexity of relationships around it. You are willing to solicit and listen to advice from others regarding finances.

Less than 5 points: You do not attach enough importance to the impact money may have on your life. This may cause you to avoid financial responsibilities and may put your future comfort and security at risk. Constantly depending on your partner to handle financial decisions creates an unhealthy inequality in your relationship.

Power and Risk

A study published in the July / August 2006 issue of the *European Journal of Social Psychology* suggests that powerful people are more likely to take risks. The authors of the study theorized that high-powered individuals often benefit when they make choices that are considered high-risk. The more power these people believe they have, the more risk they are willing to take. However, this behavior can set up an incredibly damaging dynamic. Consider, for instance, the number of scandals that regularly arise involving high-powered executives, wealthy stock-market investors, or political figures. I'm quite sure that former president Bill Clinton never believed he would get caught when he embarked on an affair with a White House intern.

Another psychological effect of constant risk taking is the impact the adrenaline rush that such behavior can provide. These thrill seekers "self-medicate," and I see in my practice their self-destruction. Individuals who are prone to addictive behavior are in danger of falling into a damaging cycle where the rush of taking the risk becomes all the reward they need. Whether or not their risky behavior is beneficial becomes secondary. And the more risks they take, the more powerful they may feel.

This type of power dynamic in a relationship can have a significant impact on a couple's shared finances. When faced with a crisis, risk takers, who generally take a "don't worry, don't plan" approach to money management, may make rash decisions that result in emotional and financial catastrophes for them and / or their partners. According to Brett N. Steenbarger, clinical psychologist and author of *Enhancing Trader Performance*, "When humans experience a powerful emotional event (and a big gain or loss in our wealth, even if it is on paper, is one) our brains don't work the way they do when we're calm. During times like these the analytical part of the brain shuts down. . . ." You need a plan to limit risk, especially at these times when your brain fails you.

To help you understand how much financial risk is present in your relationship, ask yourself these questions:

1. Do you have a plan in case of a financial emergency, such as loss of a job or a medical crisis?
2. Are there a lot of high-risk stocks in your portfolio?
3. Do you own your home?
4. Do you have multiple credit cards with high interest rates?

5. Can you easily make the minimum monthly payments on your credit cards?

6. Do you have an adjustable rate mortgage?

7. Do you have six months' living expenses set aside in case of emergency?

8. Have you ever had to take a loan from friends or family to "bail you out" of a bad financial situation?

9. Do you pay yourself first by putting money in savings before paying your bills?

If your answers to the even-numbered questions are mostly "yes" and your answers to the odd-numbered questions are mostly "no," you are living with a very high level of risk in your relationship. If the reverse is true (the even-numbered questions are mostly "no" and the odds are mostly "yes"), then you have an extremely conservative approach to financial risk.

In order to successfully navigate the power struggles that occur around money, it is important to know how comfortable both you and you partner are with financial risk. It is also important to consider your relationship's power dynamic and your personal relationship to money and power. Acknowledging these different perspectives can help you to understand where your partner is coming from when you find that you are locked in a power struggle about money.

A Warning About Money, Power, and Abuse

When the balance of power in a relationship is completely one-sided, there is a high potential for mental, physical, or emotional abuse. Money can be a tool for abuse in any of these instances. An abusive partner may begin to act in subtle ways, such as manipulating the other by focusing control around seemingly insignificant or personal spending issues, and gradually escalate to encompass far more vindictive behaviors that can inflict devastating emotional harm.

Anya had been seeing me for several months. She was afraid that her hus-
band, Dimitri, was ready to end their marriage. "I need to know what to do
to please him," she said. "How can I be the woman he wants me to be?"
Anya was a striking-looking woman in her mid-thirties. She had always
seemed to take a great deal of pride in her appearance. She had gorgeous
blond hair that was carefully highlighted. I'd asked her once what salon she
used and when she told me, I knew that it probably took a fair amount of
money to maintain her sun-kissed look. On this visit, however, I noticed that
her hair was a much darker color. When I asked her about it she told me that
she'd been using a home dyeing kit because Dimitri had told her that her vis-
its to the salon every six weeks were a selfish indulgence that was ruining
their budget. "I've had to quit the gym as well," she added. "And I guess
you can see that my clothes aren't fitting so nicely anymore." I could tell that
she was self-conscious about the change in her appearance.

On the next visit she had managed to convince Dimitri to accompany her.
He sat stiffly on the couch, making no effort to touch or connect with his wife.
As I guided the conversation toward Anya's fear of abandonment, he sud-
denly spoke up. "Why shouldn't I leave her for someone younger, prettier?"
he asked. "She barely takes care of herself. Look at her ugly hair color!"
(This is called "crazy-making" behavior—a no-win, damned-if-you-do-
damned-if-you-don't situation. Anya bought into it.)

He continued his litany of complaints. "She's gaining weight; her clothes
fit poorly; she doesn't care that she makes me look bad for choosing a wife
who is so willing to let herself go. Why shouldn't I leave her?"

On the third session, I told Anya straight out that from my perspective she
was in an abusive relationship. Dimitri was using money as a way to manip-
ulate her into a situation where he could then belittle her. Each time he saw
her self-confidence crumble a little more, he would up the ante by threatening
to leave. Anya was exhausting and demeaning herself trying to meet all of
his demands. She was brainwashed into thinking that by spending money on
herself to maintain her looks she was driving him away, when in fact, he was
cruelly preying on her fear of abandonment, amusing himself by watching her
struggle to meet his standards for both beauty and thriftiness.

Although Dimitri agreed to be tested, and was diagnosed with a chemical imbalance that was most likely the cause of his severe projection on to Anya, he refused to undergo treatment with Dr. Morrison and me. Because it was clear that Dimitri was extremely narcissistic and was not willing to take any responsibility for his behavior, and was blaming and shaming, I advised Anya to leave him. She broke off her relationship with Dimitri and is now happily married to someone else.

If you can answer "yes" to any of the questions that follow, consider whether you might be a victim of abusive manipulation, with money being used as the tool:

- Does your partner withhold or minimize the importance of money for critical care such as health care, dental work, weight control, and so on?

- Does your partner urge you to practice denial by telling you that certain things are not necessary or that you should not be indulging yourself with them unless he or she agrees to it?

- Does your partner tease you with money, for instance, promising you dinner out and then telling you it's off because you spent too much on the credit card?

- Does your partner "gaslight" you regarding money? Does he or she consistently promise to pay a certain bill but then accuse you when there is a late fee? Does your partner deny having bought new items that appear in your home? Does he or she tell you that it's your fault that there is no money in the budget, no matter what the circumstances?

- Has your partner "brainwashed" you about money? Do you question your own behavior around money? Are you unsure whether you are "worth" spending it on?

- Does your partner have sadistic behavior around money? Does he or she hint about extravagant presents and then purposely forget to get you even a card, or give only a trivial gift, for important events such as birthdays or anniversaries? Does your partner buy and flaunt expensive items for him- or herself, but pick a fight if you dare to spend money on something you want?

If you think your partner has abusive tendencies toward you and is using money as a tool, it is important to share your fears with a counselor or other trusted individual in order to protect yourself and your money. In cases where an abusive individual is controlling the money, the fallout from a breakup can cause the victim not just emotional distress, but financial ruin!

Fighting Fair

One of the most important things for any couple moving through the Power Struggle stage of their relationship is to learn how to fight fair. Discussions about money that escalate into arguments are a classic sign of a power struggle. When your disagreements about spending and saving begin to affect sex, intimacy, trust, and respect, it is vital to have techniques to allow for the *safe* expression of conflict in the relationship.

It's important to note that I am not advocating that you and your romantic partner avoid conflict in favor of polite discussions about—or around—money. In fact, in my book *Adultery: The Forgivable Sin*, I note that adultery and divorce occur more frequently in marriages when couples are *not* willing or able to fight through an issue and work out solutions. In any relationship, conflicts are inevitable and it is the way that couples work together to resolve those conflicts that influences how they relate to each other emotionally.

So, go ahead: express yourself strongly. But be sure that you are "fighting fair" by using the following techniques.

Ten Rules for Fighting Fair

1. ***Ask permission.*** Make an appointment. Say, "I want to talk to you about this month's credit card charges. Is this a good time?"

2. ***If your partner is not ready to talk, reschedule within twenty-four hours.*** If you are involved with someone who seeks to avoid conflict, he or she may stonewall, ignore, or forget your request. Make a specific appointment. "Let's plan to talk at six p.m. tomorrow."

3. ***Put time limits on fighting.*** Everyone has a personal threshold of tolerance for emotional stress. If the topic becomes too sensitive, allow for either participant to take a time-out. Be sure to announce your desire to reconnect.

4. ***Do not ignore your partner.*** Maintain eye contact, acknowledge comments, say what you need to say, and listen attentively. Turn off the television or other distractions. Do not plan a discussion for when you are out socially, at drinks or dinner, or at bedtime.

5. ***Use "I" sentences, rather than "You" sentences.*** Do not blame, criticize, or be sarcastic or negative. Take responsibility for your actions and thoughts.

6. ***Echo what you hear and validate your partner's feelings.*** Listen closely and repeat what you hear your partner saying—without reactivity or editorializing or adding your own spin. Block out your own thoughts in order to show you fully understand what he or she means. Saying, "What I hear you say is that you lost five thousand dollars at a friendly poker game because you were angry with me for canceling our dinner date?" is much less threatening than saying, "What do you mean you blew all that money

because I had to work late?" and gives your partner a chance to clearly articulate the emotional reasons behind his or her actions and can help to eliminate countless misunderstandings. Validate what your partner is saying—you don't have to agree with it, but don't minimize what your partner is saying by smiling condescendingly, rolling your eyes, or shaking your head no while he or she is speaking. Don't attack the person for what he or she is saying. Avoid thinking or saying, "But what about me?" Try to walk in your partner's shoes—to put yourself in your partner's place.

7. *Empathize.* *Feel*, or cue in to, what your partner's feelings may be. Say, "It makes sense" or "I can see how you feel that way." Say, "I can see that you must feel neglected that I was putting work before our relationship. I see that you are hurt and disappointed."

I tell couples I counsel to be sure to remember to put on their invisible emotional "bulletproof vests" before beginning a fair fight. This type of visualization reminds them that any angry words spoken during the fight cannot penetrate them. Everyone is safe from verbal darts. "Contain" the anger of your partner instead of reacting.

8. *Be honest, without being hurtful.* When used as a weapon, honesty can be cruelty. Go beyond your comfort zone to express exactly how you are feeling and what you are worried or fearful about, but choose your words carefully and keep to the topic at hand.

9. *Detach from your emotions.* When you argue, practice listening to the content but not feeling emotional in response. Erase all your thoughts; don't get defensive, angry, or hurt by the words. Some couples also imagine putting on very soft, fluffy, pillowlike gloves to remind them to "cushion their words."

10. *Before, during, and after each fight, practice attachment skills.*
Reach out and lovingly touch your partner when making a point.
Hug, kiss, hold hands, or stroke each other's hair while talking even
when the discussion becomes heated. After a particularly stressful
fight, reconnect by wrestling, exercising together, or having sex in
order to create endorphins and reverse the flow of negative emotions.

Don't worry if, for the first few times you fight according to these
rules, the discussions seem stiff and mechanical. You are working on creating a safe space for expression, validation, and healing without fear of
feeling inadequate, shamed, or judged. The goal of fair fighting is to get
the anger out. But more important, it allows you to understand the hurt
and emptiness beneath the anger (usually carried from childhood) and
have these feelings validated by your partner so that together you can
arrive at a resolution and feel more loving and connected. Making a true
effort to understand what is motivating your partner, and understanding—
from your partner's perspective—what he or she is feeling, without becoming defensive or critical, will bring about a new, deeper, and more
intimate way of relating.

After a fair and productive fight, you and you partner must practice
"stretching," implementing a specific behavior change that one person
has requested. Each person picks one to three behaviors for the other to
work on. *Remember that the changes you wish for in your partner are usually
those that are most difficult for that person to enact.* The more you "stretch,"
the more changes you will see in your relationship. For instance, if your
partner asks you to work on saving rather than splurging—and you
honestly try to practice saving money—then you will gradually begin to
modify your behavior around saving, changing the part of you that was
previously unable or unwilling to do so.

POSITIVE POWER STRUGGLE TALK

"It's so nice that we are finally taking a vacation together. But I want to make sure I have budgeted enough money."

"I'll just put expenses on my credit card."

"St. Barths is so expensive. Do you want me to pay for airfare and you can pay for the hotel and our meals?"

"Whatever. We can figure it out when the bills come."

"I'm worried that it will be more than I can afford. Would you mind if we spelled out our agreement in writing before the trip?"

"I guess that would be all right. You should know that my other girlfriends have said I'm not always consistent. But I do like to surprise people."

"I'm not good with unpleasant surprises."

"Yeah, that's what my ex-wife said, too."

When Money Talks

Tune into your internal money dialogue. If your money is telling you any of the following, especially during a power struggle with your partner, you need to talk back and put it in its rightful place:

- "You make more of me, so you should have more say about how you spend me."
- "Your partner loves me more than he or she loves you. You need to take control of me so that your partner will pay attention to you."
- "I can be a powerful tool for hurting your partner. Think of how you can use me when you want to punish or get revenge."
- "The more you can get of me, no matter what the cost to your relationship or health, the more powerful you will be."

- "The more you flash me around, the more powerful others will think you are."

Smart Heart Dialogue for Negotiating a Power Struggle

Warning: Even though you are using Smart Heart dialogues to neutralize power struggles and make discussions about the role of money in your relationship as safe and nonthreatening as possible, be aware that, for most couples just beginning to address the role of money in their relationship, these conversations will usually lead to *transitional points* in the relationship. Welcome these transitions as an opportunity for growth and increased intimacy in your relationship.

Smart Heart Dialogue for Dating Singles

Power struggles can occur at any time in a relationship. When you are first dating someone, don't assume that early power struggles mean you should break up. Working through conflicts with an understanding that fights about money are rarely *about* money can yield rich emotional benefits that may strengthen a new relationship.

Who makes the move when it comes to sex and money? Single men wonder if it's a sign of virility if they pay. They wonder, "If I make more than she makes, and I pay, will I be seen as a chauvinist? Or will she think it's romantic? Is she supposed to pay if she asks me out? If I let her pay, will she think I'm a deadbeat? Or will she think I'm very relaxed and secure? And if we split the bill, will she think I don't like her or find her unattractive?" What should be a fun and sexy first date can quickly deteriorate into an awkward power struggle when the check is delivered.

Case #1:

What he says: "Do you really need that?"

What he may mean: "Are you expecting me to buy that for you?"

The Smart Heart reply: "I don't really *need* anything, but it gives me pleasure. If I decide to get this, I'm hoping you're not going to feel resentful or be judgmental."

Case #2:

What she says: "You don't have to pay for this date. I'll split the check with you."

What she may mean: "If I pay my own way I'm not obligated to sleep with you and you're not entitled to any expectations."

The Smart Heart reply: "I appreciate your offer but I hope you don't feel like you owe me anything for taking you out. I don't want you to feel pressured. I'm willing to go as fast or slow in this relationship as you want."

Case #3:

What he says: "Whoever is paying can choose where we go."

What he may mean: "If you expect me to pay for you, then we will do what I want."

The Smart Heart reply: "I could understand from your patriarchal background that you feel that money is power. I don't equate money with this type of decision making. It's important to me that we take turns deciding how we spend our time together—no matter who is paying."

Case #4

What he says: "What do you want to do about the dinner check?"

What he may mean: "Are you assuming that I have plenty of money and that I will take care of you? Or are you the type of person who is willing to share?"

The Smart Heart reply: "I understand that there aren't any real rules about who pays on a date anymore. And I hope I have the chance to be generous with you. But I'm old-fashioned and would love it if you paid for dinner."

Case #5

What she says: "This restaurant is expensive. I'm concerned for your wallet and would like to ask you how you'd like to handle the check."

What she may mean: "I'm concerned about how much you're spending and worry you'll be resentful later if we don't go out again."

The Smart Heart reply: "It's nice of you to ask. I love it when a woman offers. I'm never sure whether my date is offended if I pay, or if she wants to be taken care of. I don't want to insult your independence, but I like to be generous, so if it's okay with you, I'll pay."

Case #6

What he says: "Do you want to split the bill?"

What she says: "I don't mind; some women feel if they pay for their share, they're not expected to have sex!"

What he says: "That's interesting. What does sex have to do with money?"

What she says: "Sometimes everything. We feel we owe you and want your approval."

His Smart Heart reply: "It's great we can talk like this; I really feel closer to you."

Her Smart Heart reply: "It's true. When a man can be open with me I feel like it starts our relationship on solid ground."

Smart Heart Dialogue for Married and Committed Couples

For couples that have been together awhile, ongoing power struggles may have become the norm in the relationship. It can be difficult to look past the surface tension to uncover the underlying triggers for these conflicts. Instead of shutting down when a power struggle surfaces, use Smart Heart dialogue to move beyond the usual money fights.

Case #1

What he says: "We can't afford to have a baby right now. We both need to keep working."

What he may mean: "I'm afraid that I can't support a family. I'm concerned that you will want to stop working and I will have too much financial responsibility. This is a huge change and I'm worried about how it will change our relationship."

The Smart Heart reply: "Having a baby is a big financial and emotional commitment and I'm nervous about it, too. There's never a perfectly 'right' time. I still want to have all the things and the time with you that we have planned for—even after the baby. Let's talk about how we can make that happen!"

Case #2:

What she says: "You said we couldn't afford a vacation to Europe and now you've bought season basketball tickets without telling me."

What she may mean: "I can't trust you and you're selfish."

The Smart Heart reply: "I know it's wrong for either of us to make unilateral decisions that involve large amounts of money. It makes me feel childish to have to ask you for permission to do something that I want to do. I need to be able to make some choices that are just for 'me,' not for 'us.' I need you to understand that just because you bring home the money doesn't mean that you control it."

Case #3

What she says: "You say that we have to save for a new house, but I want to send the kids to private schools. I wanted to go to a private school, but my parents wouldn't send me, either."

What she may mean: "I am trying to heal a childhood wound by living through our daughters. When you say it isn't important to you, I hear that you think *I* am not important to you."

The Smart Heart reply: "I'm sorry you felt deprived in your childhood. Is there anything I can do to make you feel more secure? It would be nice to send our children to private school, but I want to be able to afford a new house, too. Will you let me help you to choose which we should focus on?"

Smart Heart Jump Starts for a Balanced Power Dynamic

Once you have analyzed, understood, and rebalanced the power dynamic in your relationship using the exercises above, the following Smart Heart skills will allow you to maintain the new equilibrium and continue feeling the benefits of shared power around money:

- *Walk a mile in the other's shoes.* Honestly try to see things from your partner's perspective. Don't immediately worry, "But what about me?"
- *Look for the emotional history behind the actions.* Practicing empathetic responses will allow you to remove your own emotional reaction to the situation and help you to view your partner's actions in the right context.
- *Agree to respect each other's perceptions of power.* Identify and define the struggle. If one person thinks there is a problem, then there *is* a problem. It's that simple.
- *Fight fair, using time limits and by appointment only.* This is one of the most important rules in resolving relationship power struggles. But don't be afraid to work through conflict. Remember, it is the *polite* marriages that are most likely to fall victim to infidelity and fail.
- *Replace blame and criticism with solutions, attachment skills, and tenderness.* Predict and expect struggles and conflicts, but balance the stresses with pleasure. Use power struggles to make each of you, and your relationship, stronger and more secure.

A Contract for Financial Fidelity

In order to maintain the balance of power around love and money in our relationship, we agree to:

- *Face financial issues head-on to strengthen the relationship.* Using the rules for "fighting fair," work through tough money issues knowing that you will grow closer and more intimate by safely and openly communicating.
- *Understand, compromise, and work toward common goals.* Share your "script"—your thoughts, beliefs, and feelings about how things should go—and listen closely to your partner's. Accept coaching and don't assume your partner already knows what you want. Don't mind-read!
- *Make transactions around money feel safe.* If you can understand your attitude toward money within the context of your relationship, then you will begin to feel safe. If you feel safe, you will not have any physical or financial infidelity and you *will* have more passion.
- *Never use money as a punishment or reward.* Using money to manipulate your partner into changing his or her behavior guarantees a buildup of resentment that will inevitably explode in intense power struggles and may break up your relationship for good.

Step 3:
Divest Yourself of the Past

Understanding Your Inherited Money History

A s couples negotiate the Power Struggle stage, each conflict provides an opportunity for growth and change. These *transition* stages give the couple a chance to decide whether they should move on together or whether they should move on to other relationships. Transition stages can happen at any point in a relationship; it doesn't matter whether you are just beginning to date or have been together for years. Transition stages are usually precipitated by outside changes—things that are sometimes referred to as "life events"—such as deciding whether to move in together, get married, buy a house, have a child, change jobs, or go back to school.

When dealing with transitions in a relationship, several factors come into play. Perhaps the most important of these is your "family of origin." Simply put, this means the ways your background and upbringing influence your behavior. In every relationship choice you make, from the way you spend money to the type of partner that you choose to be with, your subconscious is urging you to repeat or avoid patterns that were present in your family during your childhood.

In *Getting the Love You Want*, his seminal book about relationships, Harville Hendrix (under whom I studied) explains that as you search for the ideal mate, you are guided by an unconscious image of a partner that has been forming your entire life. He calls the inner picture the *imago*, which is a Latin term for "image." Your imago is a composite of those people who influenced you most at an early age, most commonly your mother and father, grandparents, and sometimes siblings or babysitters or other caregivers or role models. Your brain has stored impressions of all of these people, from the color of their hair to the sound of their voices to the way they smiled and their moods, talents, and interests. Your brain also recorded your significant interactions with them. These stored impressions and interactions are both positive and negative. Your brain did not analyze this data, it simply used it to create a template that you are largely unaware of.

Dr. Hendrix explains that the motivation to find a romantic partner that matches your imago is infused with the urgency of healing childhood wounds. In other words, you will search for a romantic partner who can fulfill the positive parts of your imago as well as compensate for the areas in which you have unfinished childhood business involving formative adults.

I have found Dr. Hendrix's imago work to be very helpful in getting couples to understand their relationship dynamics around money. From a very early age, money has a role in your life *vis-à-vis* your family. And how your parents, grandparents, and other significant people in your life behaved with finances plays an important role in developing what I call the *financial imago.* Using an exercise based on Dr. Hendrix's reconstruction of your imago, you can uncover the subconscious ways in which you re-create childhood expectations and suffer childhood wounds related to the role of money in your relationship.

In my own life, I can clearly see how my financial imago affected my choice in marrying my first husband. While my father was generous with money, he was also a gambler, so there were times when money was plentiful, and times when money was extremely tight. I admired his generosity, but even as a child could sense the stress when there was not much money in the household budget. It was unsettling sometimes, not to know whether we would be eating steak for dinner that week or subsisting on spaghetti. It really depended on how well his business had done that week. Or more accurately, how well his business had done compared to how well his poker games had gone. Despite this recipe for financial instability, there was no cheapness in my family, but no boundaries, either. When we had money we had it. When we didn't we didn't. My parents' mantra was, "don't deprive yourself; don't punish yourself when there's no money—money will come; you can always make more."

When I married my first husband, I wildly overcorrected. My first husband didn't believe in credit cards. He had a lot of savings. He was ambitious. He was so worried around money that he would carry a calculator to the grocery store and tally the items as we put them into the shopping cart. If I went over the budget he would wait until we got to the register and then announce that we had to put something back. His dependence on money as a means of control probably was one of the reasons the marriage ended. When he lost his job and his earning power, he may have lost his self-confidence. When I went back to school, got a job, and began making my own money, it may have been hard for him, thus he became emotionally distant and reserved.

If I had realized the importance of acknowledging my family of origin and financial imago at the time I began dating my first husband, I might have seen that we were doomed to clash over financial matters. Now I know that when you marry, you also marry the money behavior of the person. The exercise that follows allows you to explore how your own financial imago was formed. It is based on Dr. Hendrix's Ten-Step Program for a Conscious Marriage as outlined in *Getting the Love You Want.*

Exercise: Understanding Your Financial Imago

Part 1

Imagine you have returned to your childhood home as a young child. Re-create a typical day in your home as you interact with your parents, siblings, and other important people. Imagine asking them questions about money (even if such talk was discouraged in your childhood home). Do not imagine how they might respond to you as an adult; hear their answers as if you were still a child. Remember how they respond to these queries and note your emotions in each of these interactions: abandoned, shamed, blamed, angry, sad, happy, or secure. Did your parents tell you they couldn't afford things? Did they give you everything you asked for, but expect certain behaviors in return? Were they generous with each other?

Step A: List all of the positive impressions you have of money. You don't need to note what behaviors belong to which individuals; just list as many as you can. Use simple phrases such as, "I want you to have this," "I love you and you deserve it," "Saving is responsible," and so on.

Step B: List all of the negative impressions you recall about money: "triggered fights," "worried there's not enough," "can't afford to participate," "ashamed about how my family acted around money," "used for punishment," "afraid," and so on.

Now circle the positive and negative traits that seem to affect you the most in the present. This list of circled traits is your financial imago.

Step C: Complete the following sentence: What I wanted most as a child and didn't get because of money was _____.
(This answer should be something emotional, rather than material, such as "Attention—my father was always working late.")

Step D: Complete this sentence: As a child, whenever money was discussed in my family, I had these negative feelings over and over again:_____.

Part 2

Step E: List recurring frustrations you experienced as a child that had to do with money. In one column, list the cause, and in another, list your response. For example:

Frustration	Response
Made grades to be accepted to private school, but couldn't go because of cost.	Failed classes at public school.
Wanted particular status item but was denied.	Took money from parents' wallet or purse until I could afford to buy the item myself.

Part 3

Now you will bring all of this information together to analyze how your unfinished childhood business impacts your choice of partner and relationship with money and your partner. Recognizing this hidden agenda will allow you to work with your partner more effectively during the transitional times that strain your relationship, whether married, single, engaged, or living together.

Complete each of the following sentences by filling in the information from above:

I have spent my life searching for a person who has these characteristics in financial interactions: [insert the traits you circled in step A]

When I am with such a person, I am bothered when he or she behaves in the following way when dealing with money: [insert the traits you circled in step B]

I wish that person would give me: [insert your answer from step C]

When I am insecure around money, I have these feelings: [insert your answer from step D]

And I often respond in this way: [insert your answers from step E]

You now have a map of your emotional inherited legacy surrounding money and finances. Link this knowledge to your present or your fantasy of a future partner. Have your partner complete this exercise as well. Defining and acknowledging your financial imago illuminates the hidden agenda around money that you bring to each relationship.

Because I had become aware of my own financial imago during my first marriage, when I began dating my current husband, Jeff, I was immediately aware of how his generosity filled an important ideal for me. When I first met Jeff, I was just getting back into the dating game. I had met several men, all of whom suggested that we go out for a coffee to get to know each other better. Though this was a perfectly reasonable suggestion, to me it felt as if they were unwilling to take a financial risk to get to know me—why should they pay for dinner when the relationship might not work out? When Jeff called to ask me out on a date, he immediately suggested dinner. I had vowed to be more open about money with the men I was dating and so I asked him, "Are you sure you want to buy me dinner? What if we don't like each other after the date?"

"I have to eat anyway," he said. "Why not have dinner with you?"

With his answer, Jeff assured me that he was more than willing to take a risk, both financially and emotionally. I immediately was enamored and responded to this sense of generosity.

But we still had work to do as we started to fall in love. Jeff's financial imago was very different from mine. Where my father was generous, and my mother encouraged me to always take care of myself, even if it meant splurging when money was tight, Jeff's mother was very thrifty. I remember coming home one day with two shirts that I had spontaneously bought for him. He admired both of them and then told me that I could take one back. I was hurt. Didn't he like the shirt? He assured me that he did, but it soon became clear that he was very uncomfortable accepting two shirts. His mother would only ever allow him to have one item at a time—and only if it was on sale. In his mind, he didn't even need a shirt. So while a gift of one might have been acceptable, a gift of two bordered on frivolous and self-indulgent. If I had been less aware of his financial imago, I might have felt hurt and we might have fought. Instead, I was able to talk with him to help him realize that he was worthy of receiving such a gift and that it didn't cause me any financial pain to give it to him. Now it gives both of us great pleasure to go shopping and have him pick out several of whatever he likes. He has worked out his childhood wound with me, which is why he picked me.

Your family history with money doesn't simply *create* your financial imago. This inherited legacy influences most money interactions you have. While your family money history is always with you (we will examine this in depth beginning on page 137), and clearly affects the money relationship you build with your adult partners, the life circumstances that are *triggers* for conflicts around money are equally important. When a couple is moving through a transition stage in their relationship, how they view money is usually a factor in their decision-making process.

In order to pass through a transition stage in a relationship, while avoiding the harmful behaviors associated with financial infidelity, it is helpful to identify some of the most common life events likely to provoke reasons for change in both the emotional and financial arena.

How to Successfully Negotiate the Top Ten Transitional Financial Stresses

Certain financial events are more likely to trigger transitional events in a relationship. These changes can make either or both partners in a relationship feel more vulnerable. This insecurity can manifest in many damaging behaviors, including financial infidelity. In the midst of any of these events, it is crucial to acknowledge the stressful impact they may have on your life. When you ignore or deny the issues that arise at these times you risk triggering a breakup, but more importantly, you miss the opportunity to successfully transition to a new level of communication and security in your relationship.

1. ***Becoming engaged or moving in together***. Deciding to take your relationship to the next level also means deciding what to do about commingling your finances. I want to stress again that if you cannot discuss finances with your future partner, then you are headed for trouble. Be prepared to discuss prenuptial or cohabitation agreements. Don't practice magical thinking or expect a person to suddenly change once you are living together. Before you buy—or accept—the ring or call the moving van, you *must* take the time to talk about the following: How will you handle banking and finances? Will you have separate accounts? If so, how much will each person contribute to joint expenses? What expenses will you consider "joint"? (Vacations? Luxury items? Vehicles?) Do you want to have a written agreement (a prenup)? Do you want to rent or own a home? How much debt are you willing to take on and how much debt have you already accrued?

2. ***Getting married***. Huge weddings can mean that you start your life together deeply in debt. (The first year marriage is already the hardest.) There is also the emotional stress of bringing extended families together (sometimes for the first time). If you are getting married, you should have already addressed some of the big questions above, but don't forget to think about the literal cost of a wedding. Here are some things you should consider before you set the date: How much are you willing to spend? Will family help to defray the costs? Who will pay for what? What is more important—a lavish wedding or a large guest list? Can you afford to host a large wedding? Have a rehearsal dinner? How important is an expensive dress? A large bridal party? How important is location? Decor? Would you rather have a lavish wedding or an exotic honeymoon—or both?

3. ***Having a baby***. The impending arrival of a child, whether through pregnancy or adoption, raises a host of emotional and financial issues. A surprising number of the couples I see argue vehemently

about how much money is spent on the children. Before the child arrives, be sure to discuss with your partner the short- and long-term costs of raising a child, including: Are you willing to pay for fertility treatments if necessary? How will you budget for adoption if you choose to build a family in that way? Will one or both of you return to work after the child arrives? What type of child care do you expect to need? Will you need to purchase a new, or second, car? How important is it to buy new clothing, furniture, and other things for the baby—or will hand-me-downs be fine? What will you do if the child has special needs? What kind of education do you hope to provide? If private schools, how will you budget? How do you plan to save for college? Remember, also, that bringing a child into a relationship may trigger fears of abandonment or cause resentment. Talk about what it will cost to maintain emotional closeness: Will you be able to go out for date nights? Will you be able to afford an occasional romantic getaway for two?

4. *Job loss.* The loss of a job is stressful even when both individuals in the relationship are employed. The emotional impact on self-esteem cannot be underestimated, particularly for those who tie their personal worth to their net worth. When faced with the financial stress of a job loss, it is critical for couples to work together to support each other emotionally and financially. Ideally everyone should have six to eight months' worth of living expenses put away in cash in case of unemployment. If not, the best way to deal with the stress is to avoid blame and plan together how to adjust financially. Important questions to consider include: What cash is immediately available for living expenses? What expenses are you able to cut in the short term? In the long term? What is the most practical way to search for a new job, in terms of both career and financial security? Can the other partner increase earnings to help with any shortfall? How will you present your financial situation to friends or family? Are you willing

to ask for help from family or friends? What plan can you make
to keep your credit under control while funds are restricted?

5. *Midlife.* This is an equal-opportunity crisis and both women and
   men can suffer similarly strong reactions to this life passage. When
   either partner is struggling with making a next step in life there
   are serious financial considerations that should be discussed: What
   are your plans for retirement? How do you see your life together
   in your golden years? How much help do your children expect
   from you? Are you willing to relocate? If you leave your established career, will you be able to find other work at a financial level
   that will sustain your family and/or lifestyle? Are you willing to
   make a change in your lifestyle to support a major change?

6. *Changes in earning status (retirement, promotion, etc.).* Losing a
   job is not the only reason couples can face money stress. Any
   change in income may become a catalyst for discussion, disagreement, or change. If you are facing retirement or anticipating an
   increase in income consider the following: How will your spending and saving patterns be affected? Will your control over free
   time change? How do you plan to spend free time? Are there new
   hobbies or travel plans that call for review of your existing budget? If retiring, what areas will you be saving in (clothes for work,
   lunches out, transportation expenses)? Where might expenses increase (club memberships, travel plans, social events)? If you are
   receiving a promotion or increase in salary, are you planning on
   giving yourself a material reward for your achievement (a new
   watch, an important piece of jewelry, a new high-tech toy)? Are
   there any new costs associated with your promotion? Is there
   anything you have been saving for that you plan to acquire or
   change immediately?

7. *Illness or chronic conditions.* Chronic conditions affecting mental
   or physical health—whether yours, your partner's, or close family

members'—may strain your financial resources. Take steps ahead of time to ensure that you are protected if an unexpected health issue should arise. Do you have sufficient health insurance? Do you have disability insurance? Have you planned for long-term care before you need it? What can you do if you or your partner is forced to stop working, either for a short time or permanently? If you have a child with a chronic issue are you prepared to budget for any necessary support that is not available through public agencies?

8. *Divorce.* There is no denying that divorce is expensive for both parties. Often I see couples where the man is demanding a divorce and it comes out in therapy that he feels trapped by his responsibilities to his wife and family. He may think that divorcing will allow him the freedom to selfishly pursue his own interests. He may tell me that he plans to buy a new sports car, or a boat, or admit that it has become a financial strain to support both a wife and a girlfriend and that he has decided to spend more on the girlfriend. But the truth of the matter is that cold, hard numbers don't lie. Once the costs of divorce lawyers, child support, alimony, division of assets, and so on have been calculated, many men hoping to save money by getting a divorce realize that, in fact, their standard of living is likely to go down—especially those who are planning to swap wife for girlfriend. I always tell them it is basic math: supporting two families is more expensive than supporting one. It may surprise you to find out that, for some couples I counsel, the financial costs associated with ending their marriage are high enough to cause them to decide to attempt reconciliation. Their anger sometimes is intensified by lawyers' battles and precludes them from seeing the "good" and the foundation of their marriage. I never encourage couples to stay together simply because of money or children, but some do decide to stay together using the excuse that they do not want to alter their lifestyles. Through money they can decide to see "their love." If you are considering divorce, don't forget to consider the financial repercussions: Do you have a prenup or postnup?

What expenses will arise to care for your children over the long term? Will you make or lose money on the sale of shared assets? And, perhaps more importantly—are fights over money one of the driving factors in seeking to end your relationship? (Because if they are, believe me, the fights will not end once you are divorced!)

9. *Aging parents.* For the boomer generation in particular, the care for aging parents has become a transitional stage trigger. If you or your partner anticipates having to become financially responsible for the care and well-being of your parents as they age it is important that you make predetermined decisions about the level of monetary support you are willing to commit. Be sure to consider the following: Are you and/or your siblings willing or able to help? Would your partner welcome your parents to share your home? Would you welcome your partner's parents? Are you counting on receiving an inheritance? What will happen if your parents are forced to spend their savings in their later years? Don't let family money history stop you from discussing this important topic with your parents, either. Some important questions for you to ask include: Do they have plans in place for their care as they age? Will their Social Security and/or Medicaid benefits be sufficient for their living and health expenses? Are they willing to spend their savings and investments (and your potential inheritance) on maintaining their quality of life as they age?

10. *Death.* It is sobering to think about how much money is related to death. I've heard many stories of families that were torn apart over the death of a parent and ensuing sibling squabbles over inheritance and wills. Understandably, no one wants to talk about what will happen when a loved one dies—or what will happen when they themselves are gone—but it is important to make sure that your affairs are in order. For some couples I counsel, having this discussion leaves them with a greater sense of security about

their financial future and removes some of the stresses they may feel about providing for their families. When talking about how death may affect your relationship financially consider some of the following: Are you expecting to receive an inheritance from your parents? Will you be able to live on it during retirement? How important is it for you to leave an inheritance to your children? Consider, too, that money is not the only legacy you can leave after your death. A great exercise to help you prioritize when getting your affairs in order is to draft what is called an "ethical will." An ethical will is not a legal document, but rather a very personal legacy. It is a written document that allows you to share your values and life lessons, to describe your hopes and dreams for the future, and to share blessings, love, and forgiveness with your family and friends. An ethical will can be written at any time and to anyone. It can be shared while you are still alive, or you may put it with your final effects to be read after you have died. For more information about ethical wills, go to www .ethicalwill.com.

An important point to realize in making decisions about these transitions is that each individual is strongly influenced by perceptions and preconceptions derived from their family histories. Asking the types of questions above will not just reveal how your partner wants to use money, but, if you listen carefully, you will be able to learn *why* your partner chooses to use money in certain ways.

Daniel and his wife, Caroline, came to see me when their discussions about whether or not to have a child had triggered Daniel to begin an affair and pushed their relationship to the edge. They were at the point of deciding whether or not they should separate.

"I'm not that young anymore," Caroline said. "If we're going to have a child, we have to have one soon. But Daniel won't commit."

"She doesn't seem to understand what a huge step having a kid would

be," Daniel said. "All I want her to think about is the kind of lifestyle changes we will have to make. She loves to take expensive vacations and go shopping at the mall, but that will all have to stop."

"I've told you time and time again that I'm willing to change all of that if we have a baby," Caroline said.

The more Daniel talked, the more apparent it became that he felt backed into a corner by her insistence. His wife was so adamant about her desire to have a baby that he felt like he didn't have a choice. As we continued the session, Daniel admitted that he thought that having a baby meant he would lose his freedom.

It wasn't until I asked him to talk about his family that Daniel was able to consider how his childhood had negatively affected how he perceived the interrelationship between freedom and money and choice.

When Daniel was going away to college, his mother had refused to pay for his first choice of school because his brother was going to the same college and she wanted him to find a less expensive choice. His mother told him that she would only support him financially if he did what she said. He felt that he had no choice in his future and vowed that he would always have enough money, that no one could tell him what to do or control him through money. He worked hard and became a success, but even today his mother still attempts to control him, claiming that he owes his success to her financial backing and that he has no choice but to take care of her as a way of paying her back.

When Caroline talked about planning for the expense of a baby, Daniel immediately felt as if she was trying to limit his money, thus his freedom. He began looking for ways in which he could make a choice to do what he wanted. Having an affair was a natural progression because it allowed him to both be free of responsibility and act out some of the resentment he had against his mother.

Once Caroline understood the tangled legacy of finances, freedom, and emotional responsibility that Daniel had inherited from his mother, she was able to find the empathy to forgive him for the affair. In subsequent sessions they worked at untangling the strong emotions Daniel had attached to money from the choice about planning a family together.

When you are able to recognize and respect the historical emotional context acting as the force behind you and your partner's decision-making processes, you will be able to consciously divest yourself of inherited patterns and learn to work together to arrive at a joint solution. When both partners share an understanding of each other's past experiences they are able to both initiate and participate in financial discussions, especially during times of difficult transitions when most growth can occur. Working through these challenges together reaffirms each person's courage and commitment to the relationship.

Your Family Moneygram

Change cannot happen in a vacuum. Unless you become aware of your inherited triggers around money matters, you can find your relationship stuck in an endless loop of Transition stage to Power Struggle stage to new transition to new power struggle. Eventually, deeply frustrated, but not knowing how to end the cycle, you or your partner may decide to simply end the relationship. Not just knowing *why* you or your partner reacts in a particular way to hot-button money topics but taking specific actions can help you empathize, negotiate, and compromise through Smart Heart dialogue. When you approach a discussion about money during a transition stage you will be better able to safely express your old wounds and fears and then lovingly work together to attain shared goals. You and your partner, with help from your parents, should both complete the following Family Moneygram, which allows you to uncover the repetitive patterns that you may have unknowingly inherited. Analyzing these "money scripts" that have been handed down from generation to generation can help you to change your legacy from *unconscious* to *conscious* and your relationships to money from *incompatible* to *compatible* and hand down a different legacy to your children!

This moneygram is derived from a way of charting family history known as a "genogram." The genogram, a graphic tool designed to provide a diagram of familial relationship patterns, was developed by Murray Bowen, MD, and named by Philip Guerin, Jr., MD (under whom I studied). I use the Family Genogram in my work with couples that are struggling to understand why their relationship is susceptible to affairs or other triangles involving money. The genogram allows these couples to trace patterns of abandonment, separation, distancing, and so on, in their family history. I have adapted it below for you to use as a tool for discovering patterns and opening up conversation about familial relationships to money and finance.

How to Use the Moneygram

Begin by recording information about you and your siblings. Do they have successful careers? Are any married? Have any been divorced? Any remarried? Are you aware of any financial infidelities? Has anyone claimed bankruptcy? Are they savers? Spenders? Are they risk takers or very cautious? Do any of them have financial arrangements such as prenups or trust funds?

Work backward, answering the same questions for your parents, then your aunts and uncles, then your grandparents and even great-grandparents. You should initiate discussions with your family in order to find out necessary information, even if you think you already know the answers. Don't be surprised if it is difficult to get them to open up to you about their finances and money behaviors. Ask them about expectations, disappointments, and fears. Try to find out how your family communicated about money. Learn who controls the money, who earns it, who spends it. Try to find out how they perceive marriage and money.

Don't be surprised if these conversations are challenging. Money can be a taboo topic in any relationship. In many families, part of the money legacy is associated with shame and guilt, or is too private to discuss. Be gently persistent and listen with an open mind and without judgment to what family members may share with you. Ask them what they would have liked money to mean to them in their relationship or life. In what ways would they have liked to change their relationships or marriage in relationship to money? You may find it helpful to share your reasons for asking, "My husband [or wife, boyfriend, girlfriend, or fiancé] and I have hit a rough spot in dealing with some financial issues [or are getting serious about our relationship and want to avoid money problems in the future]. We need to understand and change how we relate to each other about money and I'm hoping you can help me search for patterns in my past that will help us."

Using the chart on page 140 as a sample, note your answers in abbreviated form. You may be surprised to see certain patterns emerging. See if you notice instances in which money was part of a triangle for members of your family. For example, your parents may have grown closer over spending money on the children. On the other hand, perhaps you find a family dynamic where partners were distanced over spending money—perhaps in spending on an older family member. Consider how money acted to dilute or avoid other issues in these relationships. What do you think would have happened if money had been taken out of the equation? Has money acted as a stand-in for other needs?

These symbols allow you to note the *money behaviors* and relationship dynamics for several generations of your family. Feel free to add your own, as needed. Talk to your parents, grandparents, and other family members as you complete your Family Moneygram following the examples that my husband, Jeff, and I provide. When you have finished, create a chart (see example) to help you analyze patterns around money, love, and sex in your family history. This analysis will allow you to predict, prevent, overcome, and solve money behaviors now or in the future.

FAMILY MONEYGRAM FOR READERS

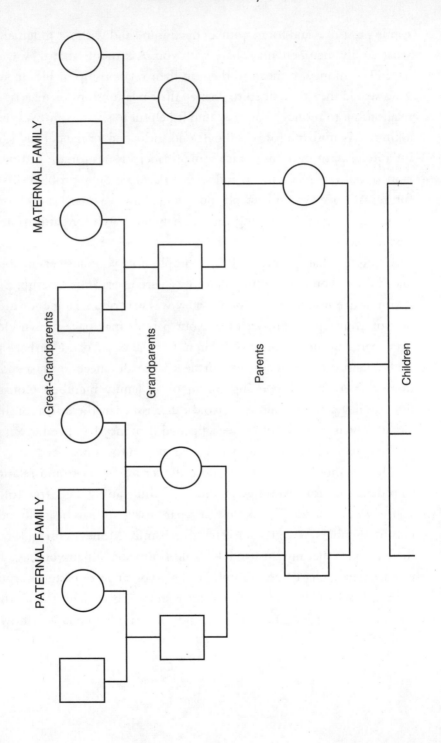

Key to Family Moneygram

□	man	/	separated
○	woman	//	divorced
C	compatible money couple	=	remarried
I	incompatible money couple	♡	happily married
FI	financial infidelity	SFI	separation because of FI
$–	spender	DFI	divorce because of FI
$+	saver	SS+D	simultaneous separations and divorces within a family which affects money
$$$	binge spender		
$++	hoarder		
$––	poor	S x I	sexual infidelity
$!	wealthy	PM	pursuer with money
$M	middle class	DM	distancer with money
PR	poor rich (does not have money, but acts and spends as if has lots)	PN	prenup
		NN	no-nup
		PTN	postnup
RP	rich poor (has money, but acts and spends as if has little)	W	workaholic
		Im	impulsive
		$☺	money for fun
WC$–	worried, cautious spender	☺–	carefree, lives for today
WC$+	worried, cautious saver	☺+	saves, lives for tommorrow
GG	generous, giving	◯	death of a parent (alters intimacy and money; form of betrayal)
⊗$	no savings		
⊗R$	no retirement fund		
⊗C$	no college fund	SOL	starting over (lost in war, Holocaust, Great Depression)
CCD	credit card debt		
NCCD	no credit card debt	IU	immigrated to U.S.
▽	magical thinker (with money)	⊡	gambler
PS	power struggler (with money)	SOW	starting over (wealthy then lost it)
R	risk taker		
L	loafer	S$	sabateur with money
UE	unemployed	MM	married for money
WH	withholding	Ⓢ	bankruptcy
___	married	⚠$	money as triangle (avoiding the "real" couple issues)

DR. BONNIE'S MONEYGRAM

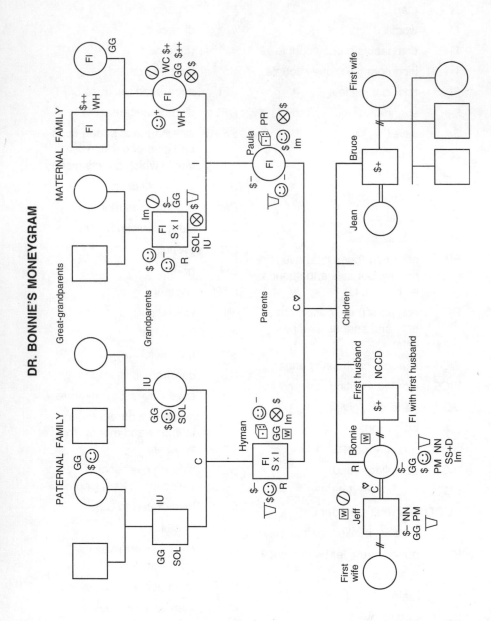

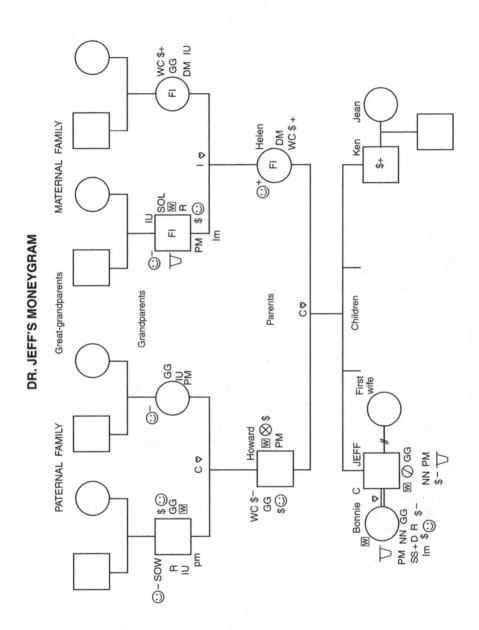

DR. JEFF'S MONEYGRAM

Analysis of Dr. Bonnie's and Dr. Jeff's Moneygrams

This chart allows you to see at a glance how you and your partner's family history of money compare. Even if you think you each have very different money styles, you may be surprised to see how much overlap there is when you study several generations of your families. As you see from my example, Jeff and I have a (rare) conscious and compatible money marriage—one where our financial imagos (the same) are different from our emotional imagoes (different)—as did several generations of our family members. What about yours? Most couples have opposite financial imagos. Use this information to open a discussion with your partner. Do you have a conscious money marriage? Most couples are attracted to each other because their financial and emotional imagoes are different (opposites attract). Can you see patterns of overcorrection or compensation that have been handed down through the generations? How has your family legacy around money affected your own relationship to money—and to your partner's money behaviors?

TRAIT	DR. BONNIE'S FAMILY	DR. JEFF'S FAMILY
Generous	Father, mother, maternal and paternal grandparents, maternal great-grandmother, paternal great-grandmother, Bonnie	Father, mother, maternal and paternal grandparents, Jeff
Money belief: "Live for today"	Father, mother, maternal grandfather, Bonnie	Father, maternal grandfather, paternal grandfather, Jeff
Worried, cautious about money	Maternal grandmother, maternal great-grandfather	Mother, maternal grandmother
Saver	Maternal grandmother, brother	Mother, maternal grandmother, brother

TRAIT	DR. BONNIE'S FAMILY	DR. JEFF'S FAMILY
Hoarder	Maternal grandmother, maternal great-grandfather	
Money belief: "You can always make more"	Father, mother, maternal grandfather, paternal grandmother and grandfather, paternal great-grandmother, Bonnie	Father, maternal grandfather, paternal grandmother and grandfather, Jeff
Money belief: "Use money for fun"	Father, mother, maternal grandfather, paternal grandmother, Bonnie	Father, maternal grandfather, paternal grandfather, Jeff
Spender	Father, mother, maternal grandfather, paternal grandmother, Bonnie	Maternal grandfather, paternal grandparents, Jeff
Money belief: "Save money for a rainy day; live for tomorrow"	Maternal grandmother, maternal great-grandmother	Mother, maternal grandmother
Money belief: "Work hard, play hard"	Father, mother, maternal grandfather, paternal grandmother, Bonnie	Jeff (with some help from Bonnie)
Workaholic	Father, mother, paternal grandparents, maternal grandfather, Bonnie	Father, maternal grandfather, paternal grandfather, Jeff
Never knew if there was money or not	Mother (as a child), maternal grandmother (as a child and an adult), great-grandmother, Bonnie (as a child)	Mother (as a child), maternal grandmother Jeff (as a child)
No savings	Father, mother, maternal grandparents and great-grandparents	Father, mother, maternal grandparents

TRAIT	DR. BONNIE'S FAMILY	DR. JEFF'S FAMILY
"Layaway" plan- save for a goal	Mother, Bonnie	
Risk taker	Father, maternal grandfather, paternal grandmother, Bonnie	Paternal grandfather, maternal grandfather
Hard worker	Father, mother, maternal grandparents, paternal grandparents, Bonnie	Father, mother, brother, maternal grandparents, paternal grandfather
Put family needs before self-interest in regard to money	Father, maternal grand parents, Bonnie (In his business, my father employed his aunt, brother, son, mother, and my first husband. He paid for his grandchildren's education, from infancy through college, and fully provided for his in-laws.)	Father, paternal grandfather, maternal grandfather, Jeff (Maternal grandfather paid for his and his wife's surviving family members to come to the United States post-Holocaust. Paternal grandfather and father each helped support his respective mother's family.)
Immigrated to the United States	Maternal grandparents, paternal grandparents, maternal great-grandfather	Maternal grandparents, paternal grandfather, maternal great-grandmother
Experienced starting over financially	Father, mother, Bonnie (After government tore down housing projects, my father's business had to be rebuilt.)	Maternal grandfather, paternal grandparents, mother (He lost most of his business due to WWII; she pawned her jewelry and lost valuable property inherited from her father.)

TRAIT	DR. BONNIE'S FAMILY	DR. JEFF'S FAMILY
Couples in an incompatible, unconscious money marriage	Maternal grandparents, Bonnie and first husband, maternal great-grand parents	Maternal grandparents
Couples in a compatible, conscious money marriage	Father and mother, paternal grandparents, Bonnie and Jeff	Father and mother, paternal grandparents, Jeff and Bonnie

When you are finished with your moneygram chart, take another piece of paper and follow the instructions below to better understand how these patterns of money behavior continue to affect your life and relationships today. Prompt your partner to recall their own Money Tree memories.

- First, list the money dialogues that have been handed down through the generations in your family and how these dialogues affected your family. *My father said, "You can always make more money."*
- Note how you have perceived these messages. *I heard: "You don't have to worry about money; there will always be plenty."*
- Take these real and perceived dialogues and match them to the money behaviors you observed in your family. *Despite my father's philosophy that there would always be money, there were often times when we did not have enough money for preferred groceries.*
- Think about what message you wish you had received. *I wish my father had said, "Even though we can always make more money, it's important to put some aside."*
- Finally, analyze how these admittedly mixed messages and actions have influenced your choice of romantic partner. In what ways, both positive and negative, have your relationships reflected these messages?

For instance, after I completed my own Family Moneygram, I noticed that the money dialogue was similar on both my maternal and my paternal side for more three generations. I inherited a strong legacy that money was for fun, to be used generously, not to be worried about. I believed that saving was not a priority, and that money would continue to flow. My family passed down the philosophy that it was important to "live for today." It is interesting to note that Jeff and I "pay ourselves first" by setting aside a portion of our income before using the balance to pay bills or purchase "treats." Due to my legacy this has proven to be the most effective method to ensure that we save.

In my first marriage, I chose a man I thought was very generous. He spent lavishly on me in the honeymoon stage, which reminded me of my father, plus he *saved* and did not have credit cards, which I admired. Looking at my family legacy, it is clear why I picked him. Once we married, however, I began to see that he was actually very thrifty. (He resented when I stopped working in order to attend grad school, practice family therapy training, and obtain my PhD because it meant I would stop being the main breadwinner and he would have to step up his financial responsibility.) Clearly, he did not share the same philosophy toward spending that I did. As a result we had many conflicts over money as I began to resent the very things I had first admired, and ultimately our marriage ended in divorce. It was during our divorce that I first became aware of the trust-shattering impact of financial infidelity. When I began to talk about divorce, my then-husband secretly withdrew all of our money from our shared bank account. At that moment, it became clear how important money was to him in the context of a relationship—and perhaps more importantly, how ultimately unimportant it was to me.

When I met my current husband, Jeff, I was aware of my financial imago and so I knew I had to ask him a lot of questions about his family's history with money. Because of the financial infidelity in my first marriage, I made sure to use Smart Heart dialogue when talking about finances and money with Jeff. I found that we shared an inherited attitude toward money and that while Jeff's mother was frugal (unlike my mother, but very much like my maternal grandmother), his father and my father shared very similar money dialogues. Because Jeff and I understand our family legacy around money, we were able to work toward a conscious money marriage.

Your Family Financial Legacy

Looking back at my family history, I see that my first exposure to financial infidelity occurred when I was quite young. I can remember my grandmother coming downstairs dressed to the nines in a brand new dress.

"Is that new, Dearie?" my grandfather asked. "It looks very nice on you."

"Oh, this old thing?" she responded. "I've had it in my closet forever. Just never had the occasion to wear it."

As a youngster, I was confused. Grandma was clearly lying. And we had always been taught that lying was bad.

When I was older and had studied family of origin as part of my training, I came to realize that Grandma—who had often told me stories of her miserly father—couldn't accept how generous Grandpa was. Even though they really couldn't afford splurges like new dresses, he was always glad to see that she had bought herself something. But despite her husband's generous nature, she continued to live in guilt and fear that she'd be "found out" whenever she bought anything she considered frivolous.

The money legacy passed down another generation, to my mother, who never wanted to ask my very generous father for money. Instead they developed a "game" where my mother would help herself to all the change that was left in my father's pants pockets at the end of the day. My father, fully aware of her sneaking extra spending money, always made sure there was cash in his pockets at the end of the day. He never mentioned it was missing, and she never had to confess to taking it.

From them, I learned the art of financial omission.

Of course, my brother and I inherited our own financial legacies. In my first marriage, I married a man who saved in a way my father never could. (In fact, my father often borrowed money from my brother, who was good at saving from the very early age of seven.)

From one generation of financial infidelity to another, our family legacy was unconsciously handed down until I learned the truth about financial infidelity and how it damages a marriage—or any relationship.

Whether it is conscious or unconscious, your financial legacy impacts your relationship. In order to forge a safe and loving connection when making decisions around money, it is important to recognize and let go of all expectations, hurts, and fears that constitute your family legacy, and may prevent you from initiating talks about money with your partner. If you were raised to believe that it is "shameful" to talk about money, you may have a particularly difficult time safely communicating with your partner about the feelings and emotions you attach to money. The following exercise is designed to help you feel more comfortable about discussing what money means to you, both in terms of your family of origin and in terms of defining the money legacy you will pass down to your own children.

Exercise: Family Letters

These letters are meant to be shared with your partner in order to help him or her understand how your family history with money has influenced your emotional responses to the role of money in a relationship and to share the legacy of financial fidelity that you hope to pass along to your children. You may decide whether or not to actually send them to your parents and children.

Letter to a parent: Write a letter to your parents telling them how the money dynamic in your household affected you as you were growing up. Recall instances where you felt punished or rewarded around money. Explain how this has influenced your current relationship with your partner when discussing or handling money. Do not blame or vent angrily: simply share the feelings—whether positive or negative—that come up when you revisit the role and power of money in your childhood.

If there is a particular incident that has special power for you, revisit it in this letter. For example, in my money letter to my parents, I recalled a confrontation between my parents over money that resonated with me for many years. It was not until I was an adult and working through my family legacy that I understood the full significance of this incident. It was prom time, and my boyfriend and I were going to both my school's prom and his. My mother took me shopping for a dress and when I found two beautiful gowns she insisted that I get both, even though they were equally expensive. When we got home, my father was furious. He wanted to know why I would need two dresses—after all, the dances were at two different schools, no one would know. But my mother stood her ground, insisting that I needed both. At the time I was confused and distressed. I could have worn the same dress, but it seemed terribly important to my mother that I have two. At the same time, my father wasn't angry with me or accusing me of being greedy, but he seemed inexplicably angry with my mother for spending so lavishly on me, rather than getting herself something.

When I shared my money letter with my parents, their responses allowed me to understand why the situation was so fraught. My mother's mother had grown up during the Depression and, as a result, was incredibly thrifty. She rarely spent money, and would never consider giving in to what seemed to her to be an indulgence. My mother told me how, in high school, she had made the cheerleading squad—an achievement she had been proud of—and when she excitedly told her mother that she would need a uniform so she could cheer at the games, my grandmother refused to buy her one. It wasn't something she "needed." From that moment on, my mother swore that she would never let money interfere with the dreams of her own children. My grandmother's withholding caused my mother to overcorrect with me and this legacy of financial infidelity continued for yet another generation as it affected my first marriage.

And my father's strong response? I learned that he was compensating for the extreme guilt he felt over an affair that he was carrying on—and that my mother likely knew about. As long as he could see that she was indulging herself—spending his money in ways that might be considered frivolous—he felt she was tacitly absolving him of his guilt.

For much of my young adult life, I had felt guilty that I had made my father angry and that I had somehow deprived my mother by allowing her to buy me two dresses. The fact of the matter was that it was not about me at all, but about the relationship between my parents and their own inherited family legacy of money. The same is true when it comes to Jeff and the story of the two shirts.

Letter to your children: Write a letter to your children telling them everything you know about how the family finances affect them. Explain how you have prioritized spending for the family. Let them know what you plan to leave them as a financial inheritance and whether or not you expect them to become financially independent. Express any hopes you have about how they might take care of you financially as you age. Write down the things you believe are positive about money. Tell them the things that you believe are negative about money. Be honest. Remember: you can choose whether or not to show this letter to your children—now, or ever.

> *Greg and his wife, Debbie, came to see me after she found out that he had been having an affair. She had been suspicious of various expenses and the amount of time he had been spending at work, but whenever she questioned him he would lie to her. She pointed out that whenever he was caught in a lie, he would immediately give her some incredibly expensive gift and make dramatic promises—none of which he ever kept—about how he would change. Debbie was ready to divorce him. She told me that she doubted she would ever be able to fill the emptiness that he claimed he felt. Over the course of many sessions, it became apparent that instead of participating in a marriage, Greg was essentially reenacting his childhood relationship with his mother.*
>
> *When his mother had found out about a string of affairs his father had carried on for most of the marriage, she divorced him and received a huge settlement. Greg was sent to live with her, but she was bipolar and treated him terribly. He admitted that he never knew if she was going to be generous and lavish him with gifts—or even whisk him away on a trip to Paris for dinner with her adult friends—or be distant and critical or ignore him, at times sending him*

off to an expensive boarding school, where she would occasionally send spectacular gifts to make up for leaving him there over holidays.

During therapy, Greg realized that he began his first affair at the same age his father was when he first cheated on his mother. After that affair, Greg began spending a lot of money on Debbie, apologizing with jewelry or exotic vacations. He also began buying large items for himself: cars, houses, and the latest technology.

As I helped him to see that he was attempting to fill himself up with money and material objects to comfort old childhood wounds, Greg was able to cut back on his workaholic hours (he would often spend fourteen to sixteen hours a day at his office) and end his latest affair. Debbie encouraged him to stop "apologizing" with material gifts and to instead spend time and emotion on their relationship.

As this case study clearly illustrates, your perception of how money was used in your childhood has a direct bearing on how emotionally loaded money is for you as an adult. Unless you are able to acknowledge your family money history, you will be unable to truly understand the role that money plays in all aspects of your relationship and how it affects romantic love, sex, power, control, and self-esteem.

When Money Talks

We all carry family legacies that influence our choices and behaviors. The generational chorus of emotional input is already a significant internal dialogue to recognize and address. Don't let your family legacy with money add to the background noise. If the money ghost of past generations starts whispering in your ear, you need to announce your independence from the financial infidelities of your family tree.

- "Doesn't your partner sound like your father sounded when he criticized your mother for spending so much on an outfit?"

- "You've been trying to get more of me your whole life. How can you just stand by while your partner just throws me away?"
- "You never had enough of me when you were growing up and you don't deserve to have me now."
- "You don't have to be financially responsible now; when your parents die you will get lots of me."

Smart Heart Dialogue for Sharing Emotional and Financial History

It is important to remember when you embark on these dialogues that the desired outcome is attachment and change in the relationship. Don't give up if the change is not exactly what you had hoped for or doesn't follow *your* personal script. You can get through the newness and continue to use these dialogues to provide opportunities for greater growth for both yourself and your partner. Relationships should not be stagnant. Welcome change!

Smart Heart Dialogue for Dating Singles

When you are beginning to date, finding out how a person's family treated money can be very revealing. Understanding the type of money habits that have been ingrained from a young age can illuminate financial behaviors that—depending on how one's family viewed money—could trigger conflict. Remember that many of these types of discussions are usually prompted by a transition in a relationship.

Case #1:

What he says: "Why are there a bunch of shopping bags stuffed in the back of the closet?"

What he may mean: "If you're hiding this from me, what else are you hiding?"

The Smart Heart reply: "I can understand your concern since money is tight. When you tell me you think that I have spent too much it reminds me of how my father used to control my mother's spending on personal items. I need you to work on helping me feel safe and not controlled, so I'll spend less."

Case #2:

What he says: "If we move in together, do we split all the bills equally?"

What he may mean: "I make more than you do and I think it would be fair to split all joint expenses on a percentage basis."

The Smart Heart reply: "Thanks for understanding that moving in together would mean my expenses would greatly increase if we split fifty-fifty. But I would like us both to contribute equally to a fund that we could use for fun and play. That way we can make shared decisions about how that money is spent."

Case #3:

What he says: "It seems I overspent while we were on vacation together. Would you mind lending me some money?"

What he may mean: "I've invested quite a bit in this relationship already by taking you out and spending money on vacations; the least you can do is help me out when I'm in a tight spot."

> **The Smart Heart reply:** "I understand how much you spent on me and I thank you for that. Since you agreed to pay for things I didn't plan on spending that much. If I knew ahead of time, I would have budgeted. Please help me by understanding this."

Smart Heart Dialogue for a Money Tree Memory

The conflict: "I need to use some of our savings to cover my mother's medical bills."

"I thought you promised we could buy a new car? Our old one is not nice at all."

The struggle: "Do you mean I should abandon my mother?"

The fear: "I'm afraid of spending all our savings on your mother. We barely have enough for ourselves. What will happen in the future?"

> **The Smart Heart Reply:** "I know you worry about money. And I know you feel like you never had enough when you were growing up. I will show you how to trust me. I don't want to abandon my mother the way my father abandoned me and I promise I won't abandon you."

Smart Heart Dialogue For Married and Committed Couples

Even though you may feel you know your partner's family as well as you know your own, you may not truly understand how ingrained family money behaviors have been passed down from generation to generation. Emotional reactions to money conflicts can often be traced back to inherited beliefs around money and finances.

Case #1:

What she says: "Is it necessary for you to review my credit card bill each month?"

What she may mean: "It feels like you're checking up on me and I feel resentful. I don't want to be in a parent/child dynamic ("Mother may I . . . ?") with you. I don't want to sneak purchases but I feel afraid that you will blame me for overspending."

The Smart Heart reply: "I love you and I am in this relationship with you for the long haul. Your needs and desires matter to me. I want you to feel safe, nurtured, loved, and heard by me unconditionally."

Case #2:

What he says: "You seem to make a big deal about our kids' birthday parties. You spend so much on them. Why do they need a big party at all?"

What he may mean: "Money is serious. It should not be used lightly for fun. We need to save it for a rainy day."

The Smart Heart reply: "I understand that you want us to have enough money for a rainy day. It reminds me of my mother's fears growing up during the Depression—she always worried that we wouldn't have enough and never let us buy things she considered frivolous. But we can celebrate important events in ways that are fun and still have enough money to live on."

> ## Case #3

What she says: "We can't afford to go on vacation with your parents again this year. Last year, they made us pay for our share of the house, even though they had invited us as their guests."

What she may mean: "Why can't you stand up to your family and stick to our plan? I can't count on you or your family to keep your word, and when I protest, you always make me do your dirty work."

The Smart Heart reply: "I know it's important to you that we always discuss changes in plans that will involve money. Even though my family can be casual about these things, I understand that you will feel better when we stick to our own plan, and I will do so. Thanks for teaching me. I can see that my family does try to manipulate me around money. But I was raised to believe that plans are made to be changed, and that being flexible around money is a good thing."

Smart Heart Jump Starts for a New Beginning

Now that you are aware of your family history with money and can identify the emotional triggers that can precipitate or escalate conflict about money, the following Smart Heart skills allow you to evaluate your reactions to financial scenarios and safely share the source of your emotional response. These tools will encourage you to be empathetic while experiencing life events associated with potential financial stresses and help you to work together to keep your relationship strong as you successfully negotiate change and reach common goals:

- *Go counterintuitive.* When you find yourself tempted to express a knee-jerk reaction to a particular financial scenario, stop yourself and instead see how it changes your relationship to react in the opposite manner. For instance, if you usually protest, "Oh, that's too expensive; you shouldn't spend that much," when your partner brings you an unexpected gift, the next time you receive a spontaneous present, instead respond, "Thank you so much. I am learning it's okay to allow myself such a treat."

- *Appreciate change.* Embrace the messiness that signals these periods of transition. Really listen to your partner's "script" and understand what that person is asking for. Talk honestly about ways in which compromise can help you resolve your issues. Don't be tied to old patterns of behavior, no matter how deeply they are entrenched.

- *Coach each other and reward each other for changes that are sustained.* Be patient when navigating a transition. If your partner continues to act in predictable, unproductive ways, remind him that he needs to try stepping outside of his comfort zone to try a new approach to a familiar situation or disagreement. Reward changes in behavior in ways that are significant to the person that has made the change.

- *Announce your triggers.* Sometimes disagreements about money can trigger sensitivity from a time before you and your partner met. When you find yourself becoming upset over how your partner is handling money, do not expect that she or he will understand why you are reacting in a particular manner. Announce how her or his behavior is affecting you.

- *Embrace the positive and step away from the negative.* When your relationship becomes particularly stressed, or arguments become heated during times of transition, be sure to remind yourself of what attracted you to your partner in the first place. Avoid focusing on the person's negative qualities and imagine how good your relationship will be when you work together and successfully come out on the other side of a rough patch.

A Contract for Financial Fidelity

In order to be conscious of—and work to avoid—harmful inherited patterns surrounding love and money in our relationship, we agree to:

- **Be conscious of each person's love and money maps.** Respect that many of your partner's opinions about money and relationships were formed well before the two of you ever became a couple. Make an honest effort to know the truth about each other's family background and how your parents and other family members dealt with emotion, fidelity, and finances.

- **Expect change and prepare for it.** Do not be anxious about changes that will inevitably occur in your relationship. Think of opportunities for change as gifts that will allow you to continue to grow closer and more intimate in your relationship.

- **Appreciate change and use it to our relationship's advantage.** Realize that each opportunity for change is an opportunity to strengthen your relationship and promote greater intimacy. Honest communication—especially about tough topics and in hard times—is important in the continued evolution of any relationship.

- **Avoid "coasting."** Don't avoid the difficult topics in order to keep the surface of your relationship smooth. Passion and turmoil often go hand in hand. Acknowledging the difficulties of a transition and coming together to arrive at a solution may not always be easy, but positive, cooperative changes will always add depth, strength, and renewed romance to your bond.

- **Continue to respond in new ways and try different solutions.** Challenge yourself to respond to your partner in unexpected ways. Ask yourself if you are locked in a pattern that prevents transitional change. Assess whether fear is limiting your responses and be willing to talk about these anxieties openly with your partner.

Step 4:
Break Up with Your Money
Letting Go of Money's Emotional Hold

Some couples find that they have become entrenched in the damaging patterns of the transition stage. This can happen in any type of relationship: dating, living together, pre-engagement, engagement, marriage, separation, or divorce. When couples become stuck in patterns of anger, resentment, or grudge holding, one or both of them begin to feel dissatisfied and trapped. They often describe their relationship as "empty." In my practice, I often see individuals who attempt to fill this emptiness by cheating on their partner, either by withdrawing emotionally, while remaining in the relationship, or by withdrawing physically by starting an affair. Often these people tell me that they began another relationship because they had "fallen out of love" and wanted to stimulate the feelings they claim are missing from their marriage or relationship.

While these people often fantasize about breaking up with their partner, they are unwilling to face the emptiness and self-reliance that is the result of a clean breakup. By seeking out an affair, they bring a third party into the relationship in the hopes of avoiding the painful feelings that accompany the end of a relationship. When this type of triangle has been created—and discovered or revealed—a breakup of some kind is inevitable, although for the patients I counsel, it is almost always temporary.

The same types of toxic patterns of behavior can arise around money or finances in a relationship. Some people are literally having an affair with their money (what I call your "money mistress"). These individuals are practicing financial infidelity by making money—how they spend it, how they make it, what it means to them—more important than their relationship. And like any affair, sometimes a breakup, albeit a temporary one, is necessary to reach a resolution.

"We had a wonderful life," Harriet said. "Ron had a good job and I was able to keep busy buying and selling art. But when he lost his job, everything fell apart."

"That's not strictly true," Ron pointed out. "Our marriage has been in trouble for years; it's just that you loved the money enough to stay with me even when things were bad."

Ron went on to tell me that he and Harriet had not had sex in nearly ten years. Their marriage was full of tension. Harriet was negative and pessimistic and treated him with contempt. When he was working, she would find an expensive hobby, such as buying artwork, and that would seem to make her feel better. And Ron didn't feel as though he was in a position to complain—after all, he had a mistress, someone who made him feel better about himself and kept an element of romance in his life. When Ron suddenly lost his job, and money became an issue for the couple, Harriet began running through a laundry list of everything that was wrong with the relationship—and with him. She wanted to divorce.

I asked Ron how he was handling the money problems and he admitted that he was simply avoiding the issue. "I won't even bother to open the bills," he said. "It's depressing to me to think that Harriet is right: that I'm worthy only of contempt because I'm not earning enough to support our lifestyle."

While Ron was avoiding the issue of their financial trouble, Harriet was using it to punish him. Every weekend, she would begin the day with pulling out all the bills and calling the bank and checking their balance. She harangued Ron about how much they owed and how little they had. In response, he would withdraw or become defensive, arguing that none of it was his fault—"not the job, not the affair"—that she'd driven him to it with her negativity.

It was clear to me that this couple was deeply entrenched in damaging patterns and I suggested to them that in order to save their relationship in the long term, it might be best for them to separate.

"We can't afford to separate or get a divorce," Harriet immediately responded. And to my surprise, Ron agreed. In my experience, when a couple says that they can't "afford" to split up, it is often an excuse! Money—or lack of it—provides a convenient reason to stay together without acknowledging their love for each other and the need to face the painful emotional work that is necessary to truly salvage the relationship.

When it comes to ending one of the relationships in a money/romantic partner triangle there are two possible resolutions: choosing to break up with your money or choosing to break up your relationship. In the case of Harriet and Ron, both were guilty of bringing a third party into their marriage. For Ron, having an affair helped soothe the emotional wounds inflicted by Harriet's contempt and filled the emptiness he felt as a result of their sexless marriage. But Ron was not the only guilty party.

It was quite clear that Harriet was involved in a triangle as well. In her case, it was her love affair with Ron's money that made it impossible for her to acknowledge the lack of true intimacy in their marriage. It was when I pointed out the fact that both Ron and Harriet had been guilty of infidelity in their marriage that they were able to begin to take steps to "break up" with the third parties each had brought into the marriage.

Exercise: Compartmentalize the Cash

As with any affair, the less time, energy, and attention you give to money, the less influence it will have over your relationships. Understand that I am not advocating ignoring your financial responsibilities or practicing magical thinking in the hopes that your money woes or conflicts will simply "get better" or "go away."

If money issues are coming between you and your partner on a constant basis, try this exercise to help you break up with an unhealthy overinvolvement with money, freeing up time and emotional energy to spend on your partner. This exercise was particularly helpful for Ron and Harriet as it forced Harriet to relinquish her obsessive focus on their finances and made Ron take responsibility in an area of the relationship he had previously been happy to avoid.

1. Pick a time to discuss bills or money. This time cannot be on a weekend, during dinner, before sex, at bedtime or while you are out on a "date." Both partners must agree to the time and place for the meeting.

2. The person who has the concern or problem begins the meeting and gets fifteen minutes to discuss bills or financial situations. The other person agrees to remain connected to the discussion, but may, if he or she begins to feel uncomfortable, ask for a time-out for a mutually agreed-upon amount of time. After the time-out, the discussion may resume for the remainder of the fifteen minutes.

3. Both partners must participate. No watching TV or taking calls. No drinking alcohol. Turn off your cell phone or Blackberry and log off of your computer.

4. Insist on shared responsibility. The person who has called the meeting must allow the other person to make suggestions and take charge of certain financial matters. For instance, if you are upset that your partner practices magical thinking by continually refusing to open credit card bills that arrive in his or her name and is ruining your shared credit rating by incurring late fees and nonpayment charges, you must allow that person to suggest a way to avoid this problem. For instance he or she must periodically take over doing *all* the bills. In turn, he or she must accept responsibility for follow-through.

5. Plan for a fun activity immediately following the discussion. Do high-energy play first, like having sex, dancing, or exercising to-

gether, then go out to dinner, watch a favorite movie, or take each other to lunch. As a result, endorphins are reversed and you feel positive and upbeat.

At first you may need to schedule several of these "meetings" per week. But as time goes by and both of you begin to compartmentalize your money issues into these time slots, you should notice a change in your ability to enjoy the time together without money issues hanging over every activity.

How to "Break Up" with Money to Save Your Relationship

When I work with couples in crisis that are trying to decide whether or not to end their relationship, I first help them to understand that in every relationship there is a dynamic between the *pursuer* and *distancer.*

Pursuers are maximizers who make emotional, impulsive, feeling-based decisions regarding money and finance. They are optimistic and charismatic, but also very intense. When taken to an extreme, their behavior feels imposing or demanding.

Distancers are minimizers who are uncomfortable with confrontation. They are often described as patient, logical, practical and are sometimes considered selfish. They don't make demands and they do not want anything to be expected of them. But they do miss their partner—after he or she is gone!

People are usually one or the other in an intimate relationship—however, they may act as a pursuer with their boss and a distancer with their mother and spouse. In order to make the relationship work, each must set aside his or her dominant behavior and work toward a *connection* by being flexible. If individuals remain rigid in their pursuer or distancer roles with regard to money it will inevitably become a *deal breaker* in their relationship.

When financial infidelity has driven a couple to the brink of a breakup, it is equally helpful to understand each person's dominant behavior around money. The quiz below will help you to determine whether you are a pursuer or a distancer when it comes to money in your relationship. You can also go back to the Family Moneygram you created in step 3, "Divest Yourself of the Past," and see if you can identify pursuers and distancers in your family history.

QUIZ: ARE YOU A MONEY PURSUER?

1. Do you obsess about being left without enough money to take care of yourself when you are old?
2. Do you overreact and make rash decisions or assumptions when discussing finances, rather than taking the time to find out the facts?
3. Do you have high expectations of your earning power?
4. Are you able to ask your parents for help with finances?
5. Do you think of the needs of others before your own?
6. Do you dislike being alone and find yourself offering to pay to ensure companionship at meals or while traveling?
7. Do you long for commitment or marriage?
8. Are you sensitive or emotional?
9. Do you thrive on having discussions about money or finances?
10. Do you feel you get taken for granted?
11. Do you feel you're not taken seriously?
12. Do you resist setting limits on spending?
13. Do you give in easily because you don't want to insult your date or partner?
14. Do you enable your date or partner to be financially irresponsible by making excuses for him or her?
15. Do you feel that it's your fault when there's a financial crisis?
16. Are you preoccupied with being betrayed financially?
17. Are you willing to take financial risks?

18. Do you make impulsive investments or purchases?
19. Do you try to anticipate others' needs and fill them before they ask?
20. Are you quick to attach to people or things?

SCORING

If you answered "yes" to 5–10 questions, you are a *moderate* pursuer.
If you answered "yes" to 11–20 questions, you are an *extreme* pursuer.

Becca wanted to talk to me about whether or not she should continue her relationship with Gary. A successful lawyer with a large and beautifully decorated apartment in New York, Becca had met Gary, a businessman from Florida, in an online dating site. They had been traveling back and forth between New York and Florida for a few months and she was having some serious questions about the relationship.

"Everything was great at first," she said. "Gary would make dinners, take me for long walks on the beach in Florida, buy me flowers for the apartment when he was in New York. But he wants us to move in together and I'm not sure."

When Gary first suggested living together, he told Becca he would move to New York, but that he thought the lifestyle was too expensive and that he would never feel comfortable spending so much of his money on rent. She tried staying with him in Florida, but found his bachelor house uncomfortable and not up to her standard of living.

I suggested that she offer a compromise, that perhaps Gary could make his home more comfortable for her.

"That's what first got me worried," she admitted. "I asked him to buy us a new bed, but he said that the mattress I wanted was too expensive, but if I really wanted to, I could buy it myself."

I encouraged Becca to talk openly to Gary about her financial situation and to ask him direct questions about his. In our next session, she was even more worried.

"He won't talk about money," she told me. "I told him how much my apartment was worth, how I had lost money after my divorce and was worried I wouldn't have enough; how I worked long hours so I could make the kind of money that let me live the lifestyle I preferred. I told him I was a generous person and I didn't expect him to completely take care of me, but that I did want a man who helped make me feel financially secure."

Gary responded by telling Becca that she was getting too "personal." She told me that on the visit in which she first discussed money, Gary continued to act romantically toward her, but began to have trouble performing sexually. "Maybe he doesn't have any money," she worried. "Maybe he's just attracted to me because of my money."

Despite Becca's underlying worries, she continued to push the issue of financial disclosure with Gary. Her pursuer style around money allowed her to be comfortable with the topic. But Gary reacted by distancing—both from the topic of money and from Becca sexually. "I'm totally willing to be transparent with you about my finances," he told her. "Once we are committed to each other."

Ultimately, Gary never reconciled his words and his actions. After hearing them argue about money over dinner, one of Gary's friends finally took Becca aside and told her, "He says he can't afford you. You have to understand, he's a nice guy, but he'll never be a provider."

Once Becca recognized the pursuer / distancer dynamic that had evolved around money in her relationship with Gary and determined that he was unlikely to change in a way that would provide the security she was seeking, she decided to break off the relationship.

QUIZ: ARE YOU A MONEY DISTANCER?

1. Do you stand still and wait for money to come to you?
2. Are you reluctant to make investments?
3. Do you say yes when you mean no—spending when you would rather not—and then feel resentful?
4. Do you provoke your date or mate with your money behaviors?

5. Do you avoid money confrontations at all costs?
6. Do you avoid planning, preferring to leave things loose and "up in the air"?
7. Do you encourage input on managing your finances, but then disregard the advice?
8. Do you assume your financial future will "take care of itself"?
9. Are you a workaholic?
10. Do you make unilateral decisions about finances?
11. Do you have an attitude, moan, or sigh when asked for money?
12. Do you feel suffocated in relationships?
13. Do you feel it's important to have your own bank accounts and credit cards?
14. Do your parents tell you what to do with your money?
15. When you have made a bad money decision, do you keep it secret?
16. Do you dislike being told what you should do with your money?
17. If you know someone needs financial help, do you try to avoid him or her?
18. When your date or partner asks about money, do you tune out or refuse to respond?
19. Do you take it for granted that your date or partner will pay?
20. Has your family disinherited you—or threatened to?

SCORING

If you answered "yes" to 5–10 questions, you are a *moderate* distancer.

If you answered "yes" to 11–20 questions, you are an *extreme* distancer.

Henry came to see me at his wife's urging. Following some significant losses in the stock market he had become very distant and emotionally remote. She was afraid that he was having an affair. When I talked to Henry, he told me that he was not having an affair, and that he was depressed, but he refused to say anything more. It wasn't until he crossed his ankle over his knee and I noticed holes in the bottom of his shoe that I was able to begin a dialogue that helped him to begin to come to terms with how his relationship with money was affecting his ability to connect in other areas of his life. Although it took Henry nearly six months to open up to me about money—in the beginning, initiating a discussion about finances would cause him to experience physical symptoms such as stomachaches or headaches—when he did begin to talk, it became apparent that he had distanced himself from money in an extreme manner.

His father had always told him horrible stories about financial ruin in their family, including a favorite uncle killing himself after he went bankrupt. As a result, Henry became very distant around money. Because he never wanted to worry about financial security, he became a workaholic, but he never enjoyed the money he made. He immediately invested everything (in case something "bad" happened) and refused to spend anything on himself. He told me that he hadn't been to a doctor in five years, because they were "too expensive."

As is common, Henry was attracted to, and married, a money pursuer. His wife tried to get him to use money for fun and pleasure. "You'll make more," she would tell him.

However, Henry's attitudes toward money eventually caused him to become distant from not just money, but emotional connections. It was important that he learn how to manage the need to relate to money in order to begin to be able to reconnect with himself, his wife, and his family.

Both Henry and Susan need to learn how to modify these dominant money behaviors to become what Dr. Thomas Fogarty would call "operators"—individuals who can balance both pursuing and distancing behaviors. A financial operator can pursue money without becoming distant to emotional connections as well as put money in its place in order to focus on a relationship. My definition of a "financial operator" is someone who is prudent, but looks for profit; a spender who also is able to save.

Types of Attachment to Money

By now you are probably beginning to understand that your personal attachment to money is formed by many influences, including your family and your dominant pursuer/distancer behavior. *Before you break up your relationship with money, it first helps to understand the type of attachment you have formed to it.*

Anxiously attached: Does money evoke feelings of insecurity? Do you feel emotionally dependent on it? Do you cling to your definition of how much is "enough" money? Does a low balance in your bank account trigger low self-esteem? If so, then you are "anxiously attached" to your money. You tend to be hypervigilant about finances and obsessively focused on how you make and spend money. When your partner's views differ from yours, you become emotionally distressed and resentful if your partner does not shift his or her views to more closely mirror yours.

Avoidantly attached: If you reject the importance of money and the influence it can have on your life, you are "avoidantly attached." You do all you can to keep your emotional reactions to money at low levels of intensity. You can be compulsively self-sufficient and unwilling to accept generosity from a partner.

Emotionally detached: A person in this situation is unable to create a stable bond with money and may be prone to binge spending, hoarding, or a disturbing combination of both. This type of extreme behavior around money can signal a history of trauma or abuse, a mental illness, or a chemical imbalance.

Securely attached: Are you able to appreciate what money can accomplish? Are you willing to place limits on what you are willing to do to acquire money? Do you respect money? Can you have fun with it? Do you believe money has an appropriate level of importance in your life and your relationships? Do you put money second to important relationships? If you answer yes to these questions, you can consider yourself securely attached to your money. You are willing to engage in interdependent financial behaviors with a partner and respect his or her financial views. Your emotions are rarely, if ever, manipulated by money.

Breaking Up with Your Money

Unless you have a secure attachment to your money and a history of safe, honest communication in your relationship, you will benefit from learning how to "break up" with your money so you can start over in a healthier relationship.

The first step is to realize the areas in your relationship where money has intruded to create a triangle. These "triangles" are easily recognized. They are some of the most common areas where couples report conflict. Just as a sexual affair causes an unhealthy triangle—husband, wife, lover—so, too, can money play a main role in perpetuating a damaging dynamic. Money, children, sex, in-laws and household chores are all common elements of these potentially volatile triangles. Consider whether you may be creating any of these common money triangles with your partner:

- **Sex/Money/Relationship:** Whenever you link sex to money, whether directly or indirectly, you set up an unhealthy dynamic for intimacy. One of my patients bragged that she never gave her husband oral sex unless he bought her an expensive piece of jewelry. Another confessed that he was so angry with his wife's spending sprees that he slept in the guest room whenever he had to pay her credit card bills. In a functional, loving, and trusting relationship, sex should never be a commodity.

- **Family/Money/Relationship:** Family legacies of money behaviors are not always contained in our subconscious minds. The very real demands of extended family members for financial support can place a strain on a couple's relationship. One couple I counsel nearly broke up over the husband's insistence that they provide extra financial support to his widowed mother so that she would not have to change her lifestyle following her husband's death. His mother made it clear to her daughter-in-law that she considered it the duty of her son to take care of her, no matter what the costs to his own family might be.

- **Children/Money/Relationship:** Nearly 70 percent of all couples experience severe relationship stress after having children. Discussions about when to have children and worries about money, (after careers are established, or certain financial benchmarks are reached), how to have children (adoption, expensive fertility treatments), and how to raise them (nannies, day care, or stay-at-home parent, public or private schools, Ivy League or state colleges) can create financial stress for couples. When a couple becomes contentious over spending on their children, their intimate relationship can suffer. Often one spouse will accuse the other of "choosing" to invest in the children rather than in their own intimate relationship. These feelings of abandonment often trigger a host of toxic behaviors.
- **Spending or Saving/Money/Relationship:** When the theory of "opposites attract" goes to an extreme a relationship becomes at risk for damaging power struggles, sneaky "payback" behaviors, and other deceits. *Couples who cling to opposing goals for saving or spending elevate the importance of money over the well-being of their relationship.* Such couples often become deeply entrenched in patterns of financial infidelity.

Hiding or denying the role money may be playing in any of the triangles above eventually has the same toxic effect on a relationship as hiding a lover would. The secrecy of your relationship to money negatively influences your relationship with your partner. You may not think you are cheating because you are not having a physical affair, but if you continue this type of secret keeping it will gradually take a toll as your attention to your *money mistress* replaces sex or intimacy with your partner.

Cheryl and Andy had planned a romantic getaway to see if they could rekindle some of the romance that was lacking in their relationship. Instead of being a spark to their love life, the trip triggered a dramatic fight and threats of a breakup. They came to see me to see if they could work things out.

"It's clear that he doesn't care about me at all," Cheryl said.

"I planned this whole romantic trip," Andy protested. "Even you agreed that we had found the most beautiful, secluded spot."

He explained how he had taken her camping, planning to romance her under the stars and lavish his full attention on her and only her. "My cell phone didn't work up there," he exclaimed. "I was there to pay attention to you and only to you."

"But you know I have a bad back," Cheryl said. "And I was practically crippled after sleeping on the ground for one night. I couldn't hike. I couldn't enjoy myself. We should have left and gone to a hotel."

"I'd already paid for the campsite," Andy said, "and all of our food for the week—including the wine that you like so much. And it wasn't cheap. Staying at a hotel would have totally blown the budget for this trip."

"So what you're saying is that your money is more important than my comfort and health," Cheryl said. "Why don't you try taking your bank account on a romantic getaway!"

Andy's insistence on sticking to his budgeted plan, even after he saw the toll that the campout was taking, not only on Cheryl's enjoyment of the trip, but her health and comfort, served to reinforce Cheryl's perception that he cared about protecting his money more than he cared about protecting her.

As I asked both Andy and Cheryl to share how they felt about the failed trip, it became clear that they were locked in a power struggle and Andy, in particular, was using his money as an excuse to control their relationship. Instead of planning a getaway they both might enjoy, he hid his unwillingness to spend a lot of money by convincing Cheryl that if she did things his way, she would command his unlimited attention.

Cheryl was hurt and angry. She interpreted Andy's reaction to her request for a hotel as proof that he was more concerned about the security of his bank account than he was about the intimacy of their relationship.

I suggested that Andy allow Cheryl to plan a low-cost getaway that she would enjoy. She would create a budget for the trip, including meals and other expenses, and Andy would approve it. In exchange for having approval over the amount they would spend, Andy would promise to leave his "BlackBerry mistress" at home and focus his attention on her. Cheryl felt nurtured by Andy's attention, and he was able to relax, knowing that Cheryl would not make any unexpected money demands.

Concerns about money can often ruin chances for connection and intimacy. It is important to realize when your attachment to your money comes between opportunities for you and your partner to enjoy each other.

For instance, after I had been dating my husband, Jeff, for about three months, he proposed we go away together. We went to St. John and were having a very romantic time. I already knew I was in love with him and I welcomed this trip as a chance to allow him to express the same feelings for me. Everything was great, until the day we were window-shopping in nearby St. Thomas. St. Thomas is famous for its duty-free jewelry shops and I could not resist the allure of the sparkling gems in the windows. With Jeff trailing behind me, I strolled into a store and began browsing.

I was having such a wonderful time trying on rings and bracelets that I did not notice that Jeff was growing increasingly quiet. The salesclerk was encouraging me to take particular pieces out into the sunlight so I could see the quality of the stones in natural light. As I admired various pieces, Jeff leaned up against a display, offering neither comments nor enthusiasm.

Finally I was trying on a gorgeous and elaborate emerald necklace and decided to draw him into my dress-up fantasies. "How do you think this looks?" I asked him.

His reply shocked me. "Do you really need that?" he asked.

I didn't really know what to say. Does anyone *really need* a thirty-thousand-dollar necklace?

We left the store and returned to our hotel, hardly speaking. Jeff made some excuse to go out on his own and I was left to consider what had just happened. Over dinner that night, I decided to use Smart Heart dialogue to uncover what had gone on between us.

"You didn't seem to enjoy the time in the jewelry store," I began. "I had hoped you'd be able to participate more. Ever since I was a little girl, I've loved playing dress-up and I couldn't resist the opportunity to play with such gorgeous things."

"You were just playing?" Jeff said.

"Of course," I reassured him. "I certainly wasn't planning on leaving there with that necklace."

"You mean, you weren't expecting that I'd offer to buy some of that jewelry for you?" Jeff said sheepishly. "I mean, I'm a generous guy and all, but . . ."

It was clear to me what had happened. While I had been trying on jewels and hoping for compliments on how beautiful I looked in them, Jeff had been huddled over in a corner, assuring his money that he would protect her from this new girlfriend.

"Next time we go into a store like that," I told him, "pretend that it's all free and if I really wanted it I could just ask the salesperson to give it to me."

Jeff laughed in relief. "I wish I'd known that at the time. Maybe I'd have tried on one of those diamond-encrusted watches. But I really didn't want to send you the wrong signals. I'd like to give you some beautiful jewels someday," he said. "You'll just have to wait until I'm ready."

I'm happy to report that the rest of our vacation was just as romantic as I had hoped it would be.

The following exercises will help you to get in touch with any possessive feelings you may have toward your money. Inappropriate focus on the importance of money can have a damaging effect on your emotional relationships. Being aware of the level of importance you place on your financial status is the first step in understanding how to prioritize the role of money in your life and relationships.

Exercise: Black Tuesday

The day the stock market crashed in 1929 lives on in history. Called Black Tuesday, the event was remarkable for devastating hundreds of businesses and individuals in a single day and was a factor in the Great Depression. As losses mounted, people's emotional responses were extreme, with reports of suicides and abandonment filling the headlines. To jolt yourself into an awareness of what your money represents to you, I want you to imagine that you suddenly have no money at all. Pick a weekend to put away your credit cards and bank cards and impose a no-spending rule. Now continue to lead your life normally—only without money. If you usually shop on the weekend, then window-shop. If you usually go out to dinner, cook a special meal at home. If you usually go out with friends, plan an activity that does not require spending. Each time you want to do something and are unable to do so without money, allow yourself to acknowledge everything you are feeling. Share these feelings with your partner. Are you panicking because you forgot to pay a bill? Are you embarrassed if friends offer to cover your share of the tab? Notice the emotions that you might otherwise try to mask with money. Note those times when you are tempted to spend. Pay attention to the things you consider necessities, and those you are able to do without.

Exercise: Withdrawals and Deposits

Day 1: Pretend you have suddenly been forced into bankruptcy. You are poor. You have nothing. No money, no investments. Take your negative fantasies to the extreme. Wallow in them and embrace the negative energy. Imagine yourself selling everything you have, being free of all your material goods.

Day 2: Visualize yourself as wealthy and with plenty of money.

Day 3 and forever after: Be consciously grateful. Each day, count the things you are grateful for.

Breaking Up with Your Partner

In some cases, financial infidelity has poisoned the relationship so fatally that a breakup seems like the only solution. For the couples that I counsel who tell me that there is no option for them but a breakup, I suggest that they first break up *temporarily* in order to fully experience the loss of ending their relationship and the subsequent appreciation of what they had. I call this temporary breakup a "Brush with Death" because it can evoke many of the same feelings of permanent loss and emptiness. If you feel like your relationship is already on the verge of ending, a Brush with Death may be the shock you need to wake up, and shake things up, and initiate positive change.

Jimmy was at his wit's end. He had stormed out on his wife, Carlotta, and their three children after his wife's last shopping binge depleted their joint savings account of over twenty thousand dollars. A hardworking construction foreman, Jimmy felt his wife was consciously sabotaging his efforts to provide for the family.

When Carlotta came in with him for the next session, she had a long list of grievances: Jimmy never talked to her about his day; he spent too much time over at his mother's house; he claimed he was too tired to help with their children when he came home from work; he didn't ever show her emotion; he was too logical and thought there was a simple answer for everything. "So I kicked him out," she concluded.

I asked her to tell me how she felt trying to manage on her own. "It's hard," she admitted. "But when the kids are asleep, and I can go online and shop, I forget about my problems for a while."

I told Jimmy and Carlotta that they needed to try a Brush with Death to help them minimize some of the sources of frustration in their relationship and encourage them to appreciate and remember the good parts of it. For three months Jimmy lived with his brother and spent time with his kids just as he would be required to if he was sharing custody after a divorce.

After the Brush with Death, both Jimmy and Carlotta missed each other enough that I recommended Jimmy attempt to woo Carlotta emotionally. They began dating and rekindling romantic feelings for each other. Both continued in therapy, individually and together with me. Carlotta was diagnosed with postpartum depression and "burn-out" and began taking supplements to balance her brain chemicals, (which you will learn more about in part 3 of this book). These treatments, along with conventional talk therapy, helped her to control her urge for shopping binges. Jimmy made an effort to put Carlotta first, before work and his parents.

Soon not only Jimmy and Carlotta were noticing a difference in how they felt about each other, but their children could see a difference in how their parents interacted. Both Jimmy and Carlotta knew they were ready to try a reconciliation when, after he dropped her back at home after a "date," their five-year-old said, "You really love Daddy, don't you? Why don't you two get married?"

Exercise: Brush with Death

Often a temporary breakup is necessary for long-term change. For most people, the fear of permanent loss is a great motivator. Whether you are married, living together, dating, or separated and unable to reach commitment, this experiential exercise is constructed in a way allow you to undergo the emotional "jolt" of the loss of your relationship, prompting you to acknowledge your fears and accept the unknown elements of the future of your relationship. This exercise is to be used *instead of* attempting to talk things through or threatening a breakup. This is not meant to be a "cry wolf" scenario, but rather a planned, thoughtful and *loving* disconnection in order to reconnect at a point of *greater emotional vulnerability and intimacy*.

- First, discuss your feelings about a time-limited breakup *before* you announce you are leaving.
- Tell your partner you are leaving and ask how he or she feels. This will allow the person being left to feel as if he or she has some control in the situation.
- Announce your intentions gently. Do not try to hurt, to inflict guilt, or to use this exercise as a means for revenge. Allow your partner to see you feel confident that this break will help repair, revitalize, and strengthen your relationship.
- Walk the walk. Once you have announced your intentions, you must follow through and leave the relationship.
- During the breakup, do not attempt to call, e-mail, text, or see your partner. Both of you must be allowed to experience the full sense of loss and realize the true depth of your feelings. Tell your partner that if either of you feels so lonely or abandoned that you're starting to shut down or have revenge fantasies, you may contact the other.
- Do not attempt to mask your own loneliness with another relationship during the breakup. This is a time for you, too, to evaluate the relationship.
- Don't "date" during your breakup or attempt a reconnection too soon. A Brush with Death breakup should last approximately six to eight weeks. Your partner may try to reconnect earlier, but be aware that this may also be a tactic to mask the pain he or she is feeling by returning to familiar and comforting patterns. Remind your partner you have undertaken this exercise with the intent of initiating clear *change. Pay attention to the person's actions*, rather than his or her words.

- When you are ready to reunite, announce your desire for reconnection. When ending the breakup and reconnecting, do so with the intent of heartfelt forgiveness and a true sense of trust. Don't go back until change occurs!

Remember that the work on your relationship is not over simply because you have reunited. If you do this Brush with Death exercise, be sure to use the techniques that follow in the rest of this book, to support the changes you have initiated.

Divorce and Financial Infidelity

In some cases, the fact is that a relationship cannot—or should not—be saved. However, I do want to caution you that threatening divorce is rarely a productive way to get your partner's attention. And holding someone hostage to get them back by using money as a weapon when threatening separation is one of the most harmful types of financial infidelity I have seen.

Marcia and Howard were in my office seeking counseling for closure as their separation period ended and their divorce decree became final. I was asking each of them to share their feelings about the behaviors that ultimately destroyed their marriage.

"I love you still," Marcia said. "I never wanted our marriage to end."

"All you wanted was to ruin my life," Howard said.

"All I wanted was for you to notice me," she insisted.

"She sold me down the river," Howard said. He explained to me how during their separation, in a fit of anger, Marcia had reported him to the IRS. As his business crumbled, she initiated the divorce. Now that his finances were in ruins, she had decided he had been humbled enough and was telling him she wanted to take him back.

"I told you I was sorry," Marcia said. "It was a rash decision."

"You can't take that back," Howard said. "I can never trust you."

Marcia sat quietly for a moment. "I'd do the same thing again, if I thought it would make you pay attention to me," she said.

When a relationship is ending and a divorce is imminent, there is no way to keep the topic of money from entering into discussions. *Statistics show that following a divorce 45 percent of women's financial situations decline, while 15 percent of men's financial situations improve.* If you are facing a divorce, be sure to take steps to legally protect yourself financially. Do not ignore the fact that money is a big part of divorce discussions. If you do not have a thorough understanding of your own *and* your partner's financial situation, you *must* educate yourself by talking to a qualified financial adviser *before* you agree to any steps in a separation or divorce.

I have counseled some couples through their divorces, in order to help them find emotional closure with the relationship, and I can say that without a doubt, those who have been able to agree upon and accept their new financial situation are able to end the relationship more amicably than those who cannot release their emotional hold on their financial picture during the marriage.

Even if a couple claims that they do not have any issues of financial infidelity in their relationship, if they decide to divorce, problems about money are the most common complaints their divorce lawyers will hear. *Breaking up is hard to do financially.* One prominent divorce attorney lists some of the most common complaints about financial infidelity he encounters:

- **Overspending.** One spouse will habitually overspend on items, with the other spouse's tacit approval. Women are known to handle their emotions financially. Wives often purchase expensive jewelry, designer clothing, or fur coats. Husbands may buy cars, boats, or high-end gadgets. While the marriage is stable, neither partner mentions these concerns, even though they are aware of the spending patterns. At the first sign of trouble, however, the lawyer hears the complaints: "I could afford that, but she doesn't need it." "For a purchase of that size, he should have discussed it with me first."

- *Secret spending.* One partner may rack up huge debt on credit cards, often building up huge liabilities on several cards. These liabilities are shared debt in a marriage. One client told his divorce lawyer how his ex-wife would buy, but not wear, expensive designer clothing. She just hid her purchases away in her closet. When he confronted her about her habit, she moved on to other secretive acquisitions—taking money and jewelry from friends whenever the couple was invited to dinners or parties.

- *Hidden assets.* Fearful that one spouse is planning to take advantage of the other's greater net worth, some individuals will "hide" assets such as stocks, real estate, or bank accounts. This kind of nondisclosure is an indicator of future issues with trust in the relationship.

- *Guilt gifts.* One woman told the lawyer about her extensive jewelry collection, built up over the years by accepting expensive and lavish pieces from her husband each time he had a new girlfriend on the side. For a number of years, she was able to tell herself that she preferred jewelry to fidelity, but eventually, the lack of true intimacy in the relationship caused the marriage to end.

- *The tax-return game.* Some spouses have no idea of their net worth as a couple. A surprising number of couples admit that one person prepares the return and the other signs without reviewing the entire document. In some cases, one spouse has forged the other's signature.

Protecting Yourself against Financial Infidelity

If you are concerned about protecting your financial interests in the event of a breakup or divorce, you should consult with a lawyer to understand how joint finances are handled in your state. There are a number of reasons to consider talking to your partner about prenuptial and postnuptial agreements.

Prenups

A prenuptial agreement is a legal contract you enter into before marriage that states how a couple's assets and debts will be divided in a fair and reasonable way in case of a divorce. Couples who don't intend or—like many gay couples—are unable to marry may want to consider a *cohabitation agreement*, which is like a prenup, only you may enter into it while you are living together, even though you are not planning to marry. In her book *The Courage to Be Rich,* Suze Orman details some of the most compelling reasons to ask for a prenup, including:

- A previous divorce where you did not have any preexisting financial agreement
- An extensive stock or real estate portfolio that existed prior to the marriage, where you want the property and its growth during your marriage to remain in your name only
- You have a career with high earning potential and wish to retain your projected future wealth
- You are expecting a significant inheritance
- You are marrying someone wealthier than you who would have greater assets to mount and sustain a legal battle in the event of divorce
- You have children from a previous marriage and want to protect their assets
- You share a business with your spouse
- You know your future spouse has debt or is prone to bad spending decisions and do not want to be responsible for future debt that may accrue in his or her name
- In the case of a cohabitation agreement: you want to live together and share some assets, but do not wish to commingle all of your financial assets

Asking for a Prenuptial Agreement

There's no getting around the simple fact that discussions about prenuptial agreements are not romantic and can be a deal breaker—they need to be approached gingerly. For couples in the throes of planning a fairy-tale wedding, it may be difficult to broach the idea of a prenuptial agreement. If you are the one who brings up the topic, you risk looking as though you have no confidence in your future spouse. If you are the one who is being asked to sign, you may feel your partner does not trust you. Therefore, it is important that you communicate the idea that a prenuptial agreement is designed to protect *both* parties.

If you have been married before, or you feel strongly about protecting assets that you are bringing to the marriage, plan a private time to begin a dialogue about how you will handle this kind of financial planning. Be specific about why you want a prenup: to protect your children from a previous marriage, to keep an inheritance in your family, or whatever it is. Point out that creating a prenup requires full financial disclosure, so there will be no money secrets as you start your marriage. Remind your future mate that this agreement will allow you both to feel secure about your financial situation and remove worries about money. Many couples find that addressing important money concerns *before* the wedding actually brings them closer and is a benefit in planning their financial future.

Finally, you don't have to be all business when talking about a prenup. Connect romantically by letting your partner know (by actions and words) that you trust him or her and that you do not plan on ending your marriage—ever.

When you have both agreed to a prenuptial agreement, make an appointment to visit a lawyer together to finalize the details. If you have very complicated financial situations, you may each want a separate lawyer to represent your interests in the agreement.

> ## *A Typical Smart Heart Dialogue for Discussing Prenups (or Other Agreements)*
>
> "I trust you and I love you. I'd like to sign an agreement before we get married (or move in together). I've been married before and have assets that I want to retain. How do you feel about signing an agreement?"
>
> "I'm happy to sign as long as I can oversee my own investments and we can have some joint assets as well. Gone are the days when the woman just deferred to the man. Is this okay with you?"

Postnups

Postnups—or postmarriage agreements—are becoming increasingly common in relationships today. They are being used as estate planning tools, as a means of protecting assets against a potentially messy divorce (some investment companies are even requiring that their top executives have executed pre- or postnuptial agreements in place to protect the firm's assets in case of employee divorce!), to amend a prenuptial agreement, or to provide security if you are reconciling after a separation.

> *Brenda and Jake were seeing me to work on reconciling after Brenda had temporarily left Jake using the Brush with Death exercise. Jake had been having a series of short (and according to him, meaningless) affairs since the beginning of their marriage.*
>
> *"I don't want him to leave," Brenda said. "I like being married to him. I like my lifestyle and I miss him when he is gone."*
>
> *"It doesn't matter to me how many times she kicks me out," Jake said. "I honestly don't know what she could do to stop me from having affairs. I like being married; Brenda's a good wife; but I need the physical excitement I get outside our marriage."*
>
> *"Well, I have an idea," Brenda said. "I want you to sign an agreement that says each time I catch you in an affair, you will deposit $250,000 into*

an account in my name only. You will not be able to touch this money if we divorce."

Jake looked astounded. "I think you might have found something that will make me think twice about cheating," he said.

"I still want a real marriage with you," Brenda said. "We have to continue to come to counseling, but at least if you sign the agreement, I'll feel I have a way out if you continue to hurt me."

While Brenda and Jake clearly had a long way to go toward repairing their relationship, her novel approach indicated that she had a pretty good sense of her husband's priorities when it came to their marriage. Brenda understood that money and power were closely linked in Jake's mind. By shifting significant amounts of money into her control, she is shifting the power in the relationship as well. Instead of appealing to romantic notions of marriage and fidelity, she approached their relationship like a business deal with an expensive noncompete clause.

Other times when a postnup might be worth considering include: when one partner has quit his or her job to stay at home with the children; when one partner has inherited significant assets or a family business; and when doing estate planning. Postnups should be discussed with each person's attorney or a financial planner with knowledge of the laws of the state you reside in.

Remember, a postnup is not an indicator of defeat in a relationship or the first step on the road to separation and divorce. If you want to discuss the idea of a postnup with your partner, approach the discussion in a collaborative way, soliciting—and listening to—your partner's input and feedback and validating his or her concerns. Be prepared to negotiate and compromise using only Smart Heart dialogue.

No-Nup

The earlier you and someone you are dating can talk about money the better. The best thing to do is to put everything out on the table and

initiate some honest discussion. If you are considering a deeper commitment such as living together (without commingling assets) or becoming
engaged, you may want to consider putting your financial situations and
intentions in writing. This type of agreement does not need to be legally
binding, but should represent your mutual commitment to take care of
the business of money matters in order to be able to essentially "set them
aside." The knowledge that you and your partner agree on fundamental
financial issues allows you the freedom to concentrate on creating the
physical and emotional intimacy and connection that is the foundation
for a real and lasting love.

*Dylan and Brandon came to me for some counseling before moving in
together. They were concerned because they had been getting along great for
the past ten months that they had been dating, but when they began to discuss giving up their own apartments and finding a new one together, they had
begun to experience serious conflicts.*

*"If we were getting married, I think I'd feel more confident," Dylan
admitted.*

*"Well, that's not an option for us right now," Brandon pointed out. "Not
that I'm even sure I'd be ready to get married if we could."*

*"So I guess I need to know how we'll protect our interests going forward,"
Dylan said.*

*Brandon looked surprised. "I thought you were mad at me because we
weren't getting married," he said. "We can figure out the money thing."*

*"If you were to try to get back at me through money, it would feel like
the ultimate betrayal," Dylan said. "I think I could deal with you having
an affair, but we can't have secrets about money if we're depending on each
other."*

"Don't you trust me?" Brandon asked.

*Dylan hesitated. "Well," he said slowly, "you did lie about your age on
your dating profile."*

*Brandon cracked up. "Well, you lied about your weight! Maybe we do
need to get everything out in the open."*

Once they had opened up the conversation about money, I encouraged Dylan and Brandon to make a list of their concerns, including: Who would do the bills? How would they split the expenses of the apartment? Should they have separate or joint accounts—or both? Did they intend to designate each other as beneficiaries in wills or on insurance policies? I asked them to put their intentions in writing after talking openly about their respective net worth, debt, and future earning potential. They drafted and signed a "no-nup" contract that laid out their expectations and left each feeling more secure about their financial and emotional future.

When Money Talks

Not all of the talking in a relationship is done out loud. If your money is telling you any of the following, especially if it's insisting that it should be more important to you than your relationship, you need to talk back and tell it you want to break up:

- "Why should you buy your date an expensive dinner? You should suggest splitting the check. We can have much more fun together in Vegas if you don't waste me on impressing her."
- "Have you noticed how much your partner spends on his parents? You work hard for me; I hope he doesn't expect that you'll use me to make up the difference in the household budget."
- "Did you see how much that necklace she was admiring cost? If she thinks you're going to buy her gifts like that, then she's not the woman for us!"
- "Did you notice how he was admiring your apartment? He says he wants to move in with you, but I think that it's *me* he's really interested in. How do you know he's not just a fortune hunter?"
- "I've been in your family for generations. You don't want to be the one that lets an outsider get their hands on me."
- "She's clearly more interested in *me* than she is in *you*."

Smart Heart Dialogue for Breaking Up

Using your Smart Heart skills can help you decide if you are with someone who needs to break up with money—or if you need to break up
with the person. Some triangles are stronger than others and communicating openly can help you see if your romantic relationship is stronger
than the bond either you or your partner has with money.

Smart Heart Dialogue for Dating Singles

> ### Case #1

What he says: "Money is not important to me."

What he may mean: "I don't deserve to make or keep
money. Other people will take care of me."

The Smart Heart reply: "I understand that money is not
important to you. I also notice that you rely on your old
girlfriend [or parents, or buddies] to finance your lifestyle. I see
that money is a priority, in that your relationships with the people you are borrowing from are taking priority over our relationship I'd love to help you with that so our relationship can
come first."

Smart Heart Dialogue for a Prenup

> ### Case #1

What she says: "Because of my potential inheritance from
my parents, I want to sign this standard prenuptial agreement. It
will protect us both."

What she may mean: "I don't want to disclose my assets to you without assurance you won't try to take them away."

The Smart Heart reply: "I understand the importance of protection. I trust you and I'm willing to lay all the 'money cards' on the table before we marry. I don't ever plan on divorcing you, but if something happened I would never want to take away what you feel is 'yours.'"

Smart Heart Dialogue for Married and Committed Couples

Case #1

What he says: "I think we should cut back on expenses; college tuition payments are more of a strain than we had anticipated."

What he may mean: "I wish you would stop your binge spending. You're acting selfish and spoiled."

The Smart Heart reply: "It sounds like you think I'm spending excessively without checking in with you. And I realize that it's a habit that my father always encouraged. But the next time I feel like making an impulsive purchase that costs more than one hundred dollars, I'll check in with you first. I do need to learn to splurge within the limits of 'our' budget, not 'mine.'"

Case #2

What she says: "I've been so stressed at work lately. Let's go somewhere exciting to kick up the romance—maybe Vegas or Atlantic City."

What she may mean: "Gambling's such a high. If I lose, it's easy enough to put in more overtime to make up the loss. And if I win, I can buy that new Louis Vuitton bag I've been wanting."

The Smart Heart reply: "I know you've been working really long hours and I'd love a romantic weekend. It's important to me that we have some time together. But we're saving to buy a house and I'd rather not take any chances with our savings. Let's just stay overnight locally."

Smart Heart Dialogue for Divorced Couples

Case #1

What he says: "I'll stop showing my anger at you and not use money as a weapon."

What he may mean: "I would like closure."

The Smart Heart reply: "I know you tried so hard; I forgive you. Let's bury the hatchet. A part of me will always love you. If you're okay with it, let's move on. I will stop using my lawyers to get at you."

Smart Heart Dialogue for Dating a Divorced Man or Woman

"I know we are in the honeymoon/magical stage of our relationship and my heart goes out to you. You were taken to the cleaners by your husband [or wife] who committed financial infidelity. It must make dating and commitment terrifying. I want to reassure you that I am a financially independent person who is debt free. I'm open to discussing how money will be handled on dates, trips, or seminars with you."

Smart Heart Jump-Starts for Breaking Up

Once you realize that your relationship is suffering from a triangle and that money is in danger of replacing you in your partner's affections (or you sense that you are in danger of shifting your emotional focus from your partner to your money) you need to act quickly and decisively to facilitate a breakup. The following Smart Heart skills will help you understand how to break up with your money (and perhaps, temporarily, with your partner) so you can consciously choose to reconnect in a newly dynamic, stronger, and more intimate relationship.

- *Understand some people need a serious jolt to shake them, wake them, and make them willing to change.* Don't be afraid to suggest a Brush with Death, or offer to break up with your money if your partner is willing do the same.
- *Acknowledge the pursuer/distancer dynamic in your relationship.* Move toward compromise and becoming flexible financial "operators."
- *Be aware of triangles.* Don't let your relationship with money control your relationship with your partner. If you are too worried about money to have fun, play, be intimate, or sexually connected, you are too involved with your money. Shift your focus to your personal relationship and work toward mutual enjoyment of each other as individuals.
- *Embrace the emptiness.* Understand what your money means to you by going without for a period of time. Recognize when you are using money to mask feelings or emotions or to fulfill empty spaces in you relationship. Don't deny what money means to you or distance yourself from financial matters.
- *Make sure movement or change is occurring.* Validate your partner's feelings during any breakup (whether with money or with a person) and remember that the reason you are *letting go with love* is to change the dynamic of the relationship.

- *If you are a hoarder, spend money once a week without guilt; if you are a binger, save money without resentment.* Don't let money have the control.

A Contract for Financial Fidelity

In order to eliminate unhealthy triangles involving money and prevent money from becoming a source of emotional fulfillment, we agree to:

- *Disconnect in order to reconnect.* When money becomes a flashpoint for provoking negative feelings or emotions, announce your need to step away from the conflict and examine the underlying reasons for the tension.
- *Stay calm during a money breakup.* If temporarily disconnecting from your money makes you anxious, share those feelings and allow your partner to offer emotional security and replace the anxious feelings with activity.
- *View temporary breakups or disconnections not as endings, but as opportunities for new beginnings.* Allowing yourself to realize the depth of your feelings during a loss will help you to appreciate the closeness of reconciliation.
- *Understand each other's need for a feeling of financial security and support each other in compartmentalizing the role of money in the relationship.* Whether this means agreeing to a prenup, creating a less formal written contract, making sure each person has a private credit card or savings account, or agreeing to waive claim to any assets that are brought into a relationship, you must strive to create a feeling of safety and security around money in your relationship. Separate how you feel about money from how you feel about the person who earns it.

Step 5:
Define the Currency of
Your Relationship

*Working Toward a "Free" Exchange of
Love and Intimacy*

Once you or you partner has successfully "broken up" with the money behaviors that have been negatively affecting the relationship—and once you have fully committed to returning to an intimate relationship with your partner—you are ready to begin the process of redefining and refinancing your relationship to both money and your partner. If you followed my advice in step 4, you have allowed yourself to fully experience and understand the emptiness that is the main driving force for financial infidelity and have identified the money behaviors that are putting your relationship at risk. Now it is time to be brutally honest with yourself, and with your partner, in order to successfully reconnect and forge new behaviors.

Determining Your Real Values

The first step is to define and acknowledge those values that are truly important in your relationship. Essential relationship values are those that do not carry a specific price tag. *Studies have shown that couples who value shared experiences over material objects are less likely to have conflict surrounding money and to express greater satisfaction with their relationship.* If you put values first, and then decide together how you will make your money work for you to align your life together with those values, you are well on the way to a conscious money partnership. Take a moment to write down those things that, for you, make life worth living. These are your core values. When temptation is seen as a challenge to their values, people are 50 percent more persistent in resisting detrimental impulses. One person may value freedom, fun, adventure, and confidence. Another may value spirituality, peace of mind, personal connection, and humanitarian acts. Read these lists to each other and talk about how you can align your expectations and experiences as a couple. Some questions you may want to ask include:

- Are we living a life that reflects our standards? Financially? Ethically? What are those standards and what steps might we take to move closer to achieving them?
- Do we define success in financial terms? Are we "successful" by our own definition?
- What makes us feel fulfilled as a couple? Are there areas in our relationship that are lacking? Can we strengthen those areas in ways that do not involve money?
- Do we like where we live? How could we make our environment more appealing without spending more money?
- Are we happy in our careers? Are there changes in our work that we could make to enhance our quality of life?
- Do we get along with (or at least understand and empathize with) both of our families?
- Do we have shared friendships that are satisfying to us as a couple?
- In what ways can we continue to improve our relationship and our lives, independent of money?
- What values matter most to us? How does money influence being able to live by these values?

Allison had been coming to see me for several months. She had been married to Paul, a wealthy real estate investor, for four years.

"I never loved him," she admitted. "I married for money. We never had

any money when I was growing up and my mother always told me that it was just as easy to marry a rich man as it was to marry a poor one. I thought maybe I'd grow to love him."

I asked Paul to come in for the next session and warned him that Allison was very close to seeking out an emotional affair.

"I know she didn't love me—that she married me for my money," he said. "But I loved her and I thought she'd learn to love me if I gave her enough things. I can tell she's getting tired of me. What can I do to make her love me?"

Neither Paul nor Allison had given any real thought to their shared values. If they had, they might have realized that love and intimacy were actually important to the both of them and Paul might have been able to fulfill Allison's need for romantic love instead of attempting to buy her affections. I pointed out to Allison that by staying with Paul simply because she wanted to be wealthy, she was committing financial infidelity. Paul, too, played his part, by accepting her gratitude for material objects in place of true intimacy.

When you marry for reasons other than love, you do not have the same glue of physical and emotional intimacy and romance to help you through the hard times. And when you lack even the *memory* of romantic, passionate love, it can be more challenging to stay motivated to work through relationship troubles. But there's no reason to give up hope, even if you don't "feel" like you are "in love" with your partner. You will, however, have to work harder at removing triangles in your relationship, especially those pertaining to money or financial security.

Once you and your partner have defined your shared values, you must consciously choose to let go of the behaviors and thought patterns that are holding you back from true connection. Each of the previous four steps in this book has helped you move toward this moment, showing you how to understand the inner needs behind acts of financial infidelity in your relationship. If you do not fully understand these motivations, you are doomed to repeat the behaviors over and over.

Letting Go of Fears

In order to reconnect with your partner and truly feel safe around money in your relationship, you must let go of any last fears you have about money.

Angelica, a very wealthy patient of mine, spent an entire session with me working through her justification for purchasing a new mattress for her bed.

"I'm embarrassed to have the man I'm dating over to my apartment," she said. "I only have an old, lumpy twin mattress. What will he think?"

Angelica had been divorced by her husband nearly a year earlier and was afraid that without his financial support she was destined to become a "bag lady." She'd been struggling to make ends meet before she had married her very wealthy former husband and was terrified that she was doomed to return to that fate. This was a woman who had received a divorce settlement of over $150 million and still needed me to give her permission to spend $2,500.

Angelica needed to let go of her fears that she would not be able to support herself. By working on the Balance Sheet exercise and practicing gratitude and abundance exercises, she came to see that she was, indeed, financially secure and was able to separate the fear of abandonment she suffered after her divorce from her fear that her money would "abandon" her as well.

Several sessions later, Angelica reported she had purchased a new luxury mattress. "I've stopped using money as a negative," she said. "Now I look at money as a route to romance and happiness. I visualize a dollar bill and think, this is to be spent. I am supposed to have pleasure with this. Once I stopped worrying about money, my sex drive and desire came back. I think I'll get a lot of pleasure from my new mattress . . . and my new boyfriend!"

I see many patients who struggle with these fears about managing money on their own. Sometimes, like Allison, they choose to stay with a partner they don't truly love. In other cases, they become, like Angelica, almost pathologically overprotective of their money and resources. *In either case, they cannot truly participate in a loving, intimate relationship with a partner until they have overcome the fear that keeps them emotionally linked to their money.*

If you cannot release these fears surrounding money, return to step 1 to see if you are using magical thinking to avoid experiencing unpleasant sensations associated with money. Then go to step 3 and examine your family legacy to see if you can gain any insight to this insecurity.

Letting Go of Greed

Today's society promotes a culture of "me, me, me." But the notion of "mine, mine, mine" in any form is detrimental to a relationship. But if your lust for money—making it, spending it, keeping track of it—overcomes the lust you should be feeling for your partner, you will encounter a major roadblock to *reconnection*. In a truly intimate and loving relationship it is important to want to *give*. Money, time, emotion—these are all valuable commodities in the currency of a good relationship. In a truly connected relationship, whenever you give, it comes back to you, and you must be willing to give freely, with no strings, resentments, or expectations.

If you cannot willingly share, go back and look at step 2 to see if you are consolidating money or objects as part of a power play and then move on to step 4 to learn how to end this unhealthy connection with your money.

Letting Go of Envy

It's difficult in our society not to succumb to feelings of *envy* where money is concerned. Sociologists have even coined "categories" of wealth. Consider the "superrich": multimillionaires who seem to have no limits on their ability to spend and acquire; the "rich rich": people who have and always will have whatever material comforts they desire;

the "poor rich": people who are characterized as wealthy based upon income, but who, when compared to the first two categories of "rich," actually appear to be lacking and act as if they don't have money by refusing to buy things and hoarding their cash. These "rich poor"—the people with "middle class" trappings—are classified as poor according to the standards of the U.S. census, who enjoy air conditioning, microwaves, three-bedroom houses, multiple color TVs, and many other comforts. In fact, according to Bill Steigerwald, in a column written for Townhall.com, of these 37 million so-called "poor" Americans, 45 percent of them own their own homes. Finally, there are the actual "poor," those people who truly cannot afford food, clothing, or shelter.

Unless you are a member of the elite "superrich," no matter where you fall on this list of income stratification, you will find others who have more than you do. It is important that you avoid falling into the trap of envying what others seem to possess and you seem to lack. This is particularly true in a relationship, where envy can make you competitive and sneaky—an ideal breeding ground for financial infidelity.

If you are wracked with envy over your neighbor's new plasma TV or your sister-in-law's McMansion, check in again with step 1 and ensure you are not practicing magical thinking that is keeping you from appreciating what you do have in your life, and then go to step 4 to break up with this damaging money behavior.

Letting Go of Self-Destructive Impulses

Use the following "money mantra" to *remind yourself that money is not a tool for punishment or a weapon of guilt*. You need to be comfortable with your money in order to be able to safely talk about it. Repeat this mantra daily as needed to remind yourself that there is nothing shameful or "bad" about how you feel about money.

Exercise: Money Mantra

It's okay to not suffer.
It's okay to be abundant.
It's okay to do better than my parents.
It's okay to have more money than I "need."
It's okay to spend.
It's okay to plan and save.

Welcoming Feelings of Gratitude and Abundance

If you are prone to envy, and your conflicts with your partner tend to center around why you don't have enough—enough money, enough houses, enough cars, enough status—it is critical that you shift your focus. Remember the list of levels of "rich" above? Instead of always feeling that there is someone who has *more* than you, begin to shift your attitude and realize that there are many people who have *less* than you. Learn to appreciate what material goods and financial comforts you *do* have in your life. More importantly, focus on what there is to appreciate about your partner and your relationship.

Exercise: Partner Affirmations

Each day list five things about your partner that you are truly grateful for. Do not list material things. You may be grateful he is healthy, that she comes from a loving family, that he is attractive, that he doesn't snore. Begin each day with these thoughts of what you most appreciate. Post this list where your partner can see it, and verbalize each of these thoughts to yourself and each other throughout the day.

Exercise: Money Affirmations

Each day list five positive things about your current financial situation that you are truly grateful for. Let go of any negative thoughts such as "not enough" or "need more." Appreciate and be grateful for what your money has done for you: "a house to live in," "good food to eat," "the opportunity to socialize with friends." Begin each day with these thoughts of gratitude. Post this list where your partner can see it, and verbalize these thoughts to yourself and each other throughout the day.

Going Back to Your Partner in a New Way

If you have instigated a Brush with Death, now that you have articulated your most important values, indicated a willingness to embrace change and risk, and taken steps toward enhancing feelings of gratitude and appreciation, ask yourself these questions to see if you are ready to reconnect with your partner around money in a whole new way:

- Do you miss your partner more than you miss your money behavior?
- Do you feel safe?
- Can you validate your partner's feelings about money?
- Can your partner validate your feelings about money?
- Can you talk about spending?
- Can you give without withholding?
- Do you "pay yourself first" by setting aside a portion of your income for savings *before* using the balance to meet your expenses?
- If you wish to be taken care of, are you willing to share with your partner what you need to feel cared for?
- If you wish to be independent, are you willing to share with your partner what you need to feel independent?
- Do you have a strong knowledge about your individual and shared finances?

- Do you both recognize your part in perpetuating financial infidelity?
- Have you both expressed sincere remorse for your behavior?
- Are you both willing to start the process of forgiving each other to make a fresh start and experience a renewed connection?

If you and your partner both answer "yes" to all of these questions, you are ready to reconnect. If you cannot honestly answer the questions above affirmatively, or you have not seen actions from your partner that back up his or her promises to change, you need to extend the breakup in order to makeup. Some people end their breakups too soon and in no time at all find themselves falling back into the same patterns of behavior that drove them to initiate a Brush with Death in the first place. Do not go back until you are truly ready.

It's too soon to reconnect if you:
- Don't feel ready to reenter the relationship—for any reason.
- Still view yourself as the victim or victimizer.
- Are still punishing each other, grudge holding, or engaging in tit-for-tat behavior.
- Are unwilling to take responsibility for your part in the behavior that caused the breakup.
- Have not seen real change or movement, or are still being sucked into a vortex of false promises.
- Feel guilty or feel sorry for your partner. People who reconnect out of guilt have a greater chance of breaking up for good.
- Feel emotionally numb and lack feelings for your partner. These may be symptoms of lingering resentment.
- Are provoking fights or arguments.

The Brush with Death exercise is not an exercise in revenge or a punishment. It is not a dress rehearsal for divorce. It is a shocking wake-up call meant to evoke deep feelings of loss. It is a *real* separation, meant to effect *real* changes in behavior and initiate feelings of appreciation and love. If, during this breakup, you and your partner cannot change your damaged dynamic, your relationship does not have enough "give" and a reconnection is not likely to be successful.

Molly had asked Ben for a Brush with Death when she found text messages from his girlfriend on his cell phone. Ben moved out and after only a month was calling Molly and begging her to take him back. He promised he'd stop seeing his girlfriend. He swept Molly away for a romantic week in Hawaii. He wined her and dined her and whispered sweet nothings. They had been home for a week when Molly found more text messages from the girlfriend on the computer. When she confronted Ben, he protested that he had kept his promise. He hadn't "seen" his girlfriend since he left for Hawaii.

Molly realized that she did not allow enough time for Ben to really feel the emptiness of the loss and to miss and appreciate her. She had listened to his words, but not looked at his actions. This time, she asked him to leave with the intent of never taking him back. She hired a lawyer and began the process of filing for divorce. She refused to see Ben or speak to him at all.

Several months later, I received a call from Ben asking if I would see him and Molly in a session. He realized that he did not want to end the marriage and was ready to show Molly that he was committed to working through their problems in therapy.

I urged Molly to give him a second chance. I had watched this same dynamic in my parents' relationship as my father continued to gamble and have affairs while promising to change. Like many of my patients, he didn't realize what he had until he lost it. It wasn't until my mother literally moved out of their home and into an apartment that his behavior began to change. When she believed he understood her clear boundaries and limits, she reconnected with him and they worked on their relationship until they had achieved a real-life love that lasted until the end of my mother's life.

The Process of Reconnection

When you end a breakup or a Brush with Death and reconnect with your partner to resume your relationship, you should be ready to embrace the idea of a clean slate and a mutual willingness to move forward into a newly defined intimacy. This transition can be frightening for some people, particularly if they are distancers. Both you and your partner have done a lot of work in understanding your personal relationships to money. In order to support the new behaviors you desire around shared finances, you must reconnect with the strong desire to institute and maintain safe, honest, loving communication on all money matters.

Initiate Positive Change

Carl and Leah are their mid sixties. They fell in love after both of their spouses had died. Being widowed had forced Leah into a financial education. "I'm not really from a generation where women were expected to deal with the money in a marriage," she admitted. "But having to raise a family on my own taught me a lot about managing the money we did have."

Both Carl and Leah had children from their former marriages, and when they decided to get more serious, both agreed that they wanted to protect their children's respective inheritances. I suggested that Carl and Leah do their Family Moneygram and begin their discussions with a clear understanding of their personal money legacies. Both had a history of poverty and fear and had compensated in their marriages. As a result, both were eager to make money a "nonissue" in their relationship.

"We wanted to eliminate the power struggle and go right to the real love," Carl said.

Eventually Carl and Leah moved in together. They agreed in writing that they would split everything—even "an apple from the store"—exactly fifty-fifty. For twelve years, Leah and Carl have kept their finances entirely separate, each contributing exactly half to the expenses of running their household. They *are not named in each other's wills, instead leaving their estates solely to their children. For Leah, whose parents scrimped and saved in order to leave her with an inheritance, it was particularly important to leave a legacy for the next generation. Both Carl and Leah feel secure and in control of their financial futures—and in the financial futures of their children.*

But as I pointed out to Carl and Leah, life and love are never exactly 50 / 50. Sometimes it's 80 / 20 or 70 / 30 or 60 / 40 . . . you get the idea. There's always a power struggle in some area. Even if they think they've got the power struggle over money solved, couples still need to learn to "stretch" for reciprocity.

And while it is true that Carl and Leah do not fight over money, they wouldn't have come to see me if they'd been able to avoid other power struggles. Nevertheless, by teaching them Smart Heart dialogue skills I was able to help them to see that the power struggles they encountered as their "honeymoon" stage ended were necessary to allow them to work through and balance the "I vs. We" couples encounter in every relationship.

Each conflict they solved with empathy, understanding, trust, and love was a gift to their relationship, allowing them to access greater intimacy and real love and strengthening the connection between them.

In many ways, Leah's clarity about her relationship and her money may be ahead of the times. In an article in *The New York Times Magazine*, Maureen Dowd characterized women entering the twenty-first century as "in a tangle of dependence and independence," resulting in an intensified "confusion between the sexes." In my practice, I have seen too many women (and some men) make decisions about money based on the notion that the love of their life will also be their financial savior. Many women who successfully managed their own financial affairs while single are still "delegating" their family finances to their husbands. Still others, no matter how successful or proficient in business they have become, believe that the men in their lives are somehow superior when it comes to managing money.

All individuals should trust their own financial acumen at least as much as they trust their partner's. Whether you are married or single you must take responsibility for financial balance in your relationships. If you are single, and moving forward in a relationship, use the following checklist to help you discuss some important money issues that could impact future financial, emotional, and physical stability for both you and your partner.

Financial Implications for Singles Living Together

If you are considering taking your relationship to the next level and living together, you may want to consult a lawyer in the state you live in to see what types of cohabitation agreements your local or state courts will uphold. This is especially important for gay couples who are not allowed to legalize their relationship in certain states.

- *Decide whether or not you will keep all or some assets separate,* at least initially, including savings and checking accounts, credit cards, real estate, and investments. *Disclaimer:* You should never use the same credit card initially in case your new partner has credit issues. Keep only a small amount in joint checking or savings until you feel more secure.
- *Decide how you will handle joint assets.* Talk about how you will divide assets if you should break up or choose to move out.
- *Decide how you will contribute to shared expenses.* Will you contribute equal amounts or will you contribute a percentage based on income?
- *Will you draft and sign a cohabitation or "no-nup" agreement?* This should include any promises you have made about financial dependency (e.g., if your partner encourages you to go back to school and promises to "take care of you" while you are out of the workforce).
- *Do you want to grant each other a durable power of attorney* to allow one partner to make financial decisions in case the other becomes unable to so for him- or herself?

- *Do you want to grant each other a health care proxy* that allows a nonrelative to make medical decisions for an incapacitated partner?
- *Do you want to provide for each other* in your wills or on your insurance policies?
- *Will you each have separate money* for guiltless luxury spending?

Put Money in Its Place

In reconnecting and reclaiming your relationship, you and your partner must agree to "put money in its place." Nothing can be more important to you than each other. To assess whether or not you are allowing money to take control of the relationship, ask yourself the following questions on a regular basis:

- Am I happy in this relationship each day?
- Is my partner happy in this relationship each day?
- Am I using money to feel happier?
- Do I love my partner the way my partner wants to be loved? Does money play into that? In what way?
- Am I using money to show love, instead of sharing physical and emotional intimacy?
- Does my partner love me in the way I want to be loved? Does money play into that? In what way?
- Is my partner using money to show love, instead of sharing physical and emotional intimacy?

Learn to Ask for What You Need

Just as you cannot be afraid to talk about money, you cannot be afraid to ask your partner for what you need from the relationship. In real-life love, you love your partner as your partner wishes to be loved, not in the way you want to love or "in the only way you can." Let your partner know when you need something from him or her, whether it is emotional, financial, or physical.

Liza and Sarah had only been living together for six months when they came to see me.

"She's so damn cheap," Liza blurted out. "I can't stand it. You know what she does to show me she loves me? She brings me a flower. Once a week. One flower. It's like she's throwing it in my face that I'm only worth a single rose. And you know what's worse? She's rich. She's got a good job and a trust fund. And all she brings me is one pathetic flower."

Sarah looked shocked. "I thought I was being romantic. You always tell me that you can pull your own weight financially in our relationship. I know you don't have the same financial advantages as I do, so I didn't want to bring you a huge bouquet every week; I thought you'd start to feel pressured to give me something."

I asked Liza if she could see how Sarah might have gotten mixed messages from her. On one hand, Liza insisted on financial equality and independence in their relationship, while on the other hand, she secretly wanted to be taken care of, but was afraid to tell Sarah for fear of seeming greedy.

Liza talked about her mother, who would punish her whenever she admitted she wanted something. "I still feel guilty if I take a cab instead of walking in the rain," she admitted. "My mother always insisted I do the cheapest thing— never the easiest, or the most pleasant, or the most fun. Always the cheapest. I know why she did it. She was withholding even though we had the money! But Sarah's got plenty of money."

I pointed out that Sarah didn't seem to be withholding with her money like Liza's mother. She paid for vacations that the couple took and always offered to pay for dinner whenever they went out. In fact, as far as I could see, their conflict wasn't about roses, or cheapness, or who had more or less money to spend. It was Liza's inability to tell Sarah when she needed to be taken care of that was the real problem because of her mother's withholdingness/punitiveness.

As Liza learned to share her vulnerability, Sarah became more comfortable with giving spontaneous gifts to show her affection—including a weekly bouquet of fresh flowers. Liza reciprocated by taking care of Sarah in ways that didn't involve big expenditures, such as planning outings to museums or movies she knew Sarah would enjoy or offering to make dinner a few nights a week.

Exercise: Mirror, Mirror, on the Wall

Seeing how people feel about money is like getting a glimpse into their soul. It's like a magic mirror that shows us our true values. Using as a model the examples I've given below, do this exercise with your partner to see how each of you views the ten things you spend the most money on.

EXPENSE	WHAT IT IS	WHY I DO IT	WHEN I DO IT	PARTNER'S REACTION
1. Home	Five bedrooms, four baths, good neighborhood	For kids; for show	When mother died	Great, I love the house
2. New-model SUV	Transportation	Neighbors have one	When I feel depressed	Why do we need a new car?
3. Dining	Eating out four nights per week	Too lazy to cook; entertaining; socializing	When I feel deprived	We're broke. I think we should cook dinner tonight

HOW I PAY FOR IT	CAN I AFFORD IT?	AM I WILLING TO CHANGE?	HOW?	IS IT FINANCIAL INFIDELITY?
Mortgage, plus home equity line of credit	It's a stretch	No	Will make changes in other area	No
New car loan	Not really	Yes	Trade in for pre-owned	Yes
Credit cards	No, not so often	Yes	Start dinner club with friends; prepare meals on weekends	Yes

Exercise: Creating a Shared Financial Relationship Vision

(Based on Harville Hendrix's Relationship Vision from Getting the Love You Want*)*

1. On separate pieces of paper, you and your partner list the things that you consider most important for a satisfying and secure financial relationship. Use the *present tense* so it feels doable when writing this list and include things that you already have (such as retirement accounts) as well as things you wish you had (such as no credit card debt).
2. Share your lists. Underline the items you have in common. If your partner has a money goal or value that you agree with but did not have on your list, add it to your paper.
3. Returning to your expanded or revised list, rate each item in order of importance from 1 to 5 (with 1 being "very important" and 5 indicating "not at all important").
4. Circle three items that are most important to you.
5. Put a check next to three items you think would be the most difficult to achieve.
6. Working together, combine your lists to create a financial relationship vision. Start with the items you agree are the most important, and toward the bottom list those that are less important. If you disagree about the importance of an item, and cannot reach a compromise that satisfies both of you, leave that item off the combined list.

Your finished list should look similar to the one below. Post it where you can both see it and look at it regularly. Use it to remind each other of your shared goals and financial values and dreams.

YOUR RATING		YOUR PARTNER'S RATING	
1	We have savings.	1	
1	We are able to practice discretionary spending separately and together.	2	√
1	We have no credit card debt.	1	
1	We have life insurance.	1	
1	We have health insurance.	1	
1	We have a high checking account balance.	1	
2	We have a retirement account.	2	
2	We have wills or trusts.	1	
2	We take regular vacations.	2	√
2	We can afford private education (if we have children).	2	
3	We invest in our careers.	3	
3	We can pay off the mortgage early.	4	√
3	We have college saving accounts.	4	√
4	We have disability insurance.	4	
5	We will carry high credit card debt in order to have what we want.	5	
5	We pay bills together or take turns.	5	
5	We meet weekly for money talks.	5	

The Good Part Is Just Beginning

Congratulations on making it this far. When you have reached this stage of reconnection, you do so with a deeper understanding of hidden and subconscious agendas that drive the money behaviors causing conflict in your relationship. With this knowledge and with the Smart Heart tools for change that you have learned along the way, you are ready to put aside money as a source of conflict, tension, or stress in your relationship. The Smart Heart methods for safe communication that you have learned to apply to money dialogue can be used in any area of your relationship to enrich and sustain intimate connection.

Now that you have the ability to approach power struggles calmly and to see money conflicts for what they really are, you are ready to take your relationship to the next level and reignite the sparks of your first passion. By restoring the magic of romantic sizzle to your love, you open the doors to deep physical intimacy that will enhance all other areas of your relationship.

When Money Talks

At this stage of the game your internal dialogue should be affirming and express a healthy relationship with your money. Write down what your money says to you and how you want to respond. Share these dialogues with your partner and ask him or her to do the same:

- "Your partner's been working hard all week. Why don't you use me to book a couples massage this weekend? I'm happy to help you relax."
- "It would be nice to get your girlfriend those diamond earrings, but I think she'd be happier knowing that you were saving for a down payment on a house for the two of you. Maybe you can treat by cooking dinner tonight instead."
- "Of course you *could* use me to buy that expensive cocktail dress for dinner tonight, but are you going to be willing to tell your husband what you've done? How will he react? Maybe it would be nicer to splurge on a good bottle of wine during the meal that you can enjoy together."

- "It's true your parents never let you spend on things they considered frivolous, but you've been excellent about following your budget and it's okay to spend this unexpected money on something that pleases you."
- "I know it's not what you'd choose, but I'm sure your partner would appreciate *this* type of briefcase, rather than the one you prefer."

Smart Heart Dialogue for Reconnecting

When you decide to reconnect with your partner, you are deciding to communicate in a different way. To encourage ongoing behavior change after a "Brush with Death" breakup, it is important that you use the Smart Heart skills you have learned throughout the book. In this reconnecting phase, as you leave reactivity to money outside of your day-to-day interactions, be sure that you are consciously reinforcing safe communication and rewarding "stretches" in behavior.

Smart Heart Dialogue for Singles or Married Couples

Case #1

What he says: "It's too much trouble to make a meal and clean up afterward. Let's just grab a quick bite out at a restaurant instead."

What he may mean: "If she nags at me to help clean up the dishes, I'm going to miss the game."

The Smart Heart reply: "I know you had your heart set on going out. We've been talking about limiting how much we go out, so we can save up for a romantic vacation. I don't mind making dinner for you because I know how much you appreciate it. Why don't I make something simple and quick and then we can clean up and watch the game together?"

Case #2

What she says: "You came home late last night, after I was already asleep. I called the office and you didn't answer. Were you working late?"

What she may mean: "I'm afraid you were out with the guys gambling. You promised not to go to any more Friday night poker games until we had our credit card debt under control."

The Smart Heart reply: "I made a mistake and broke my promise to you, but I know this is going to get better if we can talk about it. You're terrific and I know you can help me. I love you and I will not act out, take you for granted, or make the same mistake again. What do you need me to do to show I am truly sorry and will change?"

Case #3

What she says: "Gee, thanks for the bubble bath. It's quite the gift."

What she may mean: "Just how cheap are you? We've been seeing each other for a while now and I expected more than this." *Or perhaps:* "This really wasn't what I was expecting for our fifth anniversary gift."

The Smart Heart reply: "I know you were hoping for something more lavish. We both agreed it is important to us to save for a new house and that means cutting back on lots of things. I want to stick to our decision. If I could, I'd get you whatever you wanted, whenever you wanted. And I hope I can someday. But for now, why don't I run the bath and light some candles? You can relax while I scrub your back. . . . Are you okay?"

Smart Heart Jump-Starts for Reconnecting

When you are ready to reconnect with your partner and leave your relationship with money outside of the intimacy of romantic life, you need to be sure that you have the freedom to concentrate your emotional connection on the person in your life, rather than the money in your life.

- **Be knowledgeable about your money situation.** Know your net worth; understand your insurance policies and retirement and stock accounts; have a shared vision for your financial future; and support each other in maintaining financial health and financial intimacy. When you are on top of your financial situation, concerns about money behaviors and risks for financial infidelity are minimized. When both partners have equal knowledge, and use the Smart Heart tools and dialogue to talk about money, there is safety in the relationship. This sense of safety allows you to concentrate on maintaining or increasing the emotional and physical intimacy in your relationship.
- **Don't fear change.** Procrastination can hurt both your financial and your emotional relationship. If something needs to change, take the risk to move toward that change and be willing to reconnect in a new place in your relationship.

- **Commit to staying together.** There's no doubt that money affects relationships, but surprisingly, it does not matter how much or how little you have. Communicating and making decisions together about your money is what will bring you closer together. Conflicts over money can be used as a strategy to leave a relationship. Vow to close off this exit for good.

- **Problem-solve together.** Define the troubling money behavior or issue. Brainstorm ways in which the problem can be solved. Evaluate all proposed solutions. Select one solution and plan for how you will make it work. Don't be afraid to ask for support from your partner or to seek professional help together to overcome real or perceived obstacles.

- **Connect when your partner disconnects.** Don't take a temporary disconnection personally or let it hurt your feelings. Do not retaliate by becoming distant. Instead give your partner some time and then reconnect with love. Coach, support, and be emotionally available to each other so you can both become stronger and more complete by healing your wounds together.

A Contract for Financial Fidelity

In order to connect honestly and safely around money in order to nurture and sustain emotional and physical intimacy in our relationship, we agree to:

- **Remain educated about our financial situation.** Pay bills together or take turns, review budgets, understand basic financial information, know your shared net worth, and figure out how your assets will be allocated in case of death or divorce. Shared knowledge means shared power.

- **Pay attention to the pronouns.** To encourage shared goals and visions always use "ours" instead of "mine" or "yours" when talking about shared or joint finances. Have a plan to eliminate "our" debt; decide whether or not you want to invest more time at work to increase "our" income; determine how much money to save for "our" future. It's okay to have separate (but not *secret*) accounts (especially for splurges), but be sure to balance the "I" and the "We" when it comes to money in your relationship.

- **Never sneak and never lie.** You cannot be afraid to reveal a financial blunder or be secretive about an unexpected windfall. Trust is the most important ingredient in an intimate relationship. People who feel safe do not need to lie. Full disclosure of any behavior involving shared finances is a matter of trust; anything else is financial infidelity.

- **Stay focused on our values.** Remember that it is shared values, and experiences relating to them—not money goals, not material objects, not stuff you buy together—that ultimately provides the security necessary for real intimacy. Don't be influenced by social factors or envy or competitiveness when deciding what you "need." Often your material "needs"—new status cars, handbags, designer jeans—are not "necessary" at all.

- **Be clear about the issue at hand and be willing to negotiate for a realistic compromise.** Use Smart Heart dialogue tools to discuss the topic without dragging in other issues, judging, criticizing, or invalidating.

- **Be proactive rather than reactive.** Avoid assumptions based on past behavior. Realize that each time you connect you are experiencing a slightly different person. Look at your partner with a "new face" every day.

- **Put our relationship first.** Plain and simple; nothing else is more important than the two of you.

Step 6:
Refinance Your Relationship

Reorganizing Your Priorities to Reclaim Lasting Love

Having made the decision—and done the work—to reconnect with your partner around money fitness, you are now free to turn your attention to the priorities that can make your romantic relationship stronger and more intimate than ever.

In relationships damaged by financial infidelity, interactions around money have become recurring negative experiences for both you and your partner. To create an environment conducive to romance, you must reduce these negative interactions and increase positive ones. According to marriage and relationship expert John Gottman, couples in successful, functional relationships experience five positive interactions for every negative one.

Couples I counsel want to know how, with so much negative history, they can change this ratio of positive and negative interactions with their partner. I tell them that first of all, they must think that they will succeed. Positive intentions and attitudes promote positive interactions. Then I tell them that reromanticizing their relationship is partly about "tricking" themselves into thinking they are in the Euphoria (or honeymoon) stage of love again.

You may remember the description of this stage from the very beginning of the book: it is the only relationship stage where money conflicts are minimal and easily resolved—because your love for your partner is your overwhelming priority. The idea of returning to the Euphoria stage by employing a strategy of "fake it 'til you make it" may sound trite, but do not underestimate the ability of your mind's power to trigger actual chemical and hormonal changes that will reinforce passion and romantic feelings. You now have the skills and indignation to make a conscious decision to stay in love.

Another critical component of reromanticizing is to remember to use the Smart Heart techniques and dialogues to break any cycles of negativity that have become part of your dynamic as a couple.

Finally, when it comes to reromanticizing your relationship, don't make the mistake many make and wait for your partner to make the first move. Trust that both of you want to be nurtured. If you are having trouble with the idea of rekindling your sex life after a breakup, try to think of sex as a form of connection and nurturing. Use physical intimacy as another way to spark communications with your partner and you may be surprised at how quickly the flame of intense passion returns to your love life.

Couples who have been together a long time and accept each other for who they are may mistake this acceptance for predictability and may find reromanticizing particularly challenging at first. In the securely attached relationship, intimacy can become the enemy of lust. Sex is never *truly* spontaneous, even in dating, but when couples have traded passion for security, they may feel that their love life is boring; they no longer even desire to plan for sex, and complain that their relationship has lost its "spark." To rekindle the feelings of true romantic love, you must enhance dopamine, and to enhance dopamine you must have sex! *It is the couples that are most securely attached that must consciously plan to keep lust alive.*

The return of romantic feelings and sexy sizzle to a relationship doesn't happen all at once. Be patient, with yourself and your partner. Any kind of infidelity, including financial infidelity, causes a deep breach of trust in a relationship. Whether you are the betrayer or the one who has been betrayed, it is important to realize that the damage to your relationship has occurred over time. Whether you have felt financial, emotional, or physical pain, the recovery is the same. You have been hurt in stages, you forgive in stages, and you get your feelings back in stages. Be proactive and patient. Embrace the idea of both giving and receiving pleasure.

Romance Wreckers

Before you can restore romantic feelings for your partner, you must be absolutely sure that you want to regain the emotional and sexual intimacy of your early relationship. To do so, you must choose to banish any negativity toward your partner, and avoid what journalist Hara Estroff Marano calls the "ritualization of revenge"—especially when it comes to matters of money. And you absolutely cannot indulge in any grudge holding.

People who hold grudges are generally afraid of passion. They nurture small hurts and wrongs rather than taking the risk of going through conflict to arrive at a better place. Grudge holding makes them feel powerful and protected against future hurt. This sense of power allows them to avoid the risk that working on love entails. In a way they are cowards who would rather silently nurse their wounds than face a conflict that would allow their partner to dissolve the grudge. Couples who opt for "peace at any price" in a relationship will eventually develop grudges, and sooner or later, one or the other person will feel as if he or she is not being taken seriously and will walk away without the other ever knowing that anything was wrong.

QUIZ: ARE YOU A GRUDGE HOLDER?

Choose the answer below that *most often* describes your behavior or reaction to conflict in your relationship:

1. Your partner has left the sink full of dirty dishes—again. He or she has already gone to bed and you've had a long day. Do you:
   a) Leave the dishes; you'll hash this out in the morning.

b) Do the dishes and give your partner the cold shoulder over coffee.

c) Storm the bedroom and demand that your partner wake up and clean the kitchen.

d) Clean up before you go to bed—you'll be sure to mention this incident the next time you have a big blowout, but you don't want to start anything.

2. You've left your partner waiting at the restaurant for twenty minutes. Again. When you finally arrive, you:
   a) Validate your partner's frustration, apologize profusely, and promises to call the next time you get stuck at the office.
   b) Tell him or her not to be such a nag—why can't he or she just read a book and enjoy him or herself while they wait?
   c) Pick a fight with him or her before they can complain. After all, a good offense is the best defense.
   d) Listen to him or her complain, say, "Whatever," and order a glass of wine.

3. You've had a really bad week and need a sympathetic shoulder. When you complain to your partner you feel like he or she always:
   a) Takes the other person's side and claims to be "just playing devil's advocate."
   b) Rolls his or her eyes and changes the topic.
   c) Empathizes and offers advice if you want it.
   d) Says that you are much too sensitive and you need to toughen up.

4. You suspect that your partner has been sneaking money out of your joint bank account. Do you:
   a) Confront your partner and demand answers.
   b) Search his or her wallet looking for suspicious receipts.
   c) Joke that your partner must be buying you a special present and see if he or she confesses.
   d) Say nothing.

5. Your new date wants to micromanage your every move. He or she has opinions on what you should wear, how you should spend your free time, and the best way to manage your career. He or she plans all the dates and you feel as if you have to ask permission for both money and time. This makes you feel:

   a) Irritated. Who made this person the boss? It's time to question some of his or her assumptions.

   b) Resigned. You're just not as strong a personality and there's no point in constantly arguing.

   c) Introspective. Are you giving off some signals that are triggering these behaviors?

   d) Invisible. Doesn't your opinion count for anything in this relationship?

6. Your partner wants to spend the weekend with his or her mother. And the holidays. And your vacations. You always agree, but the visits are:

   a) A pleasure. You love your mother-in-law.

   b) A chore. You wish just once you'd be excused.

   c) A duty. But one you honestly have come to accept.

   d) A nightmare. Luckily you can grit your teeth and get through anything.

SCORING

If you picked mostly a's and c's, you are not likely to be a grudge holder. You and your partner may engage in some passionate "discussions" from time time to time, but generally your relationship thrives on your ability to express your feelings. In order to benefit when working through conflict in your relationship, be sure to use Smart Heart skills and dialogues and remember the Fighting Fair techniques outlined in step 2.

If you picked mostly b's and d's, you're a likely candidate for grudge holding. Relationship dynamics likely to foster grudge holding include:

- Simmering resentment from saying yes when you really want to say no
- Delayed reactions to trigger situations
- Feeling that your partner minimizes your concerns or doesn't take you seriously
- A partner who is critical, invalidating, or lacking in remorse
- Conflict avoidance
- Feeling controlled, stonewalled, or manipulated, but intent on maintaining "peace at any price," so reluctant to "rock the boat"
- Feeling as if you are not heard and are "invisible"

Grudges that go unnoticed or are ignored make it impossible to reromanticize and can lead to affairs, breakups, financial infidelity, and other forms of triangling.

Exercise: Making the Love–Money Connection

From the following list, pick out the adjectives that describe your partner's best traits around money. Write them, along with any other descriptions that you can think of, in one column. Next choose those words that describe your partner's best romantic attributes. Write these descriptions down in another column. Note if there is overlap between the two lists. (There should be. How people behave with money is often reflected in how they act as lovers.) Circle those traits that are most important to you. Have your partner do the same and compare lists.

Now consider if there are ways in which money can be used to enhance your romantic relationship. Are there traits you admire around money that you do not admire in romance? Use these lists to help you decide when to bring money *into* the bedroom with you, and when to leave it out of romance.

Sample Traits

Active	Easygoing	Innocent	Responsible
Adventurous	Efficient	Intelligent	Risk-taking
Affectionate	Energetic	Jealous	Satisfied
Ambitious	Excited	Loving	Sexy
Attentive	Expert	Loyal	Skillful
Bold	Faithful	Mature	Smart
Bossy	Fearless	Mysterious	Stingy
Busy	Fortunate	Naughty	Strict
Calm	Fun-loving	Nervous	Sweet
Careful	Funny	Noisy	Thankful
Careless	Generous	Obedient	Thoughtful
Charming	Gentle	Peaceful	Tolerant
Cheerful	Giving	Playful	Trusting
Confident	Grateful	Pleasant	Trustworthy
Curious	Happy	Polite	Unpredictable
Dangerous	Honest	Precise	Unusual
Decisive	Hopeful	Predictable	Useful
Demanding	Humorous	Proper	Warm
Dependable	Imaginative	Rational	Wise
Eager	Independent	Reliable	Withholding

Bringing Sexy Back

Once you and your partner feel safe discussing and handling money, and understand the proper place for it in your intimate relationship, it's time to put your finances to good use in restoring the sex and sizzle to your relationship. Using money the *right* way—to enhance and delight your partner—is the romantic side of financial fidelity.

When Marguerite and Jared, whom we met in discussing step 2, first came to my office, she felt as if he was controlling all of the money in the household and, by extension, trying to control her. She was sneaking money and shutting down sexually. Jared was responding by becoming even more controlling, while insisting that he was offering her equal partnership in the relationship. They were stuck in a vicious circle.

I suggested that Jared focus on Marguerite's contribution to the well-being of their family, and on how she nurtured and supported him by providing a lovely home for him to return to each day. I told him to practice attachment skills by looking into her eyes when he spoke to her, holding her hand, and verbalizing his appreciation of her nurturing qualities. I suggested that he be conscious of giving her compliments on her physical beauty as well.

On the other hand, I advised Marguerite to become educated about all aspects of their finances. She was to participate in weekly budgeting sessions with Jared as well as monthly bill-paying meetings. Eventually, I told Jared, he would transfer more of the responsibility for managing the household money to Marguerite and she would take on the role of updating him on the status of their budget.

As Marguerite became more empowered regarding their shared finances, she became more confident. I suggested that she look for ways to use extra money in the budget to reignite the romantic spark in the relationship. She was already feeling sexier, thanks to Jared's compliments and frequent physical contact. In our last session she told me how she had "kidnapped" Jared one Friday after work and whisked him off for a romantic overnight stay at a local B&B. Jared was grinning as he listened to Marguerite detail how she had organized and paid for the whole adventure.

"Now that I understand the money part of our relationship, it's easy to put the romance first," she said. "We're never going to let the money get in the way of our love again."

When you have an understanding of your relationship to money—whether you are happier spending or saving, whether you use money for a good time or save it for a rainy day—you will benefit from experiencing your partner's point of view. Nothing is more conducive to increased romance than learning how to get pleasure out of seeing your partner having a good time.

Exercise: Trading Places or "Kidnapping Your Partner"

Each of you will choose a specific day to spend together. Only one of you is allowed to do the planning for the day. This is your opportunity to turn "mind reading" from a negative to a positive. When you practice *empathetic* mind reading, you do not assume you *know* what your partner is thinking or feeling; instead, you thoughtfully and perceptively intuit what your partner would most enjoy. When you make plans, try to construct *your partner's* perfect day.

If you know that she loves a fancy lunch and window- (or real) shopping, put that on the schedule. If he likes nothing better than a day out on a boat with a cooler of snacks, then willingly pack up that picnic lunch and book that fishing charter.

The planning is easy. Now you must truly enjoy, or pretend to enjoy (remember, when first reromanticizing, "faking" is allowed) the outing. Stretch your comfort zone and refrain from complaining or negative comments. *Even if you do not enjoy the activity, appreciate the pleasure it gives your partner.* Savor your partner's delight and participate in his or her good mood. Do not make your partner feel guilty about enjoying the day and do not act as if you have more important things to do. You may be surprised at how much you end up enjoying your day together. When it is your turn to enjoy the day your partner has planned for you, don't be shy about expressing your appreciation for his or her efforts.

Attachment Skills

Most relationships can be reromanticized—no matter how disconnected you may have felt before your temporary "breakup." An important touchstone for couples are the little rituals that show affection on a daily basis. These rituals make and reaffirm memories that can energize, protect, and heal us. Certain attachment techniques can be turned into rituals that will boost your romantic connection chemically by stimulating the production of the hormone oxytocin.

Sometimes called "the cuddle hormone," high levels of oxytocin are produced by breastfeeding mothers, and scientists believe that it is this flood of hormones that encourages bonding and attachment with their baby. But the fact is, any type of touch can stimulate release of this hormone.

It is important to use ritualized attachment skills to keep the hormones flowing, especially in times of stress. These oxytocin-stimulating interactions are physiologically soothing—particularly for individuals (most often men) who are "allergic" to highly emotional conflict. Use the following attachment skills regularly to keep your desire for physical connection with your partner alive:

- Gaze into each other's eyes (for at least twenty seconds).
- Kiss (for thirty seconds minimum to stimulate immune system and increase oxytocin for bonding!).
- Cuddle in bed for twenty seconds when you first wake up and before bedtime for a dopamine rush.
- Dance close.
- Touch each other's faces, arms, and shoulders.
- Feel each other's warmth and breath.
- Hold and rock each other.
- Say tender words. Use these "verbal aphrodisiacs" for three minutes each day.
- Put your arms around each other's necks.
- Stroke or brush each other's hair.
- Hold hands.
- Embrace.

Miniconnections

Another important and similar technique for fostering intimacy is to use mundane daily rituals to deepen your connection with your partner.

Like attachment skills, daily miniconnections keep the hormones flowing and allow chemistry to do some of the work of reromanticizing. Practice the following miniconnections daily until they become a completely natural way of relating to your partner:

- Hug and kiss hello and good-bye.
- Spend at least twenty seconds cuddling when you first wake up and before bedtime to stimulate dopamine release.
- Kiss deeply and romantically for twenty seconds before you go to bed to release oxytocin.
- Think positive thoughts about your partner six times a day. This is especially important for men, who do not instinctively nurture thoughts of their partner during the day. This does not mean that you call your partner six times a day or send six e-mails a day. It means that you take time out from your schedule, no matter how busy, and focus on a positive aspect of your love and your partner.
- Have dinner together. No excuses. If you have to wait for your partner to come home, then you have to wait.
- Gaze into each other's eyes for thirty seconds when you first wake and when you first reunite.
- Use "verbal aphrodisiacs"—compliment your partner for thirty seconds.
- Offer one heartfelt and original compliment daily.

Use Money the Right Way for Romance

When you are able to talk safely about how you want to manage your finances, it is easier to spend to make your partner happy. The truth is, it doesn't matter how much money you have. You can create wonderful "fantasy dates" that are incredibly romantic and sexy without spending a dime. If you have money to splurge, use it on a night out dancing. If you're on a tight budget, choose a night at home slow dancing to a Louis

Armstrong CD. Have you decided together to splurge after you receive a big bonus? Choose dinner at a five-star restaurant where you can hold hands and kiss at the table. If you're saving up for a financial goal, choose to savor a picnic after work with homemade sandwiches. It doesn't matter if it's a day out on your yacht or a walk in the park, a weekend in Vegas or a quick overnight at a local chain hotel while your parents watch the kids. It's the effort and the positive attitude that counts.

Allison, whom we met earlier, was worried when I suggested that she and Paul try to romanticize their relationship. She had been quite clear about the fact that she had married for money—not for love—and that the more Paul wanted her to behave romantically, the more resistant she felt. Paul was eager to try to bring romance to the relationship, though I cautioned him that he would have to be patient and understanding of Allison's complex relationship to both him and his money.

When you marry for reasons other than love, you do not have the same chemical attraction and you often miss out on the Euphoria stage. Sex, intimacy, and romantic love are the glue that can help couples stick together through rough spots in their relationship. It is easier to fall back in love again than it is to fall in love with someone you have chosen to be with for different reasons.

But even Allison and Paul were able to bring romance into their relationship. Paul didn't take Allison's attachment to his money personally. He loved her and understood her family legacy. He was determined that he would make her happy by loving her in the way she needed to be loved. He gave without expectations. He used his money to treat her like a princess, and enabled them to enjoy many luxuries together. I suggested some attachment skills, such as touching and kissing her gently, that he could use to romance Allison in a nonthreatening way. He was using my advice to let hormones do some of the work of making Allison "fall in love" with him.

As he continued to give freely without expecting anything in return, Allison felt less pressure to respond by being "in love." She no longer felt guilty about her attraction to the money. Gradually a remarkable dynamic shift occurred: Allison found that Paul's money was losing its sexy allure.

Before long, she was responding to his romantic advances, and to her surprise, found herself having a passionate affair—with her own partner. Paul was patient and persistent and never judged or blamed or shamed, and now Allison gratefully says, "I finally realized: You can't sleep with money. Now our love is the closest thing to my heart."

Paul was successful in reromanticizing his relationship because he understood a fundamental rule of romance: love your partner in the ways *your partner* wants to be loved—not in the ways *you* think your partner should be loved. When you both put each other first, everyone wins!

To make sure you are showing love in an unselfish way, ask yourself the following questions:

- Do I love my partner the way he or she wants to be loved?
- Do I positively acknowledge my partner every day?
- Do we spend enough time together? (It can be quiet time or sharing activities or learning new things. The important thing is that you are together.)
- Do I fight fair? Do I allow my partner to take "time-outs" when the conflict becomes too intense?
- Do I disconnect in the evening and reconnect in the morning in a loving way?
- Do we share meals and time to talk (without the TV on)?
- Do we go to bed together so we can talk, cuddle, or make love (even if one of us has to get back up before we truly turn in for the night)?
- Do I make the effort to initiate "miniconnections" daily?
- Do we spend at least twenty minutes each day really communicating? (University of Nebraska researchers found that most couples talk only seventeen minutes *per week*.)

In part 1 of this book, I told you about Lynn and Dave. He took care of all the bills and financial matter and couldn't understand why Lynn wasn't grateful. When they came to see me, Lynn felt like Dave was constantly try-ing to oversee and manage how she spent money. While she thought it was great that he was willing to take care of things she felt disempowered and wanted him to discuss things with her. At the same time, Dave was constantly feeling rebuffed by Lynn's criticism of him. Not surprisingly, their sex life was nearly nonexistent.

"We had crazy, wild sex when we were first dating," Lynn said. "Our chemistry was unbelievable."

Now Lynn claimed she no longer saw Dave as sexy. "I think of him as the nerdy household accountant. He's withholding and controlling. He's not a sexy guy anymore."

I pointed out that Lynn was focusing on the negatives. I told her to step back and pretend he wasn't her husband—was there anything about him that would be sexy to her if she saw him as a total stranger? I suggested that she try to attract him in order to give herself a challenge and get the hormones going again.

Meanwhile, Dave had to tell Lynn that her negativity and criticism had made him afraid of rejection. He felt intimidated by her put-downs and react-ed by trying to exert more power in the financial arena. I advised him to tell Lynn when he wanted more physical closeness. They both needed to do the opposite of what their hurt feelings were telling them to do. They had to act—and not react—in order to break the vicious cycle they were caught in and cre-ate movement and change in their relationship.

And, just as important, they needed to put the fun back in their relation-ship and try to see each other as they had when they first met.

At a session a few weeks later, I noticed that Lynn and Dave were much more physically affectionate with each other and I asked how their reroman-ticizing "homework" had been going. They exchanged an intimate look and started laughing.

"We tried something," Lynn said. "It seemed stupid at first, but it real-ly worked."

Deciding to re-create one of their memories from when they were first dat-ing, Lynn and Dave went out to a club—separately. Dave arrived first and *then Lynn arrived and tried to pick him up. At first he paid her very little attention, instead flirting with the waitress and other women at the bar. As she became more aggressive in approaching him, he began offering her verbal encouragement.*

"Seriously, by the end of the night, I really wanted him," Lynn said.

"Yeah, I ended up taking her home," Dave joked.

"And the sex was great!" Lynn laughed.

Reromanticizing is not serious work. This is the fun part of reconnecting. Channeling positive early memories and finding ways to see your partner with fresh eyes can only boost the sizzle in your relationship.

Exercise: Playdates

It is important to counteract even the smallest relationship tensions with playfulness. In the stress and busyness of everyday life, many couples forget how to enjoy each other. Howard Markman, PhD, and Scott Stanley, PhD, longtime marriage and relationship researchers and developers of PREP (Premarital Relationship Enhancement Program), note that when couples don't make time for positive experiences they tend not to protect their positive experiences from conflict.

It is important for the health of your relationship that you protect positive relationship experiences from conflict and negativity, so make time for playfulness. Don't resist, don't feel foolish, and don't feel guilty about experiencing pleasure together. Laughter and joy are great relationship rejuvenators. The simple games below instill a sense of fun as well as stimulate production of mood-enhancing endorphins. When you are being silly together, it is virtually impossible to engage in conflict. Use these methods for letting off steam, encouraging lightheartedness, and spiking dopamine levels especially after tense discussions, particularly about money.

Pillow Fighting

Called *shindai*, or bed fighting, Japanese couples practice this game when they are angry with each other, believing that the excitement of the battle stimulates passion and leads to lovemaking as a method of reconciliation.

Take two old down pillows and make a small slit in them so you can let the feathers fly—literally!

Then gently begin to hit each other. You may start out venting any leftover anger or tensions from earlier conflict, but eventually, you'll begin to laugh. The physical exercise, tension release, play, and belly laughter you experience in this exercise are all healing and restorative to your relationship.

If the person who provoked the argument runs out of feathers first, he or she must kneel down, touching each of the opponent's toes, and make a "humble apology" before assuming the fetal position and allowing the victor to finish off the fight.

If the person who was wronged is the loser and wishes to withdraw from the fight, that person can throw his or her pillow down and declare, "I give in and stroke you." Then they do so as a prelude to making love!

The Merry-Go-Round

Stimulate a sense of play by taking each other's hands and whirling around the room until you are dizzy and laughing. Look each other in the eyes and embrace until the spinning sensation stops.

The High Jump

Pogo around the room to see who can jump higher. When reduced to giggles, end by leaping into each other's arms.

Monkey See, Monkey Do

Make like monkeys by jabbering, scratching, and leaping about. See who can make the other laugh first.

The Belly Laugh

Lie with your head on your partner's stomach and then tell jokes, reach your arms out and tickle them, or do whatever it takes to provoke his or her laughter. Try to keep a straight face as you feel your partner's belly jiggle your head around. Bet you can't do it!

Big Kids' Fun

Make lists of all the things you loved to do (or wished to do) as a child, such as ice or roller skating, canoeing, picnicking, blueberry picking, and so on. Choose activities from this list and discover a childlike joyfulness together. You can also list things that you enjoyed doing together when you were first dating and re-create some of those happy memories.

Exercise: Creating a Romantic and Sexual Relationship Vision

(Based on Harville Hendrix's Relationship Vision from Getting the Love You Want*)*

1. On separate pieces of paper, you and your partner list the things that you consider most important for a satisfying romantic and sexual relationship. Write these things in the *present tense* and include things that you already do (such as regular "date night") as well as things you wish you did (such as have sex three times a week).

2. Share your lists. Underline the items you have in common. If your partner has a goal or value that you agree with but did not have on your list, add it to your paper.

3. Returning to your expanded or revised list, rate each item in order of importance from 1 to 5 (with 1 being "very important" and 5 indicating "not at all important").

4. Circle three items that are most important to you.

5. Put a check next to three items you think would be the most difficult to achieve.

6. Working together, combine your lists to create your shared romantic and sexual relationship vision. Start with the items you agree are the most important, and toward the bottom list those that are less important. If you disagree about the importance of an item, and cannot reach a compromise that satisfies both of you, leave that item off the combined list.

Your finished list should look similar to the one below. Post it where you can both see it and look at it regularly. Use it to remind each other of your shared romantic and sexual goals and dreams.

YOUR RATING		YOUR PARTNER'S RATING	
1	We say "I love you" daily.	1	
1	We have sex three times a week.	2	√
1	We go on a "date" two Saturdays a month.	1	
1	We indulge in fantasy role-play monthly.	1	√
2	We give each other small romantic gifts.	1	
2	We watch a romantic movie together twice a month.	1	

2	We have "slow dance" night at home or out on the town once a month.	3	
2	We learn something new together every six weeks.	1	
2	We go away for "sexy" weekends three times a year.	2	√
4	We will send each other romantic notes or cards monthly.	3	
4	We will try risk-taking adventures such as sports together once a year.	5	
5	We will use private nicknames for each other daily.	5	
5	We will experiment with adult "toys" monthly to spice up our sex life.	5	

Brad and Shannon's relationship deteriorated during their initial visits with me. Seeking relief from Brad's controlling criticism, Shannon left him and moved in with her trainer from the gym. Brad told me how much he loved her and asked me how he could get her back. I told him it was important for him to stop trying to control Shannon and that they both should use this breakup as a "Brush with Death" to see if they would experience the deep feelings of emptiness and loss that would eventually lead them back to each other.

Without Brad's constant barrage of verbal suggestions and criticism, Shannon began to recall some of their more romantic moments. Her relationship with the trainer from her gym was emotionally empty and she soon wanted to move back home.

I suggested that they extend their breakup until both she and Brad could take positive actions to communicate in a safe and loving way. Shannon agreed to change gyms and to stop sneaking money from Brad. He agreed to be more verbal about the ways in which he appreciated her.

Together they worked on their Money Tree memories, using Smart Heart dialogue to talk about spending issues and practice attachment skills. After only a few weeks they had a breakthrough conversation in one of their sessions with me.

Shannon went first, using attachment language to validate Brad. "I want to tell you that I appreciate how hard you work and I know that you do it for us," she said.

"I really don't mind what you spend," Brad reassured her. "As long as you're not hiding it from me. You are a beautiful woman and I'm proud to be seen with you."

Shannon smiled and took his hand (the verbal aphrodisiacs were working!). "I'm happy not to hide my new outfits from you anymore. Now that you aren't making sarcastic remarks about how much I spend or how I look, I'm not afraid."

Brad responded with empathy and acknowledged his family legacy. "I never meant to make you fearful. That reminds me of how my dad acted with my mom and I don't want to behave like he did."

I was encouraged by how far they had come so quickly, and told them I thought it was time for them to end the breakup. They moved back in together and began to work on reromanticizing their relationship. Brad encouraged Shannon to go back to modeling part-time and proudly displayed one of her new photos on his desk. As he became more comfortable with verbally expressing his love for her, Shannon became more confident and receptive to romance. Within a few months of moving back in together, they were back in my office to tell me that their relationship felt "like it did when we first met!"

Never underestimate the power of romantic words and gestures in rekindling intimacy in your relationship. Don't assume your partner *knows* how you feel. If you have had financial infidelity in your relationship, it's likely that your actions have not always matched your words and your communication skills have been compromised. Compliments are sexy; intimate communication through gestures and glances is sexy; affirmations and "sweet nothings" are sexy.

If, when you first begin to take steps to reromanticize your relationship, you feel at a loss for words, try the exercises below to convey your most intimate feelings to your partner.

Exercise: Don't Speak

Spend the whole day together without saying a word to each other. You will be surprised at how much you will touch your partner and connect your gazes throughout the day. Let your eyes and arms and lips say what you are feeling without words. Write it down if it's important. Distancers will notice how much they miss conversation; pursuers will notice how little they actually have to say to be heard. When the exercise is over, don't discuss money or other triangles. Instead engage in high-energy play.

Exercise: Write a Love Letter

Even if you say "I love you" several times a day, if you do not back up your words with deeper meaning, they can begin to sound rote. Take fifteen minutes out of your day to think why it is you love your partner so much. Think about how and why you fell in love and what makes this person so special to you. Does she make you feel secure? Attractive? Is he fun to be with? Is she a wonderful parent? Does your heart still skip a beat when you see him across a room? Write down your thoughts. Be sincere; don't allow yourself to feel self-conscious about what you are expressing. Write from the heart and mail this letter to your partner. The next time you say "I love you" as you are dashing out the door, remember all the thoughts and feelings you put into writing and put those same emotions behind your daily expressions of love.

When Money Talks

Although your money had plenty to say in the first five stages, you should not allow it to interrupt here. When you listen for a money dialogue in this step, you should hear silence. Romance is all about you and your partner. A duo. No triangles allowed. In all of the earlier steps, you considered how your emotions affect your behaviors with money and learned to listen to your head. Now I want you to listen to your heart and put all the emotion into making your relationship passionate and intimate and loving.

Smart Heart Dialogue for Restoring Romance

Case #1

What he says: "Why don't we go to the mall this Saturday? I need a new suit and maybe you can find those shoes I heard you talking about."

What he may mean: "I'm really making an effort here. I know how much you love shopping and I'm trying to find a way to participate."

The Smart Heart reply: "I'd love to help you find a suit; you look so sexy when you're dressed to kill. We could also stop by your favorite neighborhood sports bar on the way home for a burger and beer."

Case #2

What she says: "I know you've been working hard lately. Why don't we go out for a romantic dinner?"

What she may mean: "I need you to pay attention to me instead of the office."

The Smart Heart reply: "I'd love to spend the evening with you. I'll have to work a bit late, let me see if my mom can watch the kids overnight and we can have a long, late dinner and sleep in tomorrow."

Case #3

What she says: "I'd love to go away for a romantic weekend. But there's just too much going on here at home."

What she may mean: "I want to focus on the sexual and romantic part of our relationship, but I feel torn by my responsibilities to the house and kids."

The Smart Heart reply: "I know you're tired from all you do—and that the kids take up a lot of your energy. I understand that you feel torn between nurturing them and nurturing our love life. How can I help you to feel it's okay to take time away from our home?"

Case #4

What she says: "I trust we can make enough money to live well, but we will live so much better if we agree that our romantic relationship comes first."

What she may mean: "Can you love me the way I need to be loved?"

The Smart Heart reply: "Love is more important than money. I don't know what I was thinking when I chose to neglect you in favor of work. I put us all in a bad situation. I realize now that there may be a lot of different jobs, but there is only one you. I promise I will spend the rest of my life making it up to you."

Smart Heart Jump-Starts for Reromanticizing Your Relationship

Once you have analyzed, understood, and rebalanced your relationship dynamic around money, it is time to go to work on rekindling the romance and passion that heightens your love. Smart Heart skills and dialogues allow you to reheat your romance and spark intense feelings of intimate emotional and physical connection.

- **Pay attention to your physical appearance.** When you feel attractive, you feel sexy. Your partner will notice. Trust me.
- **Do what works—not what you think is "fair."** Don't get hung up on tit-for-tat. Make an honest effort to do things you know your partner will enjoy. Learn to appreciate the pleasure the other takes in your efforts. Be patient and persistent and be open to your partner's gestures when he or she reciprocates.
- **Get out of your comfort zone.** Acknowledge that you may be afraid to fall back in love, trust, or be more intimate.
- **Make sex a priority.** Schedule it in. You heard me: set a time for sex just like any important appointment, or it won't happen!
- **Remember that the things you want most from your partner are those that are most difficult for your partner to give.** Change does not happen overnight. Acknowledge the efforts your partner is making in areas you know are difficult for him or her.

- **Don't panic.** Relationships are fluid and change is inevitable. Power struggles, slipups, and moments of disconnection will still happen in your relationship. Be confident that you have the skills to safely disconnect and then reconnect. Think of each reconnection as the chance for a brand-new relationship and don't let old behaviors stop it before it starts.

A Contract for Financial Fidelity

In order to channel our emotions away from money and into each other, to reconnect intimately in a physical and emotional way, and to restore and nurture the romantic sizzle of heartfelt passion in our relationship, we agree to:

- **Make a conscious decision to fall in love again.** Fidelity results from the conscious intent to remain in love. Acting "as if" you are in love will cause you to "feel" that way eventually. Your love will grow to be stronger than before.
- **Treat each other as we did at the beginning of our relationship.** Do the things you enjoyed doing when you first met— and don't be shy about adding some new fantasies! Novelty raises excitement and stimulates dopamine release. Make these activities your top relationship priority by planning them and doing them. No excuses are allowed.
- **Remember that touch is magic.** Get your hormones flowing and let chemical attraction help you rediscover romance. Physical connection—at whatever level you are comfortable with—will enhance the romance.
- **Say good-bye to old relationships with money.** There is no room for triangles in your relationship. Loyalty to each other and to your relationship is essential.

Step 7:
Invest in Your Future

The Ongoing Work of Maintaining Your Relationship

While falling in love is easy (helped along as it is by the chemistry of hormones and the subconscious preferences of your psyche), staying in love requires real commitment and intent. Maintaining honest and safe communication in a relationship—and especially around money—is not for the faint of heart, but when you have experienced the benefits of the kind of intimate relationship where you can safely talk about *anything*, you will realize that real and lasting love is worth the effort.

The Smart Heart skills and dialogues you have learned in this book are aimed at predicting, stopping and preventing financial infidelity in a relationship. But these skills can—and should—be used to improve every aspect of your relationship. Once existing or potential money problems in your relationship are identified and prevented or resolved, you will notice an improvement in your romantic, emotional, and physical relationship as well. After a while, these exercises and Smart Heart techniques won't feel like work at all. They will become a natural way of interacting with each other and the cornerstones of your truly functional relationship.

Be Aware

Don't let financial infidelity creep back into your relationship. Be vigilant about making the time regularly to assess different areas of your life and love to be sure that your relationship to money—and to each other—is optimal.

- Know what your triggers for financial infidelity are and be conscious of the toxic behavior patterns that develop in your relationship as a result. You have the skills and techniques to continually support and enhance romantic love in all areas of your relationship. Make sure you are using them.
- Don't allow yourself to slip into the love-killing interactions that relationship expert John Gottman calls "the Four Horsemen of the Apocalypse." Dr. Gottman has identified these four behaviors as having the most profoundly disastrous effects on communication in a relationship. When talking about money or finances, do not allow any of these sabotaging behaviors to enter into your dialogues: criticism, contempt, defensiveness, or stonewalling.

1. *Criticizing* partner's spending habits can quickly turn into criticizing your partner personally.
2. *Being contemptuous* of your partner's methods of managing money can become negative thoughts that are directed at your partner's personality. (For example, when your husband tells you that the budget doesn't allow for dinner out every night, you may begin to stop admiring his thriftiness and begin to focus on how stingy and withholding he seems.)
3. *Acting defensively* adds fuel to the blazing fire of discontent that one or both of you may be experiencing and contributes to a dynamic where one of you constantly feels victimized.
4. *Stonewalling*—shutting down and adamantly refusing to admit or discuss financial problems or concerns—leads to the

perpetuation of one of the six stages I have talked about earlier. Instead of moving on and into a new, exciting stage of romantic connection, you will be caught in a vicious cycle of repeating harmful money patterns, simply because you refused to acknowledge them.

Be Proactive

In the process of learning how to safely communicate about money, you have worked through a lot of emotional and historical baggage. For most couples this is a challenging but gratifying journey. When you have nurtured a real and lasting love, you have come to accept and value the differences between you. You realize that problems and challenges in your relationship are not reasons to quit, but rather opportunities to grow closer. Intimacy becomes deeper, communication more profound.

Don't become complacent. If you have a history of financial infidelity in your family history or in your current relationship, it is important to be conscious of old patterns that may redevelop around certain triggers. Once a month, take time to run through the cheat sheet of common risk factors that may trigger financial infidelity and see where you stand. Use Smart Heart dialogue to talk about any concerns before they become *real* problems. This "cheat sheet" is based on an exercise I created to help couples determine if one or the other was at risk for an affair and lets you check in and make sure that the new money skills you have acquired in the previous six steps are working in your relationship.

Keep track of your score by giving yourself points for every "yes" answer to each of the questions in each of the categories. You and your partner should each take the test individually. Remember to use Smart Heart dialogue when you talk about your scores!

Cheat Sheet

RISK FACTOR	EVENT (AND ITS SCORING VALUE)	YOUR SCORE
Milestones: Certain events may trigger old harmful patterns.	Decade birthday (−2) Promotion (−2) New home (−2) No recent milestones (+2)	
Emotional Availability: Feelings of abandonment or emptiness may trigger financial infidelity.	You or partner travels regularly (−2) One of you consistently works overtime (−2) You rely on each other for socializing (−2) New baby becomes focus of attention (−2) Both feel secure in relationship, partner meets emotional needs (+2)	
Temptation: Situations that encourage spending may lead to financial infidelity.	Binge spending and hiding purchases (−2) Spend time with friends or colleagues who spend lavishly (−2) Feel peer pressure on trips or while shopping (−1) Stick to budget no matter the circumstances (+2)	
New Friends: Keeping up with the Joneses can quickly spiral out of control.	Pressure to join country club or similar (−2) Need to drive newer car than someone else has (−2) Clothing must have designer label (−2) Constantly redecorating or purchasing items for home (−2) Peers generally in same earnings bracket (+2)	

Couples Time: Spending *time* together can help limit spending *money*. Date night encourages communication, restores passion.	Hardly any time together (−2) A few dates a month (+1) Weekly dates (+2)	
Intimacy: Frequent or daily expressions of affection, such as cuddling, kissing, or sex (especially if it's planned), keep couples connected.	Not very affectionate (−2) A little affectionate (−1) Very affectionate (+2)	
Fighting Style: It's bad to never fight. Blowouts show passion. Holding grudges puts distance between you.	Hardly ever fight (−2) Hold grudges (−2) Fight occasionally (+1)	
Years Married: It can be harder for long-term couples to make changes in their relationship. It can become harder to find the energy to do so as well. Passion fades after seven years. The first year can be rocky, too. If there was financial infidelity in a previous relationship, there is likely to be financial infidelity in subsequent relationships.	Married 7+ years or previously married (−2) Newlyweds (−1) Married 1–6 years (+1)	
Family Influence: Having families who can impact or control your money situation, whether positively or negatively, can add stress to a relationship.	One or both parents wealthy (−2) One or both parents likely to need financial support (−2) Sibling disagreement about inheritance or level of financial participation for parents' care (−1) Parents not a factor in considering long-term finances (+2)	
TOTAL		

SCORING

If your score is 5 or more you are in great shape. Keep doing what you're doing and enjoy the benefits!

If your score is 0 to 5, you are on track, but need to keep checking in with each other. Don't shy away from the hard discussions.

If your score is −1 or less, you may need to go back and review some of the previous six steps. Don't give up—take stock of your relationship stage and get to work!

Dr. Gottman's work at the Seattle Marital and Family Institute has shown that how couples interact in everyday, relaxed situations is the best indicator of how quickly they'll accept what he calls "repair attempts" and be able to reconnect after a fight. *Couples who make time for positive experiences together are better at ignoring negative input from each other.* And they must keep these positive and negative experiences separate. Gottman explains that happy couples make "love maps," or ways of knowing each other, and update them regularly.

What I refer to as "daily check-ins" help you to know what your partner is thinking, feeling, and experiencing and helps you build positive feelings of fondness for your partner—what Gottman calls an "emotional bank account"—that you can draw on in times of conflict.

Making paradigm shifts in your relationship is a matter of making small, constant adjustments, in both a proactive and a responsive way. The Ten Commandments listed below will help you keep your focus on the key dynamics of a healthy, functional relationship. Incorporate these philosophies and behaviors into your daily life and consciously practice them until they become *unconscious* ways of interacting. The benefits you and your partner will reap—financially, emotionally, and romantically—will be astounding.

The Ten Commandments for Financial Fidelity

1. Know Yourself

Before you can ask your *partner* to make changes around money, *you* need to understand your own personal money dynamic. By acknowledging the inner forces that drive your personal behaviors with money, you will open yourself to accepting and validating your partner's money behaviors. As Daniel Siegel, UCLA psychiatrist and author of *The Mindful Brain*, says, "As you further develop mindfulness you can look to your increased self-knowing as the material from which you draw empathic inferences."

In her book *The Laws of Money*, Suze Orman says, "Truth leads to wealth." This sentiment is true not just with money, but in a relationship. The key exercises in this book allow you to examine and understand the truth about your personal money dynamic: Financial Infidelity Risk Profile (page 22); Financial Personality Profile (page 29); Financial Imago (page 124); Family Moneygram (page 137); Mirror, Mirror, on the Wall (page 210); and Financial Relationship Vision (page 211).

Encourage your partner to use these tools so that you both possess the necessary self-knowledge to instinctively empathize with, validate, and understand each other's money beliefs and behaviors.

2. Accept That Conflict Can Be Good

Psychology tells us that we will gravitate toward partners who will challenge us. If you can accept that the arguments arising from these tensions are necessary to help you evolve in particular areas, and that you will benefit from this growth and change, you can learn to see each conflict with your partner as a gift—one that will enhance and deepen your love and intimacy.

Couples who avoid conflict, whose relationships are passive, rather than passionate, are doomed to break up or endlessly repeat dysfunctional cycles like adultery or financial infidelity. Relationship therapists largely agree that the health of your relationship depends on your ability to make the inevitable disagreements result in meaningful and positive change in the relationship. Studies now show that being able to engage in conflict is equally important to your physical well-being as it is to the health of your relationship. Studies have linked keeping your feelings to yourself, or "self-silencing," during a fight to numerous psychological and physiological disorders, such as depression, eating disorders, and heart disease. These risks are especially high for women who bottle up their feelings during conflict with a partner or spouse.

While men are not as affected by a couple's arguing style, researchers have found that women are influenced by whether arguments have a hostile tone or a warm one. Hostility from a partner has a negative effect on a woman's health.

Men who stonewall or show contempt when arguing can also cause a negative impact on their partner's health. In studies conducted on the "fighting styles" of married couples, Dr. Gottman and his researchers studied the facial expressions of men while arguing with their wives. Their research showed that from on the number of contemptuous expressions made by a husband it was possible to accurately determine the number of times the wife would be come seriously ill over a four-year span.

So go ahead and argue passionately over things that are important to you in the relationship. Just remember to use the Smart Heart Fighting Fair skills (page 110) and to maintain feelings of warmth and affection for your partner as you work through even the toughest money conflicts.

3. Separate the Negative from the Positive

Feeling affection toward your partner, even in the midst of disagreement, is easier to do when you generally have more positive than negative memories and feelings about that person. In his work with married couples, Dr. Gottman stresses that in successful and long-lasting relationships there is a 5 to 1 ratio of positive to negative experiences and interactions.

Learn to feel positive about the role of money in your relationship and in your life. Let go of negative money traits such as greed, fear, and envy and embrace an attitude of gratitude (pages 198–201). Appreciate what you have and use Money Affirmations (page 202) to help you feel positive about your relationship to your money.

Exercises such as Compartmentalize the Cash (page 163) allow you to *disassociate* money from the *pleasurable* parts of your relationship. If money discussions with your partner make you feel anxious or fearful, use Smart Heart dialogue to make talking about money *safe*. Remember that your brain is more sensitive to negative information—think of it as a sympathetic fight-or-flight response. When you get anxious or negative or angry when talking to your partner about money, you are sharing highly *contagious* emotions and the conflict may quickly escalate. Positively responding to your partner's irritability or criticism around money can make a difference. Instead of allowing negative emotions to spread, think of literally catching your partner's anger or anxiety in a box and closing the lid on it. Your partner can vent, but you do not react to the emotion behind the words.

Use "attachment skills" (page 227) to defuse tense deliberations and stimulate the bonding hormone oxytocin.

After money talks, be sure to reverse the flow of negative energy (a biochemical release of stress hormones) by using high-energy playdates (page 233).

4. Mind-Read—the Right Way

When done from an attitude of complacency and righteousness, "mind reading," or categorically assuming you know what your partner is thinking, is one of the most damaging mistakes you can make in your relationship—especially when it comes to matters of money. When done poorly, mind reading can wrongly attribute critical and selfish thoughts to your partner. It can incite further conflict and cause damaging misunderstandings. Do not be a silent grudge holder who always "knows" exactly what your partner is thinking (page 221). As your frustration builds, you may approach your partner in an attacking way and get a reflexive reaction rather than a thoughtful one.

Instead, make a conscious effort to "read" your partner's mind with what psychologists call "empathic accuracy." Draw on your memories, your powers of reason, and your emotions, and be aware of physical and verbal cues coming from your partner. Allow yourself to access feelings of warmth and love toward your partner, even when angry with him or her. Slow down your interactions around hot-button topics to allow for greater choice in responding.

"Good" mind reading takes practice and a willingness to put yourself in your partner's shoes. Ross Buck, a professor of communications sciences at the University of Connecticut, points out that since ancient times, people have chosen to conceal feelings from others—even to lie—in order to advance and protect their interests. Even people in the most established relationships may unconsciously struggle with the primal balance of the need to show and the need to hide their true selves.

Using Smart Heart dialogue when negotiating uncomfortable money topics allows you to practice empathic mind reading. With enough practice, you will become sensitive to your partner's inner dialogue. As you become increasingly intuitive in your daily interactions, you will achieve the level of emotional intimacy that is the bedrock of real, true love.

5. Take Influence

Research has shown that in most relationships, women are generally accepting of influence from men. In order to have a true partnership, however, *men* must be equally willing to be influenced by women. Studies show that men who take influence from their wives are happier and have happier marriages. For example, if you say to your partner, "My boss handed out unexpected bonuses for our work on that rush project. What do you think about buying some more stock for our portfolio?" and the reply is, "The money goes in the savings account, like it always does. We're not going to throw away your bonus playing the stock market," there's a clear imbalance in influence in your relationship.

Refusing to allow a balance of power in a relationship can also take a toll on the man's health. The same research that showed a detrimental effect on women's health from self-silencing also showed that how a couple argued was as important a heart risk factor for the woman as whether she smoked or had high cholesterol. Husbands who had a warm style of arguing with their wives—saying "you may not be good at sticking to our budget, but you're good at other things," for instance—lowered their wife's risk of heart disease. Women married to husbands with a critical style of arguing—"This checkbook is a disaster. You can't do anything right, can you?"—were at a higher risk of heart disease. When it comes to struggles for control in a relationship (such as those around money), it is the men who suffer.

Consider how important power is in your relationship by taking the "Do You Need to Feel Powerful?" quiz on page 103 and open yourself to accepting the influence of your partner when making decisions about joint finances.

As the person giving influence, you play a crucial role in guiding your partner to sort out his or her feelings and emotions around a particular topic. Using "good" mind reading techniques with Smart Heart dialogue, you can gently lead your partner to illuminating realizations about the motives behind his or her responses and actions. It is important, however, that you don't feel you *have* to instinctively know everything your partner thinks and feels. In the deeply connected intimacy or real-life love, what matters is not that you instantly understand each other, but rather that *you care enough to keep trying.*

6. Ask for What You Want

Being able to successfully intuit what is on your partner's mind is only half of good communication. In order to avoid the relationship-derailing trap of magical thinking ("I love him so much. I know if I don't say anything he'll decide draining our savings to play Internet poker every night is a bad idea. . . .") you need to be able to tell your partner your concerns, fears, and desires.

Asking for what you want from your partner can be as delicate as negotiating legal agreements such as prenups, postnups, or no-nups (cohabitation agreements). Or it can be as straightforward as explaining that you'd like her to wait to have dinner with you on nights when you have to work late. In either case, Smart Heart dialogue can help you address problems without escalating conflict—what Dr. Gottman calls a "soft approach" and what I call a "soft landing."

Of course it would be unrealistic to expect that you will simply get everything you ask for, but if you feel that your partner is making excuses instead of being sensitive to your needs, you can create a system of emotional IOUs and wish lists (page 80). Being able to safely tell your partner what you are hoping for, or need, from the relationship is an important step in forging lasting emotional, physical, and financial fidelity.

7. *Know How to De-escalate Arguments*

When a discussion about finances turns into an argument, or an argument about money becomes heated and hurtful, try some of these techniques for changing the climate from negative to positive and increase your chances of making it through the conflict with your happy relationship intact:

- Take a temporary break (especially men). Announce your intent to disconnect. Be sure to reconnect within twenty-four hours to finish the discussion.
- Use verbal and physical attachment skills to soothe your partner. ("I know you feel stressed when we discuss your spending. Thank you for listening to my concerns.")
- Hold hands and look into your partner's eyes.
- Turn to humor to defuse stress and de-escalate the tension.
- Find common ground. ("I know you really want to be able to buy a new house. If we can get a handle on our credit card bills, we'll be able to plan for a bigger mortgage. How can we work on this together?")

- Don't forget to draw on what Dr. Gottman calls the "emotional bank account" of a relationship—the good feelings for your partner that are created via the "mindless, mundane moments of marriage that are the makers of romance." Use miniconnections (page 228) to build up your bank of fondness and appreciation for your partner.

Know how to approach your partner after a blowout. The checklist in "Going Back to Your Partner in a New Way" (page 202) gives you important questions you need to ask when reconnecting.

8. Stay Motivated

Stay connected by sharing goals and striving to acquire positive shared experiences. Use the Dream Big questions and chart on page 71 and the Money Tree exercise on page 75 to map out important financial and relationship milestones and remind each other of your desires when tension about money starts to seep into your relationship. Creating a Shared Financial Relationship Vision (page 211) lets you and your partner define joint goals and behaviors that support financial fidelity.

Don't be afraid to dream big. Dr. Ivan Scheier, founder of VOLUNTAS, a residence retreat focused on practical dreaming and volunteerism, has developed rules for dreamers, urging them to look beyond money as a need, obstacle, or trap. I find some of his rules particularly helpful in motivating couples in their ongoing work of achieving financial fidelity:

- Know that dreams are not realized right away. Stay with your beliefs and values and don't allow inertia to erode hope.
- Avoid the "if we only had the money" mindset. Focusing on what you don't have closes you off from appreciating what you do have. Acting "as if" brings abundance, not what's in the bank.

- It's okay to look backward. Focus on how many dreams have come true in your life. Draw on romantic memories to help you through rough times.

Newly married couples are highly motivated to deepen intimacy. But studies show that a couple's ability to practice "good" mind reading and safe communication actually ebbs after the first year of marriage. Researchers theorize that these couples have become so confident that they "know" each other that they switch from the motivation to attain greater intimacy to a state of complacency. In troubled relationships, this complacency can morph into arrogance, criticism, and contempt. In believing they know everything there is to know about each other, these couples stop their relationship before it can move on to the stage of real and lasting love.

Motivated couples welcome movement and change in their relationship. They embrace each reconnection as a chance to begin the relationship anew, to see each other in a new way, and to deepen the intimacy that signals real and lasting love. And it should be noted that both men and women are often equally motivated. However, women tend to more naturally seek to pursue intimacy while men may need to put more conscious thought into the commitment to "work" on a relationship.

In the case of a relationship that needs an extreme jolt to "wake up and shake up" those involved, the Brush with Death is perhaps the ultimate motivator (page 179).

9. Understand the Pursuer/Distancer Dynamic

In the dynamic dance of a relationship, there are pursuers (those who strive for closeness and connection) and there are distancers (those who, despite a desire for connection, respond to this attention by growing remote and backing away). In a functional relationship these differences come into a dynamic balance, with each person understanding how to relate to the one's fear of abandonment (pursuer) or the other's fear of suffocation and need for space, validation, and acceptance (distancer).

When it comes to a relationship with money, individuals are also either pursuers or distancers. Whether you are a pursuer or a distancer in a romance is not an indicator of which of these roles you will fall into with regard to money. When you identify your style around money, you can begin to understand how to modify your behaviors to reach a compromise with your partner in money matters. The exercises on pages 163 and 166 can help you categorize whether you are a distancer or pursuer when it comes to money.

Whether you are a distancer or a pursuer around money, when you have achieved financial fidelity, your relationship to money is in service of your romantic relationship. Instead of focusing on materialism, which leads to the danger of comparison, envy, or greed, you strive for shared experiences that lend themselves to subjective pleasures.

Pursuers learn not to chase after money or material items to the point where they neglect their partner. They strive to put their relationship first, and to not overreact to suggestions from their partner that they feel might jeopardize their financial security. Distancers learn to use money for pleasure and romance. They come to appreciate what they have and to refine their assumptions that they cannot share their "private" thoughts or fears about money with their partner.

Understanding the pursuer / distancer relationship, as it manifests itself with both your partner and your money, allows you to contain negative feelings, inhibit reflexive reactions, and protect your love from damaging negative emotions.

10. Practice Makes Perfect

According to Dr. Markman, "Having a good relationship is a skill." When couples are able to handle conflict in a manageable way, it fosters their commitment to work at their relationship. Especially for those getting married, using Smart Heart skills and dialogues from the beginning fosters positive experience that help to prevent relationship-eroding power struggles as they make the transition from the honeymoon stage.

The Smart Heart skills and dialogues throughout this book offer you tools to assess, improve, or save your relationship. When you practice behaviors regularly, they become a natural part of your relationship. Eventually you will not be conscious that you are practicing miniconnections or attachment techniques, you will simply notice that you do not feel as angry or disconnected toward your partner when you disagree.

The latest neuroscience research tells us that adult brains continue to grow and evolve into old age. In a nutshell—you *can* teach an old dog new tricks! No matter what mistakes you have made in the past, you are able to incrementally unlearn bad behaviors.

- Practice empathic mind reading and validation daily.
- Practice fighting fair and safe communication during every tense discussion about money.
- Practice the techniques for rekindling romance. Practice *giving*. Winston Churchill famously said, "We make a living by what we earn—we make a life by what we give." Whether you are practicing giving money, time, or even understanding, you are enriching your own life and relationship. An August 2007 *20/20* piece touted the "helper's high," an increase in the neurotransmitter dopamine that made people who gave monetarily feel happier, live longer, and have a stronger immune system.
- Practice commitment—to your financial plan and to your relationship.

Learning new behaviors around money is just as challenging as any other kind of behavior modification. But changing the damaging patterns of financial infidelity can pave the way to a relationship rich in real and lasting love and is well worth the effort. Suze Orman says, "Nurture a healthy relationship with money. What happens to your money affects the quality of your life and the lives of all those you love. Do what is *right* and not *easy* with money." (Emphasis mine.)

If you do what is *right* for your relationship, your new behaviors will eventually become *easy*. Gradually, all of this practice will stop feeling like work. Your relationship with money and with your partner will feel good. The deep connection of physical, emotional, and financial intimacy will feel *natural*. You will have reached the stage of real and lasting love and achieved financial fidelity.

Smart Heart Dialogue for Real and Lasting Love

No more examples! At this point Smart Heart dialogue should be the way you communicate on a regular basis. Smart Heart dialogue creates the glue when the relationship is new and there is no history to fall back on. It also acts to renew and revitalize the passion of securely attached couples. Using Smart Heart dialogue, you can verbalize the meaning of the unspoken messages behind the statements or questions that used to provoke anxiety. Disagreements become conversations where you both gently help each other discover what you really wish to say. Tension gives way to compromise and decisions are made based on how they will improve your relationship. Conflict is an expression of the passion that you have reignited and no longer a cause for concern. You know that each reconnection will strengthen your love.

Smart Heart Jump-Starts for Real and Lasting Love

There is no way to jump-start real and lasting love. It's a journey, not a destination. The previous six steps and "Ten Commandments" provide a wealth of tools that allow you to continue to move forward on that path. When practiced daily, Smart Heart skills and dialogues become natural ways of interacting. Attachment skills and miniconnections keep endorphins flowing and spark the euphoric feelings of the "honeymoon stage." Real and lasting love isn't hard if you are prepared to be passionate and accept change.

A Contract for Real and Lasting Financial Fidelity

When you put all the terms of all the contracts in steps 1 through 6 together, you have a comprehensive road map to lasting financial fidelity. The thirty "terms" of the contract listed below are summarized from each of the previous six steps. Don't expect to be able to incorporate all of these at once. Start with the first one and add one new rule each day for a month. Review the steps as needed. Understand that each of you will find different terms harder to comply with and be prepared to support each other in order to successfully "stretch" to implement new behaviors. You *have* the tools and the knowledge!

To achieve lasting financial fidelity, you and your partner must commit to working together (and separately) to fulfill all of the terms shown here.

1. *Increase your financial compatibility.*
2. *Make budgeting a top priority.*
3. *Avoid keeping score with money.*
4. *Agree to review shared finances on a regular basis.*
5. *Avoid magical thinking around money.*
6. *Practice fact-finding, instead of mind reading.*
7. *Face financial issues head-on to strengthen the relationship.*
8. *Understand, compromise, and work toward common goals.*
9. *Make transactions around money feel safe.*
10. *Never use money as a punishment or reward.*
11. *Be conscious of each person's love and money maps.*
12. *Expect change and prepare for it.*
13. *Appreciate change and use it to your relationship's advantage.*
14. *Avoid "coasting."*
15. *Continue to respond in new ways and try different solutions.*
16. *Disconnect in order to reconnect.*
17. *Stay calm during a money breakup.*
18. *View temporary breakups or disconnections not as endings, but as opportunities for new beginnings. When talking is not working, do the walking (temporarily).*

19. *Understand each other's need for a feeling of financial security and support each other in compartmentalizing the role of money in the relationship.*

20. *Remain educated about your financial situation.*

21. *Pay attention to the pronouns you use when talking about shared money.*

22. *When it comes to money matters, never sneak, never omit, and never lie.*

23. *Stay focused on your values.*

24. *Be clear about the issue at hand and be willing to negotiate for a realistic compromise.*

25. *Be proactive, rather than reactive.*

26. *Put your relationship first.*

27. *Make a conscious decision to fall in love again.*

28. *Treat each other as you did at the beginning of your relationship.*

29. *Remember that touch is magic.*

30. *Say good-bye to old relationships with money.*

PART III

The Biochemical Component

The Brain–Body Connection

For some individuals, especially those who exhibit dramatic forms of financial infidelity such as gambling or binge shopping, an important component of changing damaging money behaviors is understanding and correcting the biochemical factors that may be driving or supporting these relationship-destroying habits.

Throughout this book I've talked about the chemical reactions we have in our bodies, brains, and nervous systems that affect how we relate to others. When people first fall in love they experience a hormone surge (what most lovers refer to as "chemistry") that propels them through the euphoric honeymoon stage of their relationship. Later, in the power struggle stage, when conflict enters the relationship, their nervous systems react to a flood of "fight-or-flight" neurotransmitters.

Stress can affect the way you feel about your partner and your romantic life. Positive experiences can trigger feel-good endorphins that encourage you to associate certain events with pleasure. *The balance—or imbalance—of your hormones or neurotransmitters has an enormous impact on your behavior and even on your romantic attraction to your partner.*

As more sophisticated diagnostic tools are employed to study brain function and response, more information comes to light about the complex interactions of body and brain. Patients with clinical symptoms, that is, those individuals exhibiting observable, diagnosable behaviors, can have their brains analyzed by various imaging systems, including MRI (magnetic resonance imaging), CT (computed tomography), SPECT (single photo emission computed tomography), PET (positron emission tomography), and EBT or BEAM (electron beam tomography). These scans are used by an increasing number of psychiatrists and psychologists to analyze brain disorders, behavior syndromes, addictions, memory impairment, and other cognitive functions. Ongoing evidence from this "brain mapping" research is constantly adding new information to theories of attraction, addiction, depression, impulse control, and other behaviors that may play a role in ongoing infidelity and financial infidelity and other behaviors prevalent in the couples I counsel.

Another area of study contributing to our understanding hormone-driven imbalances is looking at the correlation between sleep deprivation and brain function. Study after study has shown that lack of sleep leads to poor judgment and hinders decision making. Researchers at Duke University found that subjects who placed bets in a gambling task after staying awake for twenty-four hours showed higher brain activity in areas associated with "wishful thinking" as well as reduced emotional response to loss. The need for sleep increases activity in the nucleus accumbens, a region of the brain that signals possibility of reward.

Most Americans are chronically sleep deprived—whether because of anxiety, work responsibilities, or a new baby—and it is no surprise that many find themselves seeking gratification or reward through late-night impulse shopping on eBay or overspending on items from the all-night shopping networks.

The opportunity to participate in risk / reward activities is available around the clock, thanks to computer sites that offer gambling, gaming, or even alternative universes. Online virtual worlds such as Second Life allow people to seek out gratification through projected experiences that create brain arousal and simulate a perceived sense of secure attachment.

Another study, from researchers at the University of California–Berkeley and the Harvard Medical School, published in the October 23,

2007, issue of *Current Biology*, concludes that sleep deprivation heightened emotional response by causing a rewiring of the brain's circuitry. In sleep-deprived participants, the amygdala (a brain structure involved in emotional response) "seems to be able to run amok," causing these subjects to experience uncontrolled emotional swings.

Still other scientists have shed light on the brain—body connection by looking at how food and nutrients may affect our moods and emotions. Dr. Michael Gershon, chairman of the Department of Anatomy and Cell Biology at Columbia University and author of *The Second Brain*, has spent years studying the role of the enteric nervous system, which manages all aspects of digestion. In his research on this system, which he terms the "second brain" or "little brain" because of its self-contained network of neural circuitry, neurotransmitters, and proteins that operates autonomously from the brain in your head, Dr. Gershon has established a direct relationship between emotional stress and physical distress in the gastrointestinal system. The release of serotonin from the gut (where 95 percent of the body's serotonin is housed) keeps the brain in the skull informed on what is happening in this "second" brain. When the gut releases too much—or too little—serotonin, people experience both mental and physical reactions.

It is interesting to note that some patients who have curbed their tendencies to overeat by undergoing gastric bypass surgery report developing another addictive behavior, such as binge shopping or alcohol or drug use, in the wake of their surgery.

There is still another association between what goes on in your abdomen and what goes on in your head. In my practice, and in my work with Dr. Jeffrey Morrison of the Morrison Center in New York City, I have found that hypoglycemia, or low blood sugar, contributes to behaviors associated with infidelity. Many people who practice infidelity and financial infidelity behave in the cyclical ways associated with out-of-control blood sugar. When there are large fluctuations in the balance of glucose in our systems, a cascade of biophysical events causes our bodies to produce more adrenal hormones. When suffering from a low blood sugar event, some individuals lack clarity and are unable to make logical decisions. For individuals with compulsive behavior (such as binge shoppers or gamblers) the physiological need to raise their glucose level is misinterpreted as a material need and triggers a cycle of harmful behaviors.

I have also had patients come to me complaining of insomnia. They are able to sleep for only a few hours at a time. Some of them have turned to online shopping or gambling as a way to "self-soothe," hoping to calm their feelings of restlessness and instability. When tested, many of these individuals have shown a tendency to episodes of low blood sugar. Three or four hours after a meal, their blood sugar will drop precipitously and disturb their sleep patterns. Because they misinterpret their bodies' signals and because low blood sugar causes a predisposition to poor decision-making, it is easy for them to fall into damaging behavior patterns.

Science has shown that the health of our bodies and our brains depends on the ebb and release of these critical chemical compounds. There is no doubt that chemical imbalances can alter and affect our behavior and relationships and that it is important to maintain their proper equilibrium for both emotional and physical health.

Understanding Neurobiological Reasons for Imbalance

The human brain is a remarkable structure and scientists continue to learn more about it almost daily.

Researchers such as Daniel Siegel, MD, and Allan N. Schore, PhD, have integrated findings from neuroscience, development and attachment theory, and psychoanalysis to explain the influence of secure attachment *from birth* in promoting the wiring of healthy brain circuits by reducing levels of stress hormones, including cortisol. The reduction of these hormones allows the frontal cortex to develop in ways that promote optimal management of stress responses.

At one time it was thought that the human brain created these crucial neural pathways and connections early in life and then spent a lifetime strengthening those same pathways. However, recent research has shown that the brain's "plasticity," or ability to change and create new neuronal connections, continues throughout your life. *The attachment skills, miniconnections, and Smart Heart skills and dialogue in this book, as well as talk therapy, all contribute to brain change and growth, helping to creating secure attachments, particularly when money is the stressful trigger.*

The brain regulates both physical and social aspects of your behavior via a complex communication system of neurons, cells that use naturally occurring chemicals (neurotransmitters) to communicate information to neighboring cells.

In my work with couples in crisis from various forms of infidelity, I consult with Dr. Jeffrey Morrison of the Morrison Center. Together we have developed a protocol for regulating the biochemistry and behavior of individuals who exhibit addictive and other damaging behaviors. These individuals often show a high correlation between financial infidelity and other cheating or risk-taking behaviors such as affairs.

While the biochemical testing panel and supplement protocol Dr. Morrison administers helps to illuminate and regulate hormonal and neurotransmitter imbalances, it is important to remember that the patients who enter this program are actively seeking a solution and are willing to support their regimen of supplements with my individual and couples counseling. If the individual doesn't *want* to change, nothing is going to make a difference in his or her behavior.

To understand how an imbalance in neurotransmitters can affect your behavior, it is helpful to have a simple understanding of the way in which the brain governs body and mind.

There are three main parts of the brain, all housing different structures that influence emotional and physical behaviors. The *forebrain* (or *cerebrum*) generally governs problem solving, abstract thinking, and decision making. The *midbrain* controls reflex actions as well as some voluntary movements. The *hindbrain*, which consists of the upper part of the spinal cord (or *medulla*), the brain stem, and the *cerebellum*, is responsible for cardiac, respiratory, and vasomotor systems.

There are certain areas of the brain that are of particular interest to psychologists and psychiatrists because it is the communication between these structures that influences emotions. When it comes to dealing with extreme behaviors of addiction, infidelity, and impulsive or poor decision-making, it is helpful to understand the areas of the brain that may be involved.

- The *frontal lobes* control planning, reason, trust, and fantasy, and your ability to construct memories. Because of this, optimal functioning of the frontal lobes is considered to be the key to long-term relationships.
- The *orbitofrontal cortex (OFC)*—a part of the frontal lobe that has been the subject of much recent research—governs decision-making, especially in response to reward and punishment. The OFC may also play a part in self-inhibition and empathy. A June 2007 study in the *Journal of Socio-Economics* showed a relationship between prefrontal cortex dysfunction and credit card debt and poor financial management.
- The *limbic system* is comprised of structures from the forebrain and the midbrain and is buried deep inside the brain. Working together, these structures control emotion, emotional responses, hormonal secretions, mood, motivation, and pain and pleasure sensations. Two important structures in the limbic system are:
- The *hippocampus*, which is located next to the amygdala and plays a crucial role in emotion. Damage to the hippocampus, which communicates with adrenal and pituitary systems, can reduce your ability to distinguish safe situations from dangerous ones, inducing a state of constant anxiety and leading you to seek out situations (such as affairs or financial infidelity)

that make you feel safe but are actually dangerous. Studies have shown that individuals suffering from post-traumatic stress disorder (PTSD) have measurable shrinking of the hippocampus.

- The *amygdala*, which is in the midbrain and is crucial in decoding and communicating emotion to other responsive areas. It influences arousal, controls autonomic responses associated with fear, regulates emotional responses, and triggers hormonal releases.
- The *medulla*, or brain stem, functions as the distribution center for serotonin to the brain. When there is a serotonin imbalance, individuals can suffer from chronic depression or bipolar disorder.
- The *ventral striatum* and the *nucleus accumbens* help the brain process satisfaction and happiness. These structures are associated with evaluating risk, reward, and gratification. When the nucleus accumbens is unable to process dopamine properly, individuals may turn to addictions such as gambling, alcohol, drugs, or overeating in order to stimulate pleasure responses.

The brain uses neurotransmitters to quickly and smoothly exchange information between its parts and the parts of the body they regulate. Serotonin, dopamine, glutamate, GABA, and acetylcholine are all neurotransmitters.

For individuals prone to addictive behaviors, especially those that I see because of adultery and financial infidelity, correcting existing imbalances in specific neurotransmitters and hormones helps to regulate their behavior and creates an opening for additional therapeutic work to resolve and repair their damaged relationships.

Key Biochemical Markers

When studying the brain chemistry of an individual prone to addiction or the risk-taking behaviors of physical or financial infidelity, certain biochemical markers are evaluated for imbalances.

Hormones

Testosterone: This sex hormone, associated with traditional "male" traits, is present in both genders. High levels of testosterone may contribute to aggression. Individuals with high testosterone are generally direct, decisive, competitive, and ambitious.

In her research on attraction and compatibility, Dr. Helen Fisher has noted that high-testosterone individuals—whom she identifies as "Directors"—have little regard for money and far more interest in how they will manipulate or control the system. These individuals are likely to view money as a tool or a means to a specific end.

Estrogen: Considered the "feminine" sex hormone, high-estrogen individuals generally have strong verbal and "people" skills and are strongly social, with imaginative, well-connected brains.

According to Dr. Fisher, these "Negotiator" individuals prefer long-term financial planning, although they may spend unrealistically when driven by ideals or compassion.

DHEA: Dehydroepiandrosterone is a prohormone related to the production of both testosterone and certain types of estrogen. It is related to stress management and decreases as you age.

Cortisol: This adrenal hormone is released in response to stress. In the short term, elevated levels of cortisol can help accelerate metabolism and manage stress. However, when high cortisol levels are sustained over the long term, individuals may begin to feel tired, depressed, and anxious—in short, "burned out." According to Dr. Morrison, what many individuals term a "midlife crisis" may in fact be a case of their stress hormones having been elevated for so long that they are no longer able to respond to day-to-day stresses as they were meant to. People typically experience this type of burnout as a result of having no mental downtime in which to give their brain a break from stressful stimulation.

Prolonged stress and overstimulation of the adrenal system can result in an individual who feels "numb" and most times feels out of love with their partner and their self. This decreased ability to perceive physical and emotional pain or pleasure often causes these patients to characterize themselves as "dead" inside. In order to feel "alive" they often seek out self-stimulation and "self-medication" through compulsive behaviors such as overeating or alcohol or drug abuse; sexual infidelity such as affairs or addictions to Internet porn; or financial infidelity such as gambling or binge spending.

In our society of unlimited choice and emphasis on excess, the constant pressure to live above our means in a race to accumulate material possessions can lead to an ongoing state of stress about financial debt. Individuals who have suffered this kind of hormonal "burnout" may react by drastically changing their spending habits.

Oxytocin: What I like to call the "cuddle hormone," oxytocin is an important component in sexual behavior and attachment in both men and women. It is a natural stress reducer, creating feelings of contentment, calm, and happiness.

Vasopressin: This hormone is produced in the same area of the brain as oxytocin and is associated with addictive behavior, aggression, and risk taking. In men it is associated with territorial response, sexual behavior, and defensive reaction. Men who have high levels of vasopressin, in particular, often indulge in dangerous self-destructive behavior, like adultery or forms of financial infidelity.

Neurotransmitters

Neurotransmitters are chemical messengers that carry messages to our brain and nervous system, informing us how to react to particular situations or stimulation. The neurotransmitters most influential in behaviors such as adultery and financial infidelity are:

Dopamine: This neurotransmitter affects brain processes that control movement, emotional response, and the ability to experience pleasure and pain. When feelings of pleasure or excitement, such as those caused by thrill-seeking activities like binge spending or gambling, cause a flood of dopamine into the system on an ongoing—rather than occasional—basis, the dopamine receptors in the brain increases to take up the additional chemicals. As the number of receptors increases, they become less sensitive to the dopamine and desensitization occurs. This condition, called tolerance, leads an individual to seek greater and greater thrills in order to stimulate the increasing amount of dopamine needed to trigger the feelings of pleasure he or she has come to crave. This lack of appropriate hormonal response can cause these individuals to become depressed; they may complain of feeling as if they have fallen out of love with their partners, or drastically seek to change their situation to cause new stimulation.

Dr. Fisher's research identifies high-dopamine individuals as "Explorers," people who are risk taking, novelty seeking, spontaneous, compulsive, curious, creative, and charismatic. They may be spontaneously generous with money, but have an addictive personality that may lead them to take risks or gamble. These individuals may be stimulated by instability and view loss as a challenge.

Serotonin: This neurotransmitter regulates many functions, including appetite, sleep, memory and learning, temperature regulation, mood, cardiovascular function, muscle contraction, and endocrine regulation. Low serotonin levels have been linked to mild and severe depression and symptoms such as anxiety, apathy, fear, feelings of unworthiness, insomnia, and fatigue.

Dr. Fisher identifies high-serotonin individuals as "Builders," people who may be described as loyal, conscientious, rule following, and detail oriented. Builders are planners and may be frugal with their money and apt to budget effectively.

Histamine: Often associated with allergic responses in the body, levels of this neurotransmitter influence mood, appetite, sleep, and thought. High-histamine individuals may be prone to depression, anorexia, bulimia, binge shopping, gambling, adultery, and high libido. Dr. Morrison's research has shown that those who are high in dopamine are often high in histamine. People who exhibit low histamine levels may be prone to anxiety, depression, lack of sex drive, and low motivation.

GABA: Gamma-aminobutyric acid is a neurotransmitter that controls mood by influencing areas of the brain associated with anxiety. People with low levels of GABA may feel anxious, and a Yale University School of Medicine study has linked abnormally low levels of GABA with panic disorders.

PEA: Phenylethylamine is sometimes called the "infatuation chemical." This neurotransmitter, along with dopamine, saturates your nervous system when you are infatuated, causing feelings of ecstasy and stimulation and a lowering of defenses. Imbalances of this neurotransmitter may contribute to binge spending and risk-taking behaviors.

Epinephrine: Also known as adrenaline, epinephrine works with cortisol to control reactions to stress or fear. The fight-or-flight response, which prepares your body to face a perceived danger or threat, is regulated by epinephrine.

Norepinephrine: Also called noradrenaline, this neurotransmitter communicates with the sympathetic nervous system, the part of your nervous system that responds to short-term stress. Along with epinephrine, norepinephrine increases heart rate and blood pressure and tells your body to mobilize in response to challenging situations.

When your nervous system is functioning optimally, your sympathetic nervous system will kick in to power you through stressful situations. Once the stress has passed, the parasympathetic nervous system is stimulated and acts to reverse the reaction. For people who are suffering from post-traumatic stress disorder (PTSD) or unusually high levels of daily stress, these two nervous systems can shift out of balance for extended amounts of time—with debilitating emotional and physical results.

Any number of physical conditions or emotional stresses can affect your biochemical balance and result in damaging behavioral patterns. *If your life is dramatically out of balance, you feel you have fallen "out of love" with your partner, or you feel "numb" or "dead" to emotional or physical stimulation the problem may be that you are out of sorts with your biochemical self.* Your problem may be related to out-of-whack blood sugar, chronic sleep deprivation, the use of medications that can stifle emotions and feelings of romantic love, or an imbalance of specific neurotransmitters, hormones, and biochemical reactions.

Rob and Melinda came to see me because Melinda wanted a divorce and Rob couldn't understand why. He had not had an affair or hurt her in the marriage in any way. The only reason Melinda could give me was that she was "tired" of her husband. She claimed that she "couldn't feel anything for him anymore."

When Melinda came in for a session on her own, she confessed she was worried about her impulsive overspending. She would go shopping almost daily and buy several expensive outfits. If her husband questioned her, or picked a fight, she enjoyed the binges even more. "I thrive on drama!" she would exclaim. If I saw her right after one of her binges, she would rave about her purchases:

"I just bought the most gorgeous shearling coat. It's perfect!" or "Don't you adore these earrings? I had to have them!"

I paid particular attention to this behavior. The next time I would see her for a session, I'd ask if she was enjoying her new purchases. Every time I asked, she'd wave her hand dismissively and tell me that she'd never even taken them out of the bags once she arrived home. She admitted that she had a closet full of clothing and accessories, most with tags still attached.

"Once I get them home, I find I'm already tired of them," she said. "I just don't care about them."

It was no surprise to me when Dr. Morrison tested Melinda and informed me that she had very low levels of dopamine. In cases where there is an extreme imbalance of certain neurotransmitters, an individual will often complain of having "no feelings."

After Dr. Morrison prescribed a regime of supplements to help regulate these levels and we continued our work, Melinda reported that she was able to control her spending. She said she felt like she was "falling in love" with her husband again. "I realize now that I didn't have any emotion to give; money was how I expressed my feelings." Melinda said. "But now I realize that even with all the gifts and spending in the world, if there's not love and connection, the relationship will feel empty." With her brain chemistry rebalanced, I continued to work with both Melinda and her husband, successfully using behavior modification therapy to show them how to repair and improve their relationship.

People who are highly impulsive, like Melinda, have been shown to be big spenders. A University of Minnesota study showed that impulsive subjects spent up to five times as much as those with higher levels of impulse control. The people I see who are inclined to make these impulsive purchases are equally inclined to impulsively dispose of the items they have bought. I have heard stories from women who, upon hearing their husbands complain about tight finances, particularly around tax time, rush back to department stores with bags full of high-priced clothing items and makeup, which they return in order to reduce their credit card bills.

Financial Infidelity as an Addiction

When I am talking to some of the couples I counsel about their feelings when beginning an affair, they often use descriptions like "sexual chemistry" and "irresistible attraction." Some even compare their craving for their lover to an addiction. They can't get enough. They feel high. Their descriptions verge on sounding like passages from a romance novel. And yet, there's some validity to their clichés. In fact, studies have shown that certain repetitive or addictive behaviors both are caused by and contribute to fluctuations in the mood-stimulating neurotransmitters in our brains.

The neurotransmitters we talk about above—dopamine, serotonin, norepinephrine, and epinephrine—and hormones such as oxytocin and vasopressin are associated with depression and euphoria. If the levels of these important brain chemicals are imbalanced, an individual is likely to feel depressed, and may behave in ways to stimulate—or simulate—the feelings induced naturally by the release of these neurotransmitters in the brain. Patients I counsel are often seeking to duplicate the euphoric feelings of "falling in love." They are trying to re-create their feelings with adulterous affairs, out-of-control shopping, or risk-taking behaviors like gambling. The satisfaction they feel from this "quick fix" can set them up for unrealistic expectations for an ongoing state of energy, arousal, and euphoria.

In counseling couples where one individual seems compelled to seek out hurtful affairs or commit financial infidelity, even as they express remorse over the effect their behavior is having on their relationship, I will often explore whether, for them, *the thrill of pursuit, conquest, and the fulfillment of their fantasies* is actually indicative of an addiction. In these cases, or in those where there is a family history of addictive behavior such as alcoholism or drug abuse, adultery, or gambling, analyzing the levels of the key neurotransmitter associated with depression and addiction can give me insight into their situation. Many patients I see have a constellation of these addictive behaviors. They may drink *and* gamble *and* engage in extramarital affairs. They often tell me that they have tried to stop all of these behaviors on their own, but find themselves slipping back into them or even adding new damaging behaviors. I tell these patients that because it is very difficult to exhibit self-control when dealing with addictive-type behaviors, it is important that they do not take on more than one self-control challenge at a time. And in the meantime we can manipulate, even balance their neurotransmitter levels (which are initially determined by heredity) through supplements, medication, biofeedback, or talk therapy.

Just as an individual may turn to an illicit love affair to provide the biochemical feelings of connection and experience the thrill of a new romance, over and over again, so, too, they may turn to risky financial behavior for stimulation. Even if they stop the love affair, they may not have the self-control to stop the risky financial behavior.

The reason is that the behaviors that stimulate these feelings can easily become addictive. For instance, for any addict, the choice to self-medicate in any number of ways—with alchohol, medications, sex, or money—can begin with a desire to relieve stress or mute depression. The addiction then progresses to a preoccupation with where their next "fix" will come from, and often involves a strong desire to create rituals around obtaining the "high." This preoccupation becomes a compulsion—to use drugs or alcohol, or to have sex, or to shop—followed by depression and despair as the effects wear off, leading to the start of the cycle all over again.

Joseph Frascella, director of the Division of Clinical Neuroscience at the National Institute on Drug Abuse (NIDA), defines addiction as "repetitive behaviors in the face of negative consequences, the desire to continue something you know is bad for you." The three most common types of "habits" that can slide into "addictive behavior" that I see in relation to financial infidelity are gambling, binge spending, and hoarding.

Two million adults are thought to be pathological gamblers. Another four to eight million are considered "problem" gamblers. A Stanford University study identifies one in twenty Americans as compulsive shoppers.

The individuals that are prone to gambling and binge spending may also seek to take risks in a socially appropriate way by working in a high-stress, thrill-intensive job such as a Wall Street trader, a surgeon, or a courtroom attorney. The buzz from their victories is usually immediately followed by a new stressful situation and a chance to professionally "gamble" so that they can triumph yet again.

Other people may exhibit financial infidelity as a result of *transference*. In psychological terms, transference refers to the redirection of feelings, fears, or emotions onto a new object or situation.

Gambling

With all the financial infidelity I revealed in my Family Moneygram in step 3 of this book, it probably wouldn't surprise you to find out that both my mother and my father were gamblers, although in very different ways. My father was a high-stakes poker player; my mother was a fan of Atlantic City slots and bingo.

Although both of them gambled, they did it for different reasons. My mother, who was constantly worried about her weight, would have the urge to gamble whenever she was on a diet. The more she deprived herself of food, the more she sought to stimulate herself with quarter slots or bingo.

For my father, his gambling, just like his extramarital affairs, was linked to thrill-seeking behavior and magical thinking.

While it took a major shock (my mother's use of the Brush with Death exercise) to jolt my father out of his thrill-seeking ways, my mother would seek outside help to control her impulses to gamble. She would leave for the casinos with a budgeted amount of money. If she ran out and wanted to spend more, she would call my father and ask if it was all right. This was not a new behavior. When I was young, she would take me shopping and continue to purchase things for me until I told her I didn't need any more and insist that she stop.

This is not uncommon behavior. Studies have shown that trying to take on more than one self-improvement task at a time (losing weight and quitting bingo) actually creates more of an urge to eat or gamble. A recent study from the University of Minnesota links attempts at self-control with increased impulse spending. A group that was told to practice thought suppression spent more money than those whose thoughts had been unconstrained. To minimize the urge to overspend, or gamble, individuals often seek outside help by asking permission to continue with the behavior.

Gambling is a pervasive financial infidelity and one that afflicts the population without regard to age, race, or gender. In fact, women are more likely to become addicted to gambling than men. College students and senior citizens also fall into a high-risk group. With the proliferation of online games, poker nights, and even senior bingo, it is easy for an individual with an addictive personality to fall into the vicious trap of compulsive gambling.

Binge Spending

While everyone has engaged in "retail therapy" from time to time, for some shoppers, the compulsion to buy can lead to financial and relationship ruin. In our materialistic culture, feelings of envy can kick our evolutionary drive to compete into high gear. And for some individuals, "keeping up with the Joneses" can spiral into an addictive behavior of acquiring.

> *Stan and Laura came to me when Laura told Stan she wanted a divorce after he filed for bankruptcy. While the stress of bankruptcy often triggers a relationship crisis, it soon became apparent that Stan and Laura's issues were more complex.*
>
> *Laura revealed that she had been spending forty to fifty thousand dollars a month—charging high-ticket items to credit cards that she had applied for, as well as to credit cards linked to Stan's business. Because she handled the bookkeeping for the household and the business, she was able to keep her spending a secret from Stan.*

"I suspected something was wrong, but I was afraid to confront her," Stan admitted. "It took her six years to get her to agree to marry me and during that time I learned not to push her or she would shut down and shut me out."

When Stan was forced to sell his business to cover their crushing debt, Laura vowed to change her spending habits. Just a few months later, Stan found out that Laura had listed their house for sale in order to cover outstanding debts. With his trust in his wife shattered, and their finances in ruins, Stan filed for bankruptcy, whereupon Laura accused him of hiding assets and threatened divorce.

Laura's behavior was so extreme that I sent her for a full medical and psychiatric workup. When the results came back, she was diagnosed with bipolar disorder. Her spending had signaled manic periods and with medication to regulate her behavior, she was able to continue counseling with me to address the emotional issues of abandonment and lack of trust that were intensified by her brain disorder.

Hoarding Money

Compulsive hoarding is often associated with obsessive-compulsive disorder (OCD) and may affect up to two million people in the United States. Compulsive hoarders exhibit three core features: failure to discard objects due to severe anxiety about loss; excessive acquisition, sometimes resulting in uncontrolled buying sprees; and excessive clutter to the point where their homes and workplaces cannot be used. Studies show that 81 percent of hoarders have health problems. In compulsive hoarding, brain abnormalities (some shrinking of, or an unusual shape to, the frontal lobe) can be seen and measured.

While most of my patients who are committing financial infidelity do not exhibit all of the components of compulsive hoarding as it applies to a psychiatric disorder, many do exhibit some of the tendencies related to it. These individuals will sneak and hide money or purchases, keeping their acquisitions a secret from their partners. Many of them admit that they hoard money because of fear of loss, childhood deprivation, or to stave off anxiety about the future. Those who exhibit the most severe money-hoarding behaviors will also describe their behavior as having an addictive component—the thrill of acquiring in secret versus the risk of losing, or having to return, the money.

Mike and Wendy came to see me after Mike threatened to file for a divorce after discovering Wendy had been stealing money from the store he owned and managed. For more than a year, she had been taking cash from the register. "I told her I thought someone had been stealing from the store," Mike said. "But every time I talked about installing video cameras or using a private investigator, she would talk me out of it. She told me that it was too expensive—a waste of 'our' money. She'd convince me that maybe I'd just miscounted the register total."

After he found a shoebox full of neatly bound piles of bills in the back of Wendy's closet, Mike was angry and felt he had no reason to trust his wife. "She stole and she lied," he said. "How can I forgive her?"

"I just felt safer, having the money put away somewhere," Wendy explained. "At first, I just wanted to have a little extra security, in case some-thing went wrong with the business. After a while, I couldn't stop taking the money. I would feel excited when I took it and no one noticed, and then I would get worried that I didn't have enough."

As I continued to counsel Mike and Wendy, I learned that the two of them often "relaxed" by going to the casinos in a nearby town. Mike didn't feel he had a problem with gambling; he assured me he would often walk away from the slots or tables after he'd lost his budgeted amount. But Wendy did not have the same level of self-control. She would often gamble until Mike demanded that she stop or physically took away her cash and credit and debit cards.

It soon became clear that Wendy's financial infidelity was rooted in an addictive pattern of behavior. While she sought additional help for her addic-tion disorder, she and Mike were able to continue to work with me to under-stand the underlying causes of her "stealing" from the store. They were able to slowly begin the process of rebuilding trust and a loving relationship.

For all my patients exhibiting extreme cases of financial infidelity combined with addictive behaviors, treatment involves medical intervention to balance their biochemical profile, recognizing their addiction for what it is, breaking patterns that trigger their addictive behavior, cutting off their access to the money that fuels their addictive habits, seeking support from their spouses and friends, and an ongoing and intensive course of professional therapy.

Warning Signs of Addiction and Financial Infidelity

"Addiction has a specific definition: you are unable to stop when you want to despite [being] aware of the adverse consequences," according to Dr. Nora Volkow, director of the National Institute on Drug Abuse. "It permeates your life; you spend more and more time satisfying [your craving]."

The danger is when the damaging behaviors associated with financial infidelity start out as habits, but slide into addictions. If you recognize any of the following warning signs in yourself or your partner, you may want to consider whether one of you has an addiction that is causing financial infidelity in your relationship:

- Maxed-out credit cards
- Applying for new credit cards constantly
- Cash missing or unaccounted for
- Hoarding cash, objects, or things
- Secret withdrawals from joint accounts
- Unexplained credit card bills or transfers or charge book to "buy time"
- Unexplained selling of investments (stock, bonds, etc.)
- Refusal to discuss finances
- No sense of spending or debt
- You depend on others to help you control your spending
- Excessive betting on "harmless" things like golf or office pools

- Lack of empathy
- Giving up one thing, but substituting another (transference)
- Constantly overspending your budget
- Uncontrolled spending disguised as "business," such as purchasing stocks or other investments, even when you are losing substantial amounts of money

QUIZ: ARE YOU AT RISK FOR ADDICTIVE FINANCIAL INFIDELITY?

If you can answer "yes" to three or more of the following questions, you may be predisposed to financial infidelity as an addictive behavior:

1. Do you spend money when you are depressed in order to feel better?
2. Does shopping give you a "rush"?
3. Do you experience high levels of anxiety before making a purchase?
4. Do you have "shopping bulimia"—binge shopping by purchasing things you cannot afford or do not need and returning them after your shopping high wears off or the bills come in?
5. Do you have a history of addiction (adultery, gambling, drug addiction, alcoholism, sex addiction) in your family?
6. Do you find yourself thinking constantly about the next thing you are planning to buy?
7. Do you shop compulsively, purchasing multiples of the same item?
8. Do you hide your shopping sprees from your partner?
9. Have your shopping habits substantially increased your debt (high credit card balances, drawing against home equity loans, etc.)?
10. Do you "charge back" items on your credit cards, denying you have made purchases or returning things you have purchased, as a method of managing your bills and "buying time"?

11. Do you avoid opening credit card statements, or paying your bills, even if you have the money to do so?

Dr. Vokow characterizes addiction as ". . . a medical condition." I, too, consider adultery and financial infidelity a disease and an epidemic. In fact, I have called my theory the "biochemical craving for connection." *Early* loss, stress, and separation can cause a cascade of emotions and trigger the impulse to self-medicate later on in life. If you suspect you have a money-related addiction, you may need professional help and long-term support and may wish to seek individual counseling as well as participate in an addiction recovery program. In addition, supplements, medication, and talk therapy can address the pathology of the disease, and couples therapy with an emphasis on behavior modification may help to heal the wounds the addictive behaviors have caused in your relationship and teach you and your partner how to regain trust and repair intimacy.

A Final Word: The Case for Financial Fidelity and Lasting Love

*F*alling in love can be an emotional roller coaster, albeit a thrilling one. Turning that euphoric connection into a stable, functional relationship is a task
tailor-made to evoke insecurities and deeply buried issues. Throwing money into
the equation makes it even more charged. Yet it's perfectly understandable that
talking about money is such a loaded issue for so many people. Today's culture
creates many external factors that contribute to financial stress and anxiety in any relationship.

Gender roles around money are breaking down—with census data
showing that more women than men (32 percent versus 25 percent) are
attending and graduating from college, and that women in their twenties
working full-time in the nation's largest urban areas are earning more
than their male counterparts. Women are running their own businesses
and gaining economic clout. In two-income households, one quarter of
women now earn more than their husbands.

Divorce is causing financial hardship for both men and women.
Boomer singles are beginning to date after years of marriage have
ended—many with the painful memory of financial infidelity fresh in
their minds—and are navigating the tricky terrain of love and money
with a whole new perspective and desire for financial transparency.

Everywhere you turn, you are inundated with cultural messages to
make more money, buy more things, and flaunt more wealth. Consumers
struggle with an excess of choices, and at the same time, the cost of living

and raising a family is outpacing the earning power of these individuals. With a socioeconomic structure where the rich are ranked in a hierarchy from "superrich" to "poor-rich," and the middle class is struggling to simply make ends meet, it is no surprise that financial infidelity is at the root of the unraveling of many relationships.

And yet there is *hope*. The couples that come to see me don't always know their relationship is suffering from financial infidelity. Often they are convinced that they have "fallen out of love." Eager to find a blame-free excuse to avoid the hurt and conflict that comes with growing love into a real and lasting intimacy, they attempt to mask their fears and hurts by seeking instant gratification—using money or affairs in a desperate bid to fill the emptiness they feel. What I tell these couples is what I'm telling you now: "Falling in love is easy. Staying in love takes courage and effort." But it is definitely worth it, as my parents, my patients, and my husband and I can attest.

In this book I have given you the Smart Heart skills and dialogues you need in order to predict, prevent, uncover, and end financial infidelity. As you have worked through the seven steps here in this book, you and your partner have learned the tools necessary to undertake a rewarding voyage of self-discovery. As you have learned how to communicate safely, openly, and honestly about the role of money in your life and your relationship, you have strengthened the trust and intimacy in your relationship and have begun to heal the wounds caused by financial infidelity. If you are newlyweds, you now have the skills to travel the road of a committed partnership, facing any money conflicts together with love and understanding.

Reclaiming the feeling of the romantic love you first experienced—and all the thrilling, sexy sizzle that comes with it—is possible when you make a *conscious* decision to commit to concentrate on restoring the magic of your intimate relationship *on a daily basis*. Real life love doesn't just "happen." You and your partner have to *make it happen!* You must be willing to do whatever it takes, to put your relationship first, and to hang in there and keep your love alive, through bad times as well as good.

The couples who reach real-life love and financial fidelity and enjoy a conscious "money marriage" are those who have made it through the power struggles and come out the other side with a deeper understanding of how each person needs to be loved. In my book *Make Up, Don't Break Up*, I offered a Smart Heart vow for all couples. When facing the triggers for financial infidelity or negotiating a power struggle or difficult transitional phase, remember to share these words with your partner: *"I will connect with you, detach myself from my own thoughts and emotions, so I can hear you and walk in your shoes."*

Real-life love makes life worth living. You are joyful in your relationship because you accept each other as you are, and lovingly coach one another to become better, more satisfied, and more fulfilled. Practicing financial fidelity can make you wealthy in your love and in your bank account.

Remember that the path of least resistance rarely, if ever, leads to financial fidelity and real-life love. As Franklin Delano Roosevelt famously said, "The only limit to our realization of tomorrow will be our doubts of today." Don't lose faith in this process. Learn to see money problems and challenges as gifts—opportunities to bring you closer together. With persistence and belief, anyone can reclaim the sexual and emotional connection they crave with their partner, and anyone can banish financial infidelity from their relationship. You have the tools, and the Smart Heart skills and dialogues that you need to succeed, right here in your hand so financial infidelity cannot bankrupt your relationship!

BIBLIOGRAPHY AND SOURCES

Interviews

Helen Fisher, PhD
Jeffrey Morrison, MD
Stanford Lotwin, Esq.
Sunny Shulkin, LSCW, BCD
Mark Shulkin, MD

Books

Bach, David. *The Automatic Millionaire: A Powerful One-Step Plan to Live and Finish Rich*. New York: Broadway Books. 2004.

Bach, David. *The Automatic Millionaire Workbook: A Personalized Plan to Live and Finish Rich . . . Automatically*. New York: Broadway Books. 2005.

Bach, David. *Smart Couples Finish Rich: 9 Steps to Creating a Rich Future for You and Your Partner*. New York: Broadway Books. 2002.

Bach, David. *Smart Women Finish Rich: 9 Steps to Achieving Financial Security and Funding Your Dreams*. New York: Broadway Books. 2002.

Bach, David. *Start Late, Finish Rich: A No-Fail Plan for Achieving Financial Freedom at Any Age*. New York: Broadway Books. 2005.

Bach, David. *The Finish Rich Workbook: Creating a Personalized Plan for a Richer Future*. New York: Broadway Books. 2003.

Bass, Howard L., Rein, M. L. *Divorce or Marriage: A Legal Guide*. Englewood Cliffs, NJ: Prentiss Hall. 1976.

Byrne, Rhonda. *The Secret*. New York: Atria Books. 2006.

Collins Stephens, Deborah; Speier, Jackie; Cristini Risley, Michealene; Yanehiro, Jan. *This is Not the Life I Ordered: 50 Ways to Keep Your Head Above Water When Life Keeps Dragging You Down*. San Francisco: Conari Press. 2007.

Dubin, Arlene G. *Prenups for Lovers: A Romantic Guide to Prenuptial Agreements*. New York: Villard. 2001.

Eaker Weil, Bonnie, PhD. *Can We Cure and Forgive Adultery?: Staying Not Straying. Understanding Our Biochemical Craving for Connection*. West Conshohocken, PA: Infinity Publishing, 2004.

Eaker Weil, Bonnie, PhD. *Adultery: The Forgivable Sin*. Poughkeepsie, NY: Hudson House. 2003.

Eaker Weil, Bonnie, PhD. *Make Up, Don't Break Up: Finding and Keeping Love for Singles and Couples*. Avon, MA: Adams Media. 2000.

Eaker Weil, Bonnie, PhD. *How Not to (S)Mother Your Man and How to Keep a Woman Happy?: A Simple Guide to Falling and Staying In Love For Both Men and Women*. West Conshohocken, PA: Infinity Publishing. 2004.

Ehrenreich, Barbara. *Nickel and Dimed: On (Not) Getting By in America*. New York: Henry Holt. 2002.

Eker, T. Harv. *Secrets of the Millionaire Mind*. New York: HarperCollins. 2005.

Gottman, John, PhD. *Why Marriages Succeed or Fail . . . and How You Can Make Yours Last*. New York: Simon & Schuster. 1995.

Henri-x, Harville, PhD. *Getting the Love You Want: A Guide for Couples*. New York: Harper Perennial. 1988.

Huffington, Arianna. *On Becoming Fearless . . . In Love, Work, and Life*. New York: Little Brown and Company. 2006.

Mellan, Olivia. *Money Harmony: Resolving Money Conflicts in Your Life and Relationships*. New York: Walker & Company. 1994.

Orman, Suze. *Women & Money: Owning the Power to Control Your Destiny*. New York: Spiegel & Grau. 2007.

Orman, Suze. *The Road to Wealth: A Comprehensive Guide to Your Money*. New York: Riverhead Books. 2003.

Orman, Suze. *The Money Book for the Young, Fabulous & Broke*. New York: Riverhead Books. 2005.

Orman, Suze. *The Laws of Money: 5 Timeless Secrets to Get Out and Stay Out of Financial Trouble*. New York: Free Press. 2004.

Orman, Suze. *The Courage to Be Rich: Creating a Life of Material and Spiritual Abundance.* New York: Riverhead Books. 2002.

Pond, Jonathan D. *You Can Do It! The Boomer's Guide to a Great Retirement.* New York: Collins Books. 2007.

Siegel, Daniel J., MD. *The Developing Mind: How Relationships and the Brain Interact to Shape Who We Are.* New York, London: Guilford Press. 2001.

Siegel, Daniel J., MD. *The Mindful Brain: Reflection and Attunement in the Cultivation of Well-Being.* New York, London: W.W. Norton & Co. 2007.

Sutton, Garrett, Esq. *The ABC's of Getting Out of Debt: Turn Bad Debt into Good Debt and Bad Credit into Good Credit.* New York, Boston: Warner Business Books. 2004.

Vaknin, Sam, PhD. *Malignant Self Love: Narcissism Revisited.* Prague and Skopje: Narcissus Publications. 2006.

Articles

Allison, Julia. "Dating the Single File." *Time Out New York.* August 30–September 5, 2007.

Allure. October 2007.

Boyd, Andrew. "Dating Now." *Marie Claire.* October 2007.

Brown, Harriet. "The *Other* Brain Also Deals With Many Woes." *The New York Times.* August 23, 2005.

Caldwell, Christine. "Caring for the Caregiver." *Psychotherapy Networker.* September / October 2007.

Carey, Benedict. "Do You Believe in Magic?" *The New York Times.* January 23, 2007.

Chatzky, Jean. "Shopping for Happiness? Here's What to Buy." *Money Magazine.* April 2007.

Chu, Kathy. "Breaking Up Is Hard to Do Financially." *USA Today.* September 28, 2007.

Dowd, Maureen. "What's a Modern Girl to Do?" *The New York Times Magazine.* October 30, 2005.

Estroff Marano, Hara. "Love Lessons." *Psychology Today.* Mar/Apr, 1997.

Farrell, Greg. "The Enron Whistleblower Who Wasn't." *USA Today.* October 12, 2007.

Fiske, A. John. "Couples' Finances, Upfront and Personal." *The Boston Globe.* December 29, 2005.

Gengler, Amanda. "The Urge to Lose Money." *Money Magazine.* March 1, 2007.

Kluger, Jeffrey. "What Makes Us Moral." *Time.* December 3, 2007.

Lemonick, Michael D. with Park, Alice. "The Science of Addiction." *Time.* July 16, 2007.

Loftus, Mary. "Till Debt Do Us Part." *Psychology Today.* Nov / Dec 2004.

Matthews, Kathryn. "Romance Rehab." *O Magazine.* May 2007.

Max, Sarah. "Financial Infidelity." *Tango.* Fall 2007.

Murphy Paul, Annie. "Mind Reading." *Psychology Today.* September / October 2007.

Newsweek. "Women and Power" Issue. October 17, 2007.

Norris, Floyd. "High and Low Finance: Rethinking Risk's Role in Bosses' Pay." *The New York Times.* October 12, 2007.

Ordonez, Jennifer. "Tying the Financial Knot." *Newsweek.* April 9, 2007.

Parker-Pope, Tara. "Marital Spats, Taken to Heart." *The New York Times.* October 2, 2007.

Richard, Joanne. "For Love and Money." *The Toronto Sun.* July 2003.

Rosenbloom, Stephanie. "Boss's Memo: Go Ahead, Date (With My Blessing)." *The New York Times.* October 11, 2007.

Sainai, Kristin. "More Powerful Willpower." *Allure.* November 2007.

Shivani, Vora. "When Money Doesn't Talk." *The New York Times.* January 14, 2007.

Singletary, Michelle. "Financial Infidelity: Fought About and Lied About, Even When Not Talked About, Money Makes Couples Mad." *The Washington Post.* February 11, 2007.

Tierney, John. "The Whys of Mating: 237 Reasons and Counting." *The New York Times.* July 31, 2007.

Tugend, Alina. "Envy, Anxiety, Secrecy, Taboos: The Subject Must Be Money." *The New York Times.* February 3, 2007.

Tyre, Peg. "To Catch a Cheat." *Newsweek.* October 15, 2007.

USA Today. Money. December 24, 2007.

Ventura, Michael. "Confessions of an External Romantic." *Psychology Today.* March–April 1977.

Voss, Gretchen. "The Starter Husband." *Marie Claire.* September 2007.

Williams, Alex. "Putting Money on the Table: With Rising Incomes, Young Women Discuss the Pitfalls of 'Dating Down.'" *The New York Times.* September 23, 2007.

Studies

Lott, Deborah A. "Brain Development, Attachment and Impact on Psychic Vulnerability." *Psychiatric Times.* Vol. 15, Issue 5. May 1998.

Singh, Supriya. "Money, Marriage and the Computer." *Marriage & Family Review*, Vol 24, No. 3-4, 1996.

Spinella, Marcello, Yang, Bijou, and Lester, David. "Prefrontal Systems in Financial Processing." *Journal of Socio-Economics.* Vol. 36, Issue 3. June 2007.

Sullivan, Teresa A., Warren, Elizabeth, Westbrook, Jay Lawrence. "Bankruptcy and the Family." *Marriage & Family Review,* Vol. 21, No. 3-4, 1995.

Van Boven, Leaf. "Experientialism, Materialism, and the Pursuit of Happiness." *Review of General Psychology*, Vol. 9, No. 2, 2005.

Television and Radio

Oprah, November 2007.

The Today Show, October 15, 2007.

20/20 "Doing Good and Feeling Better: Why Giving Back Could Make You Happier . . . and Healthier." August 20, 2007.

Voice of America Broadcast, August 6, 2007 with Olivia Mellan and Dr. Bonnie Eaker Weil.

Web Sites

www.2-in-2-1.co.uk Kaye, Bryce. "Marital First Aid Kid: Sneaky Spending Behavior."

www.about.com "Personal Finance for Unmarried Couples."

www.careerjournal.com Zaslow, Jeffrey. "Financial Infidelity: When It's OK to Shop Behind Your Spouse's Back" from the *Wall Street Journal* online. March 31, 2006.

www.cnnmoney.com Regnier, Pat and Gengler, Amanda. "Men, women . . . and money." March 14, 2006.

www.cnnmoney.com Sahadi, Jeanne. "Will Your Money Fights Lead to Divorce?" March 15, 2006.

www.creditcard.com

www.gottman.com The Gottman Institute.

www.investmentnews.com Shindler, Lisa. "Postnups Becoming 'New' Prenups." June 18, 2007.

www.ivillage.com

www.lawyers.com "New Survey Finds Common Financial Infidelity." October 11, 2005.

www.manangement-issues.com Amble, Brian. "Why Powerful People Take More Risks." September 19, 2006.

www.sciam.com "Can a Lack of Sleep Cause Psychiatric Disorders?" October 23, 2007.

www.sciencedaily.com "SRI Medication Effective in Treating Compulsive Hoarding Patients." October 25, 2006.

www.scoop.co.nz "Financial Infidelity? Is Honesty the Policy?" January 31, 2006.

www.smartmoney.com

www.smartmoney.com McGregor, Jena. "Love & Money." February 9, 2004. Todorova, Alesksandra. "The Six Financial Mistakes Couples Make."

www.washingtonpost.com Vedantam, Shankar. "Salary, Gender and the Social Cost of Haggling." July 30, 2007.

ABOUT THE AUTHOR

Bonnie Eaker Weil, PhD, has been an internationally acclaimed relationship therapist for thirty years and is the author of several books, including *Make Up, Don't Break Up: Finding and Keeping Love for Singles and Couples* (Adams Media, 2000), *Adultery: The Forgivable Sin* (Hudson House, 2003), *Can We Cure and Forgive Adultery?* (Infinity Publishing, 2004), and *How Not to (S)Mother Your Man* (Infinity Publishing, 2004). She specializes in counseling couples on the verge of a breakup, teaching them how to work through pain and anger to repair and strengthen their relationship. Dr. Bonnie has a phenomenal 98 percent success rate in keeping couples together in committed, loving relationships and is one of America's best-known relationship experts.

She has been named by *New York Magazine* as one of the city's *top* therapists, and *Psychology Today* named her one of America's *best* therapists. She has appeared on *Oprah* five times, was featured in a three-day series on the *Today Show*, a four-day series on dating and money for *A Current Affair* on the Fox network, and in a CNN documentary on infidelity. She is a frequent expert on Fox TV, CNN, ABC, CBS, and *NBC News*. Dr. Bonnie has been a featured guest of *The View*, *20/20*, and Fox's *O'Reilly Report*, as well as Fox's *Fox and Friends*, and appears as a contributor and expert consultant on top talk shows around the country.

In the past year, Dr. Bonnie has been interviewed for articles on divorce and relationships published in *The New York Times* Style Section (Dec. 2005) and Home Section (March 2006). She has discussed divorce, infidelity, and relationships in articles in *People, Glamour, Marie Claire, Ladies Home Journal* ("Can This Marriage Be Saved?" column), *Cosmopolitan, Family Circle, Good Housekeeping, Redbook, Time Magazine, Men's Health, Details,* and *First for Women.* She has also been featured in articles in *USA Today,* the *New York Post, The New York Times, Daily Mirror* (London), and *Toronto Sun.*

Her first book, *Adultery: The Forgivable Sin,* has sold over one hundred thousand copies and been translated into six languages: French, Spanish, Japanese, Chinese, Russian, and English. Dr. Bonnie also consulted on the adaptation of the book for television. The movie *Silence of Adultery,* starring Kate Jackson, was produced for the Lifetime channel and is now available on video.

Dr. Bonnie is rated Number 1 on Yahoo's Love and Sex Chats and is a favorite on the iVillage.com board for "Adultery: the Forgivable Sin," where she chats with couples from around the globe who are trying to put their relationships back together. She has also taught seminars on male / female communication at the 92nd Street Y in New York City and has conducted seminars at both Canyon Ranch in Arizona and The Learning Annex of New York. A five-DVD series, *Falling in Love and Staying in Love for Singles and Couples,* featuring Smart Heart skills and dialogues for dating, couples, adultery, divorce, children, financial infidelity, and reromanticizing, is available through her web site.

Dr. Bonnie is featured in the DVD series *Falling in Love and Staying in Love (For Singles & Couples),* including the DVDs: *Financial Infidelity; Adultery, It's Not Your Fault; To Divorce or Not to Divorce;* and *Smart Heart Dialogue.*

Dr. Bonnie has helped thousands of singles and couples who have benefited from her diagnostic and therapeutic skills. She has an active practice offering office visits, phone therapy, consultations, and seminars where she shares her insight and unique tools, exercises, and dialogues to help couples move through pain and anger to save their relationships.

A NOTE TO READERS
FROM DR. BONNIE

Thousands of singles and couples have benefited from the safety of the Smart Heart skills, tools, and dialogue they've learned from me in seminars, consultations, and therapy sessions, both face-to-face and by phone. I welcome you to share this wisdom and experience with me.

I can be reached at (212)606-3787 for more information regarding singles and couples, personal appearances, therapy sessions, lectures, and seminars.

You can also reach me through my web sites:

www.docbon.com

e-mail: info@doctorbonnie.com

Dr. Bonnie's introductory companion DVD, Financial Infidelity, is available on www.docbon.com. Learn how to utilize the "Smart Heart Money Love Language & Dialogue" skills and continue your journey of discovery.

INDEX